America's Grand Hotels

BE A TRAVELER - NOT A TOURIST!

OPEN ROAD TRAVEL GUIDES SHOW YOU HOW TO BE A TRAVELER – NOT A TOURIST!

*Whether you're going abroad or planning a trip in the United States, take Open Road along on your journey. Our books have been praised by **Travel & Leisure**, **The Los Angeles Times**, **Newsday**, **Booklist**, **US News & World Report**, **Endless Vacation**, **American Bookseller**, **Coast to Coast**, and many other magazines and newspapers!*

Don't just see the world – experience it with Open Road!

ABOUT THE AUTHOR

Julie Fenster is a historian who divides her time between New York City and DeWitt, New York. She is the contributing editor for the upcoming *American Heritage History of the United States* (Viking). Fenster is the author of Open Road Publishing's *Boston Guide*; *Everyday Money* (Literary Guild); and three books on automobile history. She contributes to a variety of publications, such as *American Heritage, The New York Times* and *Muse Magazine* for children; her piece "The Longest Race" for *American Heritage* won honorable mention in the book *Best Sports Writing of 1997*. Another recent honor was the Audio Publishers Association 1997 award for Best Original Script for *Zeus: A Thunderbolt From the Sky*.

Fenster has published a half-dozen articles on the subject of historic grand hotels, an American invention, and has also written about historic restaurants.

BE A TRAVELER, NOT A TOURIST - WITH OPEN ROAD TRAVEL GUIDES!

Open Road Publishing has guide books to exciting, fun destinations on four continents. As veteran travelers, our goal is to bring you the best travel guides available anywhere!

No small task, but here's what we offer:

• All Open Road travel guides are written by authors with a distinct, opinionated point of view – not some sterile committee or team of writers. Our authors are experts in the areas covered and are polished writers.

• Our guides are geared to people who want to make their own travel choices. We'll show you how to discover the real destination – not just see some place from a tour bus window.

• We're strong on the basics, but we also provide terrific choices for those looking to get off the beaten path and experience the country or city – not just see it or pass through it.

• We give you the best, but we also tell you about the worst and what to avoid. Nobody should waste their time and money on their hard-earned vacation because of bad or inadequate travel advice.

• Our guides assume nothing. We tell you everything you need to know to have the trip of a lifetime – presented in a fun, literate, no-nonsense style.

• And, above all, we welcome your input, ideas, and suggestions to help us put out the best travel guides possible.

America's Grand Hotels

BE A TRAVELER - NOT A TOURIST!

Julie Fenster

OPEN ROAD PUBLISHING

This book is dedicated to Tony.

1st Edition

Portions of this book appeared originally in *American Heritage* magazine.
Front cover photo courtesy of The Palmer House Hotel, Chicago, Illinois; top back cover photos courtesy of Historic Hotels of America, Washington, DC (top back cover image, Plaza Hotel, New York City; bottom back cover image, Jefferson Hotel, Richmond, Virginia).

TABLE OF CONTENTS

Contents

Contents

Contents

Contents

Contents

Contents

Contents

1. INTRODUCTION

To stay at a historic hotel is to take a vacation within your vacation, or better yet, a vacation within your business trip. The surroundings will flirt with your imagination, whether the place is a convincing copy of a Renaissance palazzo or the real old West in a rustic mining-town hotel. Just to walk in the door is to be jostled out of the here and now.

Historic hotels are in the midst of a glorious heyday. Across the country, hundreds have been rescued and restored over the past 20 years, thanks to the financial climate, the resurgence of downtowns, and a long-overdue reaction against standardized accommodations.

A generation ago in the 1970's, most vintage hotels were either boarded up or long gone. Even those that were still in business were apt to be tired and worn, or modernized beyond recognition. Travelers who adored grand hotels were limited to a mere handful of them around the country. The Waldorf-Astoria in New York, the Pfister in Milwaukee, the Fairmont in San Francisco: only a few hotels were old and all the more loved for it. However, because the ones that survived were such extraordinary properties, people began to get the idea that a historic grand hotel was necessarily a palace or a "grande dame," as they are often called, those sumptuously decorated big-city hotels. Yet that just isn't so.

Big city palaces have small town cousins. As a matter of fact, times have been even harder on little, old hotels than on big ones and so it is just in the nick of time that many smaller places are now being restored to their original grandeur, whatever it may have been. Even a place with nine rooms can be a superb grand hotel.

With all the restoration that has been going on, you now have a choice across the country of hundreds of grand hotels, if you know where they are. Now you do – *America's Grand Hotels* is the first complete guide. By using it, you can enhance your travels with a memorable hotel in any region and nearly any city. The excitement of staying in a grand hotel is that it is so much a part of a certain time and a specific place, and so we give you a personality profile of each hotel, along with all of the detailed information you'll need to book your room.

America's Grand Hotels was written to tell you about the most attractive and intriguing places to stay, wherever you travel. You'll see just a little more of a city or a town through the windows of a historic grand hotel.

2. OVERVIEW

This is a snobby book, make no mistake: not just any hotel is a grand hotel. There is a whole chapter on what a grand hotel is, but right at the start, we'll tell you what it isn't. It isn't a bed and breakfast created out of a mansion. Besides, you have to tell the proprietor of a B&B your life-story and, even worse, hear theirs. That isn't true at a grand hotel.

A grand hotel isn't an inn that grew out of a tavern. Anyway, you can't tell an inn that you forgot your tie, or your wedding dress or the cage for your rattlesnake, and expect them to go get you one. You can at a grand hotel.

Most of all, a grand hotel is not an apartment building, or anything else, later converted into a hotel. This specification is essential, though it unfortunately rules out swell places like the Pontchartrain (apartment building) in New Orleans and the Bel-Air (real estate office) in Los Angeles. However, to build a grand hotel is a creative effort. To make a conversion is a business decision. We draw the line in this book.

All of the hotels in *America's Grand Hotels* have been restored to modern standards of comfort and safety. They feature clean rooms, decorated with traditional furnishings, in antiques or reproductions. All were either personally inspected by the author or her associates, or are recommended by state tourist boards. This is our way of saying that we have not included any substandard hotels, however historic they may be. We sincerely believe that you will find that the cleanliness and personal safety considerations of every hotel in this book are the equal of any modern hotel.

Conveniences vary: that is the glory of a non-standardized hotel. As noted in the text, a very few still do offer rooms with the bathroom down the hall, but every hotel listed in the book gives you the option of a private privy. As to telephones and televisions, some places pride themselves on having three phones in each guestroom (one in the bathroom) and some pride themselves on having none at all. The ones that do not have telephones and televisions are not being chintzy: they sincerely want the guests to have a historic (and relaxing) experience. These and other amenities are noted for you, in each entry.

Historic hotels are surprisingly inexpensive, in many cases. A marvelous room in a small town hotel is often less than $50. Even in big cities, there is no premium for staying in a "palace," when rooms are commonly less than $125. The rates quoted in this book should be used as a general guide. In reality, the cost of a room goes up and down, depending on predictable factors (such as the season) and unpredictable ones (such as the number of conventions in town on any particular date).

Be sure to ask for a "historic" room when you book reservations. Some hotels have modern towers or additions, and some offer different types of room accommodations, ranging from the quaint to the modern.

We offer this book as a complete guide ... however, the fact is that there are approximately fifty hotels in New York that qualify. Washington and Los Angeles also have a relative abundance of great old hotels. We decided to limit those cities to approximately four examples, up and down the spectrum as to cost, so as to leave space in the book for the fullest range of locales.

Anyone with comments on the hotels listed herewith, or with nominations for our next edition, is invited to write to the author in care of the publisher at: Open Road Publishing, P.O. Box 284, Cold Spring Harbor, N.Y. 11724. All letters will be answered.

3. THE GRAND HOTEL

An American Invention

The era of the grand hotel began in 1827, with the gala opening of the **Tremont House** in Boston. It was so radically new throughout that the most succinct description came from an English minister who hated it. Everyone else just gushed.

The Tremont House was one of the first buildings ever constructed as a hotel, and it was certainly the first one so carefully planned, with 170 guest rooms, all of them private. Breaking with the custom of receiving overnight guests in a barroom, it met them with a spacious lobby, alongside other public rooms – a massive dining room and even a library – in a classical style. Then there were the gadgets: the Tremont started a hotel tradition by making an attraction of itself, an exposition of brand-new technology. The public rooms shone with gaslight. The guest rooms had locks on the doors. There were eight indoor toilets. And in the rooms, guests could call for either water or a bellboy just by pushing one of two buttons on the "electro-magnetic annunciator." The electro-magnetic annunciator tripped a small disk in the main office, indicating the room and request.

The Reverend George Lewis, however, looked past the clever part of the Tremont and recognized the even more cunning sum of its achievement: "You live in a crowd – eat in a crowd, sitting down with fifty, a hundred, sometimes two hundred at table, to which you are summoned by a sonorous Chinese gong. The only place of retirement is your room, to which you have your key."

The Tremont House calculated an effect and then controlled it, artificially stirring the activity in the public rooms, even while offering a respite above. It was the world's first hotel in the modern definition: You lived in a crowd, but your room had a key. That suited the nineteenth century so well that a generation of hotels unabashedly copied it and even made sure of the details by adhering to a book called *A Description of the Tremont House With Architectural Illustrations.*

The Tremont outlasted most of its imitators, and then outlasted its era; it was demolished in 1895. Of all the hotels that have been torn down, burned down, or blown up in this country, the Tremont House is the one that I wish had been saved. I'd be there when they turned on the lights at dusk; I'd wait around one sitting room or another for the sonorous gong, but mostly I'd be in my room, annunciating for water every two minutes or so, electro-magnetically.

Even today, the Tremont House would seem new; ambition that powerful can't age. It would have a good chance of surviving today because historic hotels matter as they never have before. They matter to their cities, which regard them proudly as permanent figureheads, "palaces of the people," in the phrase coined in the 1830's. They matter to investors, because it costs less to restore a luxury hotel than to build a new one, especially with the benefit of tax credits put in place in the early 1980's. Most of all, they matter to travelers, who can find in them just about anything, good or bad, except that blend of the two, standardization.

The Three Characteristics of a Grand Hotel

As an invention, the grand hotel is designed to accomplish a tricky act: to bring people together and yet give them their privacy. The lobbies and lounges, the meeting spaces and guestrooms, room service and bellhops, even mezzanines and balconies are part of the machinery. Inside a grand hotel, you can choose your level of sociability by minute degrees, with ways to be invisible, even in the company of thousands. Or likewise, to demand attention and receive it.

A grand hotel is an indoor extension of its town: the public is allowed inside, and that is a profound part of the invention. A person can make use of a grand hotel without paying anything – that's not true of a club, not of a restaurant, and certainly not of any other private business. The open doors represent a very unique aspect of the grand hotel: it has a covenant with the town around it to welcome any self-respecting citizen who wishes to come in – if only to read a newspaper or to people-watch. A grand hotel belongs to the public.

Third, a grand hotel is a flight of ego. Someone, far back in time, woke up with an idea of *exactly* how the perfect hotel should look and operate. Sometimes the person was a professional hotelier, but much more often, he or she was nothing of the kind. Sometimes the idea and the enthusiasm come from a group, all of one mind. From the Palmer House in Sauk Centre, Minnesota, to the Waldorf-Astoria in New York City, there isn't a hotel in this book that wasn't launched with the expression, "No expense was spared." And no expense was spared, whatever the numerical cost of construction, in the sense that the people behind each of these hotels pushed their own resources and creativity to the very limit.

A grand hotel should not be mistaken for a building – it is an idea that was built.

4. THE PACIFIC

"The cupola also had a very practical purpose. Each day, the Chinese chef of the dining room would climb onto the "Widow's Walk" with his telescope and watch for the arrival of the steamships travelling the coast. His assistant, situated at the waterfront, would meet the ships, canvas arriving passengers and signal the chef how many guest rooms, meals and hot baths to prepare."

– From *The Upham Hotel: Celebrating 125 Years*

ALASKA

Anchorage
ANCHORAGE HOTEL   1936

939 W. Fifth Ave., Anchorage 99501. Tel. 907/272-4553; 800/544-0988. 26 rooms. Rates (seasonal): rooms, $85-189; suites, $105-209.

When the Anchorage Hotel was built in 1916, it was Alaska's biggest and best hotel. Will Rogers and Wiley Post stayed there for two days in 1935, just before taking off for Fairbanks: a flight that ended in the tragic crash that killed them both. In 1936, the Anchorage Hotel added an annex, which is now the entire hotel. (The original 1916 tower was absorbed into the Hilton Hotel, next door, and little remains of the vintage architecture.) The Anchorage is a small hotel with a quiet atmosphere; although it's within a block of the Cook Inlet, the rooms with the best views look up at the mountains.

Amenities: Complimentary continental breakfast, local newspaper; in-room mini-bar, satellite television, hair dryer.

Dining tip: Breakfast is the only meal served at the hotel, but a variety of restaurants are within a block.

Location notes: The Anchorage Hotel is downtown; the Fifth Avenue Mall is two blocks away and Cook Inlet is one block away.

Juneau
WESTMARK BARANOF HOTEL   1939

127 N. Franklin St., Juneau 99801. Tel. 907/586-2660; 800/544-0970; Fax 907/586-8315. 193 rooms. Rates: $65-220.

There are those who say that the reason Juneau became Alaska's capital city was that it had the Baranof. It may be true. And it may be practical: every capital needs at least one chamber in which legislators can speak out of order. The Baranof was the first grandiose hotel in Alaska, and one of the last of this type built anywhere, with marble columns and plush carpets, and a purposefully old-fashioned idea of style. It is a comfortable hotel that seems to be busy all the time.

Amenities: Room service; business services; free parking; in-room satellite television.

Dining tip: The Bubble Room is named after a painting, "The Bubble Lady," that hung in the room when it was called the Latchstring Lounge.

Location notes: The Baranof is in the historic part of downtown Juneau.

Ketchikan
NEW YORK HOTEL   1925

207 Stedman St., Ketchikan 99901. Tel. 907/225-0246. 8 rooms. Rates: $49-54.50

None of the million dollar – or even $80 million – restorations described in this book are more impressive than that of the New York Hotel, on the Ketchikan Creek in Ketchikan, Alaska. The first owners, George and Yayoko Shimizu, built the New Yorker in 1925: a two-story clapboard building with a storefront cafe facing

Creek Street. You can still see one moment of the construction with perfect clarity: where the whole kitchen makes an abrupt zig-zag to get around a big rock. (*Always* move the rock before starting the kitchen.) The Shimizus left the deed to the hotel to their daughters, who never changed a thing, not even the old rule forbidding taking baths any day but Saturday. By 1985, though, the business was all finished and no guests came anymore. The building remained, but even it was leaning forward wearily. Time had changed anything it could, from the roof down to the pilings.

Fred Ochsner bought the New Yorker and devoted six years of his own time to it. First, he replaced the pilings: no simple task. After further repairs to the exterior, he reduced the number of guestrooms to eight from 18, equipping each with a private bathroom. "He studied old windows and copied their details," according to a hotel brochure, "those little blocks of wood underneath that allow windows to sweat and drip in wet climates without rotting them out. He saved every scrap of wood that could be reused. He saved and patiently cleaned and restored original doors and woodwork, hardware and light fixtures. He sanded, stained, painted and decorated."

In 1991, the New York opened again for business. Fred Ochsner is proud to say that he is only the second owner it has ever had.

Amenities: Rooms have telephones, cable television, antique furniture and clothes-presses.

Dining tip: The Cafe has an antique, carved bar-back, thought to have been salvaged by the Shimizus from a saloon that closed during Prohibition.

Location notes: Ketchikan is Alaska's most southeasterly city. The hotel is situated downtown, adjacent to shopping and dining.

CALIFORNIA

Berkeley
THE DURANT   1928

2600 Durant Ave., Berkeley 94704. Tel. 510/845-8981; 800/238-7268; Fax 510/486-8336. 140 rooms. Rates: rooms, $109-149; suites, $212-334.

"I came with college 'on the brain,'" Henry Durant told a colleague in 1873, describing the day, 18 years before, when he arrived in Northern California determined to start educating the whole state, as soon as possible. Durant was a Yale man, who went on to an undistinguished academic career, working as a tutor: perhaps that left him free to bolt for the coast in 1855, with an early retirement and high intentions. He found wealthy people, who were inclined to give money, but it took decades of meetings – and other delays – before the University of California finally emerged.

Durant was the very man who picked out Berkeley's hillsides as the site for the campus. He even had a short term as its first president, although the trustees soon found out that he was better suited to starting a college than running one. Nonetheless, by way of tribute, the Hotel Durant was named for the man without whom Berkeley's median I.Q. would be much lower today. It is vaguely Bavarian-looking inside, with plain white walls and wood-beam ceilings and mouldings. The rooms are traditional in decor, and most overlook either the University of California campus or the San Francisco Bay.

Amenities: Complimentary continental breakfast; valet parking; business services; room service.

Dining tip: Henry's Publick House serves American food in an English atmosphere.

Location notes: The Durant is two blocks from the University of California campus.

THE SHATTUCK   1910

2086 Allston Way, Berkeley 94704. Tel. 510/845-7300; 800/237-5359; Fax 510/644-2088. 175 rooms. Rates: rooms, $69-100; suites, $100 and up.

The Shattuck Hotel is an Edwardian-era hotel, with a leaded glass entryway, arched windows and Corinthian pillars in some of the public rooms. It has been refurbished with a mixture of traditional and contemporary furnishings: there is little danger of being confused about what year you're in while here. The location is excellent, a block from the University of California campus.

Amenities: Complimentary continental breakfast; health club pass; business services.

Dining tip: The dining room serves Southwestern cuisine.

Location notes: The Shattuck is downtown, adjacent to shops and restaurants. It is within a block of the Berkeley campus and a BART station.

Columbia
CITY HOTEL   1871

P.O. Box 1870, 22768 Main St., Columbia, 95310. Tel. 209/532-1479; 800/532-1479; Fax 209/532-7027; web, www.cityhotel.com. 10 rooms. Rates: $75-95, including breakfast.

In 1857, a hotel called the What Cheer House opened in Columbia, California. Cheap John Louis' auction rooms were on the second floor, though they were soon replaced by the Columbia Opera House – and one hopes that there were those who noticed the difference. By the end of the 1860's, though, Columbia's gold mines were petering out and its heyday was over. As to the What Cheer, a fire swept through it in 1867; a replacement was built in 1871, soon renamed the "City Hotel." Columbia meandered through the following century only as a place to be picked over by smalltime goldminers, pouncing on specks.

The whole town of Columbia remains a well-preserved monument to the Gold Rush days of the mid- and later 19th-century. In fact, the 1954 movie *High Noon* was filmed in Columbia. The City

Hotel is now itself an artifact, left over from time and owned by the state. Two stories in brick, overlooking a shady, uncrowded street, the hotel is faithfully but simply furnished. Both the City Hotel and the Fallon Hotel (see below) are operated as part of the Hospitality Management Program of Columbia College.

Amenities: Air conditioning; private bathrooms, but showers down the hall; pay phone in the lobby. Complimentary breakfast, and sherry hour for guests.

Dining tip: The City Hotel dining room claims to have one of the finest wine-lists in the state.

Location notes: The hotel is within the Gold Rush town of Columbia, about 140 miles east of San Francisco.

FALLON HOTEL   1857

P.O. Box 1870, Columbia 95310. Tel. 209/532-1470. Rates: $55-95, including breakfast.

The Fallon House was built as a place for miners to live, to meet and to keep up their hopes. But the Fallon also represents the history of entertainment in the typical Gold Rush town of Columbia: in 1886, a simple music hall was built to adjoin the hotel. By the end of the century, it was a legitimate theater, and in the 1920's, it gave way to the dance craze and then to the movie craze. For the past 50 years, however, the hall has reverted to its dignified role as a stage, and a respected local group keeps it lit through most of the year.

Rather plainer than the City Hotel and just down the street from it, the Fallon House is a brick building with stark white trim. It is under the same management as the City Hotel.

Coulterville
HOTEL JEFFERY   1851

One Main St., Coulterville 95311. Tel. 209/878-3471; 800/464-3471. 21 rooms. Rates: rooms, $59-74; suites, $99-173.

The Jeffery was started in 1851 as a hotel for people who were on their way to Yosemite. It survived the years and remained in the same family by catering to prospectors, tourists, pioneers, politicians and anyone else who happened by in the High Sierras. The hotel is a three-story building, in white and blue, with a portico across the second story and a garden in the back: shady places to while away an hour.

Amenities: Free parking.

Dining tip: The Magnolia Saloon and Grill is the hotel's dining room.

Location notes: The Hotel Jeffery is in the historic town of Coulterville and walking tours are available. It is 135 miles to San Francisco and 31 miles to Yosemite.

Eureka
THE EUREKA INN   1922

518 Seventh St., Eureka 95501. Tel. 707/442-6441; 800/862-4906; Fax 707/442-0637. 105 rooms and suites. Rates: rooms, $110-250; suites, $250.

The town of Eureka faces the Pacific Ocean in Northern California, generally surrounded by redwood forests. In 1920, the more ambitious citizens decided that Eureka possessed just about everything ... except a decent hotel. And so a public stock subscription was tendered in order to raise money for one. The new Eureka Inn was Tudor in style: best of all, to a Eurekan, it had lots of redwood inside. The Inn opened in 1922, expanded once in 1925, and was a longtime success. By the 1950's, though, it needed work – basic structural upkeep, and such profits as it generated would not cover new expenditures.

The hotel seemed doomed to close, until a local resident named Helen Barnum decided that if the town had needed the hotel in 1922, it still needed it in 1960; she bought a controlling interest in the Eureka Inn and invested her own money to restore it. The townspeople built it, but Barnum saved it. More recent owners have added 1990's innovations, such as a Monday cigar club, without taking away the 1920's ones, such as a shoeshine stand in the lobby.

Amenities: fitness center, some rooms with fireplaces; handicap-accessible rooms; meeting facilities.

Dining tip: Live jazz music is a specialty of the hotel's Palm Lounge.

Location notes: The inn is five blocks from Eureka's Historic Old Town District.

LaJolla
LA VALENCIA HOTEL   1926

1132 Prospect St., LaJolla 92037. Tel. 619/454-0771; 800/451-0772; Fax Z619/456-3921; Telex #183959. 100 rooms. Rates: rooms, $170-370; suites, $400-675.

The La Valencia Hotel was built in 1926 on an enviable site overlooking the Pacific Ocean from the town of LaJolla. It started out as a comfortable California ramble of a building, settling rooms against each and the outdoors, and expanded through its first twenty-five years into several additions, a tower and even another hotel next door.

It was an expensive hotel from the first, charging $10 per night at a time when a fine hotel elsewhere might charge $2, and it depended heavily on the Hollywood community, about 120 miles to the north. The first wave of famous guests included Greta Garbo and John Gilbert, Charles Chaplin and Mary Pickford. However, even in the Depression, the hotel refused to slip from its level of service; the original owners lost control in 1936, but even then, La Valencia's reputation remained secure, a place of polished tiles and comfortable chaises. At most hotels, guests steal things from the rooms – a number of pieces at La Valencia were actually sent by loyal guests, who felt sure that a certain antique was just exactly what some room or corner needed.

According to a booklet written by Bruce Dexter, a communal jigsaw-puzzle in one of the lounges represents the fact that "every visitor to the hotel added a little something of themselves, to help form the overall picture of La Valencia." (One guest had her chauffeur filch the whole puzzle in her determination to finish it, even at home; she returned it later.) During World War Two, Dexter noted, guests were expected to take their turns on the roof, watching for the planes of an enemy attack.

The town of LaJolla has grown all around the La Valencia in the past forty years. Now a downtown hotel as much as a beach hotel, La Valencia certainly helped to set the atmosphere of what has developed into a very sophisticated community.

Amenities: individually decorated rooms, television, VCR, views of the sea, gardens or town, room service, concierge, spa, swimming pool, gym and sauna, meeting facilities.

Dining Tip: The Sky Room, La Valencia's *haute cuisine* restaurant, only has twelve tables, all overlooking the water.

Location notes: La Jolla is about 15 miles north of San Diego.

Los Angeles
BEVERLY HILLS HOTEL   1912

9641 Sunset Blvd., Beverly Hills 90210. Tel. 310/276-2251; 800/283-8885; Fax 310/281-2905; web, www.beverlyhillshotel.com. 203 rooms, including bungalows. Rates: rooms, $275-350; suites, $625-3,000; bungalows, $595-3,050.

The sparse tract of land between northwest Los Angeles and the beach at Santa Monica was called Rancho de las Aguas when Burton Green purchased it in 1906. Green's newly formed company, Rodeo Land and Water, had plans to build a new community on the land, something like sunny, ultra-exclusive Pasadena, only even sunnier and more ultra.

The first thing the company did was build was a hotel – no, the first thing the company did was rename Rancho de las Aguas "Beverly Hills." The second thing it did was build a great hotel to accommodate prospective residents and to demonstrate just how enticing the rubbly hills could be, once they were developed. The hotel was built of stucco in the California-mission style, with three towers, and turrets on the corners of the three-story building. The exterior was painted pink. Set on the rise of a hill, the Beverly Hills Hotel opened May 1, 1912 to command its unbuilt empire.

Initially, the Beverly Hills development was supposed to be far above and well beyond the reach of people working in Hollywood's burgeoning movie business, which was still rather cheap and nasty in 1912. However, movie-star salaries soared in the later part of the 1910's, as great movie studios moved west from New York or grew from nothing in and around Los Angeles.

Meanwhile, the Beverly Hills Hotel, managed by an astute hotelier named Mrs. Margaret Anderson, was proving to be a bigger success with oldline Easterners than was the town around it. Many people arrived intending to buy a winter house, but contented themselves instead with a stay in one of the hotel's bungalows. That didn't help the local real estate market. Inevitably, the new town changed its opinion of movie-folk ... especially rich ones. Mary Pickford and Douglas Fairbanks Jr. broke the trail between Hollywood and Beverly Hills, and they were followed by other stars, including Will Rogers. When Rogers was elected mayor of Beverly Hills in 1923, the inauguration ceremony took place on the grounds of the hotel.

The Beverly Hills Hotel has been intertwined with the movie business ever since: every star's next door neighbor. Katharine Hepburn jumped into the pool fully clothed after a tennis game – actually, it being Hepburn, she dove. Spencer Tracy, who drank hard and played polo hard, was one of a crowd of players for whom the famous Polo Lounge was named in 1940 (formerly it was the much less manly "Le Jardin.") Of all the gossip that is repeated about celebrities and the Beverly Hills Hotel, however, the strangest is the saddest, that Howard Hughes would direct room-service waiters to deliver his food to a tree outside his bungalow. When he was sure he was not being watched, he would sneak out and take it.

Mrs. Anderson, the hotel manager, took advantage of an option to purchase the Beverly Hills Hotel in 1920, paying $500,000. She sold the property for five times that amount just before the Stock Market Crash in 1929. Ultimately, the Bank of America was the owner throughout most of the Depression, and one of its executives banded together with stars (including Loretta Young and Irene Dunne) to buy the Beverly Hills Hotel in 1941. The value of the hotel has done almost nothing since but increase: 12 acres of groomed gardens, 21 bungalows and the original main building, along with its rather undistinguished later addition. (The most recent purchase price was $176 million.) From the first, the Beverly Hills Hotel has aspired to that atmosphere known as "casual elegance," but an even more rarified atmosphere has settled in about the place recently, as it became a hub for the movie industry: the atmosphere of casual power.

Amenities: Concierge; 24-room service; complimentary limousine service, shoeshine and daily paper; business services; swimming pool; tennis courts; in-room three telephones; fax machine and printer; marble bathrooms fully fitted, including for example, electronic drapes.

Dining tip: The Fountain Coffee Shop is original to its 1949 soda-fountain appearance. (And one is almost as likely to spot a celebrity there as in the vaunted Polo Lounge.)

Location Notes: The Beverly Hills Hotel is two blocks from Rodeo Drive, and 20 minutes by car from the Los Angeles airport.

REGENT BEVERLY WILTSHIRE   1927

9500 Wilshire Blvd., Beverly Hills 90212. Tel. 310/275-5200; 800/545-4000; Fax 310/274-2851. 275 rooms. Rates: rooms, $295-450; suites, $495-5,000.

The Beverly Wiltshire has been staring right down Rodeo Drive since before the first Giorgio bag plopped into the backseat of a Mercedes SL. It is a substantial hotel, in Italian Renaissance style, that has never gone out of style, despite being itself governed by tradition rather than fashion.

Amenities: Business center; Concierge; swimming pool; full spa; in-room dual lines, dataport, hair dryer; mini-bar, fax machine on request. Each guest is greeted with a serving of fresh strawberries and brown sugar

Dining tip: The dining room serves haute cuisine, influenced by the health and diet considerations that are ever-present in Beverly Hills.

Location notes: There are 123 restaurants within walking distance of the Beverly Wiltshire, and at least as many shops. The hotel is about a half-hour from LAX by car.

CHATEAU MARMONT   1929

8221 Sunset Blvd., Hollywood 90046. Tel. 213/656-1010; 800/ 242-8328; Fax 213/655-5311. 63 rooms and bungalows. Rooms, $205; suites, $265-1800; bungalows, $285-900.

The beauty of the Chateau Marmont in the olden days was that it was in Hollywood – and it wasn't. Tucked just off the main drag of the Sunset Strip, it always looked like a movie set, a chateau indeed, with stony turrets and porticos. For years, Broadway actors and actresses, writers and musicians, automatically booked themselves into the Chateau Marmont. A hotel that sat in the California sun, so obviously daydreaming of the Loire Valley, or someplace, appealed to "creative types" from back east. They didn't feel as though they belonged in Hollywood, either, and swore they wouldn't stay long. But sometimes it seems that anyone who *can* stay in Hollywood ends up doing so. Look at the Chateau Marmont.

By the 1970's, though, when the Chateau's own glamour had grown stale, it became a cliché for old Hollywood. Going there was like walking through lost footage from *Sunset Boulevard*. But then, Hollywood loves a cliché, and so the Chateau Marmont was eventually rediscovered, beheld as glamorous all over again. New management in 1990 refurbished the public rooms, without masking or particularly updating the cool, quiet decor of the castle. Guestrooms and bungalows received a firmer hand; they are undoubtedly modern, but with retro furniture still somehow befitting a 1929 castle. As ever, the Chateau Marmont can be the most public place in town, or the most private and quiet. It just depends on what kind of star you are. Or want to be.

Amenities: Valet parking, pool, 24-hour room service and shoeshine, fitness room, in-room VCR, safe and mini-bar; complimentary cell-phone.

Dining tip: The hotel's dining room is open all day and serves California cuisine.

Location notes: The Chateau Marmont is on the west side of Hollywood, near the town border with Beverly Hills. It is about six blocks away from the cluster of studios in Hollywood.

THE GEORGIAN   1933

1415 Ocean Ave., Santa Monica 90401. Tel. 310/395-9945; 800/ 678-8946; 310/451-3374; e-mail, goergian@earthlink.net; web, www.georgianhotel.com. 84 rooms. Rates: rooms, $165-200; suites, $285-315.

The Georgian is a beach hotel along Ocean Avenue in Santa Monica. It is one of the best locations around, across the street from the pier and the beach. Santa Monica's eclectic shopping and restaurant "promenade" is just two blocks in the other direction. An eight-story building in early art-deco style, it still retains its gentle lines in some of the interior rooms. But the light mood of the beach is its real signature.

Amenities: Concierge; valet parking; shoeshine; in-room coffeemakers; mini-bars.

Dining tip: When the hotel opened, it had a bar popular with movie stars, including Clark Gable and Carole Lombard. The hotel calls it the "Speakeasy" and serves breakfast there.

Location notes: The Georgian is across the street from the beach in Santa Monica.

THE HOLLYWOOD ROOSEVELT   1927

7000 Hollywood Blvd., Hollywood 90028. Tel. 213/466-7000; 800/ 950-7667; Fax 213/466-9376.; web, htp//www.hotelchoice.com. 358 rooms; 65 cabana rooms. Rates: rooms, $119-169; suites, $299-1,200. The Roosevelt is a Clarion Hotel.

By the mid-1920's, Hollywood was awash in two things: spare cash and visitors on the hoof. Charles Toberman, a local business-man, put the two together in his mind and envisioned a grand hotel for the town (officially a part of Los Angeles, but busily forging a life of its own). Toberman gathered movie moguls and a few actors, including Mary Pickford and Douglas Fairbanks Sr., in an investment group, and started work on a hotel smack in the heart of Hollywood.

The Roosevelt was built in the Spanish Revival style, a way of using the space and light to cheerful effect: in the public rooms the walls are cream white, it is the ceilings that do all the fascinating. The Roosevelt was the backdrop for many premieres, since it is across from the Chinese Theatre formerly owned by Sidney Grauman. The hotel itself was the stage for the first Academy Awards presentation in 1929. Probably every movie-star, along with every second-banana, bit player and trick-horse, attended at least one function at the Roosevelt Hotel over the years: Hollywood was their company town and the Roosevelt was its hub. Marilyn Monroe often chose to stay at the hotel, in one of the cabana rooms that overlook the pool; a good choice still for someone who wants both privacy and company at the same time.

Amenities: Valet parking; business center; Olympic-size swimming pool; exercise room; in-room safe, hair-dryer, iron, coffeemaker, and mini-bar.

Dining tip: The Cinegrill books nationally known cabaret acts.

Location notes: The Roosevelt is in Hollywood's business district, across the street from the famous Chinese Theater. It is about 6 miles from downtown Los Angeles.

Monterey
MONTEREY HOTEL   1904

406 Alvarado St., Monterey 93940. Tel. 408/375-3184; 800/727-0960; Fax 408/373-2899. Forty-five rooms. Rates: rooms, $129-159; suites, $189-229.

By 1980, the Monterey Hotel was still a beautiful building – even under layers of appalling wallpaper, sloppy paint and plywood. Somewhere under all of it, nonetheless, there was a stunning hotel. Carl Johnson, head of a company called Vintage Hotels, happened to be walking past it one day in 1982, when he caught a glimpse through the front door and sensed the potential. The Monterey was built in 1902 with a Beaux Arts exterior, and a sedate, woodsy interior. Johnson was certainly right about the property's potential, but, in a miscalculation typical in the historic hotel business, he rather underestimated the effort of resuscitating it. Scheduling a six month renovation in his mind, he bought the hotel ... it was three years before the Monterey was ready to re-open. Johnson's pride and joy was the original Hammond elevator, with its gilt-edge caging: it was a marvel in 1902, and it is still one today. The current owner went even further, refurbishing Johnson's renovation, while making the guestrooms quite contemporary.

Amenities: Complimentary breakfast and afternoon refreshments; cable television, valet parking, in-room dataports.

Dining tip: Breakfast is the only meal served at the hotel.

Location notes: Fisherman's Wharf is a five-minute walk from the Monterey Hotel; the Conference Center is one block away.

Nevada City
NATIONAL HOTEL 1852

211 Broad St., Nevada City 95959. Tel. 916/265-4551. 43 rooms. Rates: rooms, $42-68; suites, $96-124.

The National Hotel is a handsome mid-Victorian Hotel, filled with antiques, some of which have been in place almost since the beginning, a long, long time ago.

Amenities: Free parking; swimming pool; in-room telephones.

Dining tip: The ornate back bar in the saloon was originally in the dining room of the Spreckels mansion in San Francisco.

Location notes: Nevada City is about 60 miles from Sacramento and 90 miles from Reno.

Pasadena
RITZ-CARLTON HUNTINGTON HOTEL   1907
1401 S. Oak Knoll Ave., Pasadena 91106. Tel. 818/568-3900; 800/784-3748; Fax 818/568-3700. 387 rooms. Rates: rooms, $185-310; $400-2,000.

Pasadena is the most eastern city on the west coast, and the Huntington was built at the height of its popularity with very rich sun-seekers from across the continent. It is a large hotel set in its own 23-acre park, a leisurely place even though it is less than a half-hour's drive to downtown Los Angeles or Beverly Hills. The Huntington is nothing if not spacious, with clubby, English-style rooms; many of the guestrooms open onto a terrace or balcony.

Amenities: Valet parking; concierge; exercise spa; swimming pool; tennis courts; 24-hour rooms service; in-room refrigerator/mini-bar, marble bathroom.

Dining tip: The dining rooms offer a low-calorie menu called Fitness Cuisine.

Location notes: The hotel is in a residential section of Pasadena.

San Diego
HORTON GRAND   1886
311 Island Ave., San Diego 92101. Tel. 619/544-1886; 800/542-1886; Fax 619/239-3823; web, www.hortongrand.com. 132 rooms. Rates: rooms, $119 and up; suites, $218 and up.

The Grand Horton Hotel and the Brooklyn Hotel were both brand new in 1886, and not too far from one another in the fledgling town of San Diego. Yet, if they had been people, not hotels, it is safe to say that they would have had nothing to say to each other. The Grand Horton was Viennese in personality, ornate and haughty. The Brooklyn was Victorian in a rugged way, and Western to the core. They would have been shocked to learn that they were going to be married, very late in life.

Both hotels had started to slide, even by the 1910's, when they weren't really very old. The Brooklyn was being called "The

Brooklyn-Kahle Saddlery Hotel," which certainly kept it from being confused with any other saddlery hotel, but the fact was that it had become a mere afterthought to the business on the first floor. The Grand Horton was in far worse shape: it was a whorehouse. In the 1970's, they narrowly avoided destruction and were sold for $1 each. New owners had them carefully dismantled, and stored in a warehouse. In 1986, they were reassembled, amazingly enough. Now they are together forever whether they like it or not, in a hotel re-opened as the Horton Grand.

Whatever remained of the interiors was augmented with period furnishings, so that the atmosphere is Victorian and rooms individually decorated. The owners have a good deal of wit in treasuring bits of the hotel's double-past. "Sunshine," the papier-mache horse who made the saddle-store a local landmark, now graces the lobby – of what some may wish to think of as the Horton Grand Saddlery Hotel.

Amenities: Historical tours of the hotel are given Wednesdays at 3 pm. Free airport shuttle; business services; valet parking.

Dining tip: The hotel's Sunday brunch is served in its open-air courtyard.

Location notes: The Horton Grand is a landmark of the lively Gaslamp Quarter.

U.S. GRANT   1910

326 Broadway, San Diego 92101. Tel. 619/232-3121; 800/237-5029; Fax 619/232-3626. 280 rooms. Rates: rooms, $155-195; suites, $275-1,500.

In 1895, Mrs. Fannie Grant purchased a hotel in downtown San Diego and ten years later, she began building a replacement for it, to be named after her late husband, Ulysses S. Grant. The hotel was largely her son's project, but he proved to be only slightly better at managing money than his father – who was often broke. With delays for refinancing, the hotel finally opened in 1910. It was the city's most deluxe hotel, and one of the biggest, with over 400 rooms.

Light in color, the U.S. Grant has two six-story wings, joined by a low center section which is dominated from the back by a temple-like tower. The design was unusual, but it seemed to open the massive building up to the San Diego skies. The interiors were rather subdued, and they were extensively remodelled in the late 1920's, to reflect a European flamboyance. As the U.S. Grant transformed itself into a convention hotel during the 1950's and 1960's, it left more and more of its past behind. In 1982, it was at a turning point, ultimately closing for the renovation that would return it to its heyday again. It reopened in 1986.

Amenities: Concierge; valet parking; 24-hour room service; in-room dual telephone, mini-bar, coffee-maker.

Dining tip: The Grant Grill has always been a popular chop-house in San Diego.

Location notes: The U.S. Grant is across the street from the Horton Plaza Shopping Mall and the Civic Center.

San Francisco
THE FAIRMONT   1906

California & Mason Sts., San Francisco 94106. Tel. 415/772-5000; 800/527-4727; Fax 415/415/781-4027. 600 rooms. Rates: rooms, $199-349; suites, $500-8,000.

The Fairmont Hotel was just about to open when it was gutted by the fire that followed the San Francisco Earthquake of 1906. The pristine white building was supposed to complement the mansions with which, if not for the fire, it would have shared Nob Hill. Even so, the Fairmont represents their style. For years, it had its own terraced lawns leading down the crest of a hill to a swimming pool, where guests lounged and watched the boats go by in the bay. In 1962, the configuration closed in, as a new tower took the place of the pool (one small patch of lawn remains between the two buildings.

The rooms in the tower, by and large, have the best views. However, the best thing about the tower is that it leaves the main building to remain all of one piece (mostly an oversized piece): five-foot-wide windows that can be opened with a pinkie; hallways that are wide, high-ceilinged, and soft enough for a quiet game of football; and the staircase to the lobby. There are elevators, of course, best used for going up, but that Fairmont staircase is the perfect invention for going down. Massive as it is in white marble, it does not crassly march into the lobby; it insinuates itself, expertly. You can stand just out of sight and spy on the people in advance or make a grand entrance, entirely aware and seemingly oblivious.

Amenities: Garage; complimentary ride to financial district; exercise room; valet; 24-hour room service; in-room dataport.

Dining tip: You can go up in the tower for a meal with a view of the Bay at the Crown Restaurant. The Top of the Mark at the Mark Hopkins hotel across the street from the Fairmont, is a cocktail lounge with traditions going back to World War Two.

Location notes: The Fairmont is on the crest of Nob Hill.

PALACE   1909

2 New Montgomery St., San Francisco 94105. Tel. 415/512-1111; 800/335-3589; Fax 415/543-0671. 550 rooms. Rates: rooms, $300-360; suites, $500-3,000.

The first "Palace Hotel" in San Francisco was a basement flophouse for hundreds of Chinese workers in the Barbary Coast. As a building, the second Palace Hotel was more accurately named; built in 1875, it was the second largest hotel in the world, with conveniences in every room. Richard D'Oyly Carte was so impressed by it that he resolved to build an American-style hotel where it was needed most – overseas. He went home and opened the Savoy Hotel in London in 1889.

In 1906, on the morning of the San Francisco earthquake and fire, the guests at the Palace thought they had escaped, even as the building was still shaking. Out on the sidewalk, though, as a guest recalled, "the air was filled with falling stones." Six hours later, as the fire swept up Market Street, one of the last telegraph messages to come out of the city during the calamity read, "Back of the Palace Hotel is a furnace." In the aftermath, a looter was hanged off a beam protruding from the entrance of the Palace; meanwhile, at the corner, a singer on tour from the Metropolitan Opera was in hysterics and practicing random snippets of song. Even as a burned-out hulk, the old Palace was full of diversions.

The new Palace Hotel, which opened in 1909, was never quite forgiven for not being the old Palace Hotel, for daring to replace the irreplaceable. That was misguided loyalty. The Palace has been recently restored with terrific integrity. The workers buffed the whole place to a shine, without taking away the patina of its years.

The heart of the hotel is the Garden Court, one of the most beautiful rooms in the country. And when one is in it, it is hard to remember the others. Somewhere just short of the sky, there is a delicate leaded-glass ceiling, with pillars leading out of the marble floor to it. The Garden Court has an Edwardian look: the potted palms, the judicious use of gilt, and an unharried arrangement of furniture. The hotel knows what it has: the Garden Court is used daily for breakfast, lunch, tea, cocktails, dinner, dancing and late supper.

Amenities: Valet parking; indoor swimming pool; 24-hour room service; business center; in-room dataport.

Dining tip: The Garden Court serves some recipes from the opening days of the hotel, including for example, raspberry crepes.

Location notes: The Palace Hotel is located in midtown San Francisco. It is two blocks from the convention center; four blocks to Union Square, and two miles to Ghirardelli Square.

THE ST. FRANCIS   1904

335 Powell St., San Francisco 94102. Tel. 415/397-7000; 800/228-3000; Fax 415/774-0124. 1,115 rooms. Rates: rooms, $195-345; suites, $225-1,700. The St. Francis is a Westin Hotel.

The "St. Francis" is nothing if not sturdy, surviving not only the famous Earthquake and Fire of 1906, but the intervening 20th century, as well. Presiding over the epicenter of the city, Union Square, the hotel just kept growing even as other hotels its age were fading off the scene, temporarily or permanently.

The St. Francis started out in 1906 with about a hundred rooms, but today it has more than ten times that number. It is possibly the hardest working hotel in the country, seeming at times more like an outpost of Grand Central Station, with crowds of individuals and groups almost constantly swelling through the bevy of lobbies, which range from the palatial to the airport-ish. The hotel has just completed a restoration costing $50 million, which is a lot of money. Yet, the hotel had a $50 million restoration only ten years ago. That is a short lesson in the reality of keeping a turn-of-the-century hotel in shape to accommodate thousands of people day in and day out.

Amenities: Concierge; business center; in-room dataport, mini-bars.

Dining Tip: On the 32nd floor of the tower is a nightspot called Club Oz, where the dance floor is decorated by views of the city.

Location Notes: The St. Francis is on Union Square, adjacent to shopping. It is about five blocks to Nob Hill: straight up.

THE STANYAN PARK   1904

750 Stanyan St., San Francisco 94117. Tel. 415/751-1000; Fax 415/668-5454; web, www.stanyanpark.com; e-mail, info@stanyanpark.com. 36 rooms. Rates: rooms, $99-145; suites, $185-225.

Golden Gate Park, which is a couple of miles from the bridge of the same name, was San Francisco's first official recreation area, with its own beach. People stomped out there even before there were roads, and long before there were museums, stadiums and horseback-riding rings. However, once those attractions began to be developed in the 1880's, Golden Gate Park became a veritable resort for San Franciscans and even more farflung visitors. Boarding houses and hotels began to spring up on Stanyan Street, the park's east border.

To all of that, Mr. Harry P. Heagerty was rather oblivious. He owned a saloon on Stanyan with a crackerjack location: it was tucked right next to a ballpark, the Haight Street Grounds, in which the California League played baseball. However, when the League moved to a bigger Grounds in 1897, Heagerty had no choice but to turn to the tourists, soon replacing his saloon with the best hotel on the street. "Their ornamentation was classical in vocabulary, but not in placement," said the Department of the Interior of the architects, in placing the hotel on the National Register of Historic Places. That means, perhaps, that it is a swell building, but it doesn't quite look like anything else. It is three stories, distinguished by a fanciful turret on the corner and there are guestrooms within the turret. Many of the rooms overlook the park.

The Stanyan Park Hotel has been restored with a commendably gentle sensibility regarding Victorian style, using some antiques, reproduction furniture, and soft colors.

Amenities: Complimentary breakfast; in-room television and telephone. All rooms have private bathroom.

Dining tip: The hotel only serves breakfast and afternoon tea, both of which are complimentary for guests.

Location notes: The Stanyan Park Hotel is located across the street from Golden Gate Park; it is within six blocks of the University of California at San Francisco or the University of San Francisco (and the old Haight-Asbury "hippie" neighborhood), and about two miles to the Civic Center. The hotel is on bus and trolley lines.

YORK HOTEL   1922

940 Sutter St., San Francisco 94109. Tel. 415/885-6800; 800/808-9675; Fax 415/885-2115; web, www.citysearch.com/sfo/yorkhotel. 96 rooms. Rates (seasonal): rooms, $129-149; suites, $175-210.

In the movie *Vertigo*, Kim Novak played – not to spoil it for those who haven't seen the movie – a couple of characters, the second of whom had a swell apartment in San Francisco. The character could have anything she wanted, as long as she dyed her hair and wore somebody else's clothes. But what the viewers never found out was that the apartment-house depicted as hers in the movie was in reality the York Hotel – *pretending* to be an apartment house. The York Hotel was built in 1922, and *Vertigo* was not its first brush with glamour.

The hotel housed one of the city's popular speakeasies, according to the stories. The former speakeasy, now called the Plush Bar, is a cabaret, noted mostly for its stained-glass ceiling and for booking big-name acts on weekends. The rest of the hotel is much more subdued, however, with a bright and airy lobby, painted yellow and accented by classical columns and cornices in white.

Amenities: Complimentary continental breakfast; valet parking; exercise room; concierge; in-room dataport, safe, mini-bar, coffee-maker.

Dining tip: Breakfast is the only meal served at the hotel, though there are myriad ethnic restaurants within a four block radius.

Location notes: The York is five blocks from Union Square; six from Grace Cathedral and 10 blocks from Chinatown.

San Jose
HYATT SAINTE CLAIRE   1926

302 S. Market St., San Jose 95113. Tel. 408/885-1234; 800/492-8822; Fax 408/977-0403; web, http://www.hyatt.com. 187 rooms. Rates (seasonal): rooms, $230-260; suites, start at $270

The Sainte Claire was designed by the same architectural firm responsible for the Beverly Wiltshire (see above), a group far less rooted in the region than most West Coast firms. The exterior of the Sainte Claire is more typical of its time, the 1920's, than its place, California. Presiding over downtown San Jose from a corner location, it is a six story brick building with classical details, fanning away from its main entrance on the corner.

The guestrooms, on the other hand, are undoubtedly rooted in San Jose – and are absolutely state-of-the art. They have computers fully stacked with software, along with printers and modems and other things that grow like crops in the Silicon Valley, which happens to be just outside the window. The public rooms downstairs at the Sainte Claire are handsome and pristinely maintained, combining marble floors and wood paneling. The main lounge has a feature that is state-of-the-art in many a historic hotel: a couple of armchairs, looking into the fire.

Amenities: Shuttle to San Jose airport; valet parking; 24-room service; concierge; fitness center; in-room feather bed, computer, printer/copier, safes, iron.

Dining tip: The hotel restaurant serves Italian cuisine.

Location notes: The Sainte Claire is located in downtown San Jose, adjacent to many shops and restaurants.

Santa Barbara
FOUR SEASONS BILTMORE   1927

1260 Channel Dr., Santa Barbara 93108. Tel. 805/969-2261; 800/ 332-3443; Fax 805/969-4212. 234 rooms. Rates: rooms, $360/450; suites, $750-1900.

The Biltmore was planned as a hotel, but designed to resemble a hacienda. It doesn't rise up high, it rambles, instead, and nowhere is it taller than the average palm tree. Insinuated into gardens and terraces, the buildings that make up the hotel are constructed in white stucco with red-tile roofing. The Santa Barbara Biltmore was opened by John Bowman, the head of a chain of hotels named for "Biltmore," the famous Vanderbilt estate in North Carolina.

The location, along the curve of the beach, yet part of downtown Santa Barbara, allowed the property to double as a resort and as the city's grand hotel. Neither was much in demand, however, in 1936, when the Biltmore empire was worn down by the Depression and the Santa Barbara property was sold on the courthouse steps at a sheriff's auction, for about $500,000. It was an ignominious moment for the $2,000,000 property. Nonetheless, the new owner was ideal: he was Robert Odell, a hard-headed hotelier with a soft spot for the Santa Barbara Biltmore. Odell operated it at a loss for the following 35 years, as though he were willing to support the delicate creature ... but only if it were perfect. He gained a reputation as a demon boss, but if he were a perfectionist, at least he paid for the privilege. The Biltmore has had several different owners since Odell, but none have made substantial changes to the hacienda. They couldn't even if they wanted to: Santa Barbara has its own strict rules about redevelopment.

Amenities: Concierge, swimming pool, business facilities; health club; in-room fax, ceiling fan, hair dryer; shoeshine.

Dining tip: The Biltmore's Sunday brunch is estimable, including fresh shrimp, clams and seafood, home-baked breads and desserts, Belgian waffles and even a table devoted to stir-fry. It costs $39.95

Location notes: The hotel is on the ocean-edge of downtown Santa Barbara.

MONTECITO INN   1928

1295 Coast Village Rd., Santa Barbara 93108. Tel. 805/969-7854; 800/843-2017; Fax 805/969-0623. 60 rooms. Rates: rooms, $185-225; suites, $265-625.

According to the legend, Lorenz Hart wrote his 1936 lyric, "There's a small hotel, with a wishing well ... not a crowd of people, who wants – people?" about the Montecito Inn. To try and corroborate even without rushing to a book of annotated Lorenz Hart: it is true that the Montecito Inn is a small hotel. It is true that it had a wishing well. But as to there not being a crowd of people, that depends on who it is that makes for a crowd.

The Montecito was built in 1927, a pet project sponsored by Hollywood movie stars, including Charles Chaplin and Roscoe ("Fatty") Arbuckle, the scandal-ridden comedian. In fact, both of them were scandal-ridden comedians, but they were also among the original backers of the Montecito. The people in the first crop of guests were their buddies: Norma Shearer, Janet Gaynor, Gilbert Roland, Wallace Beery, Marion Davies, Conrad Nagel, Lon Chaney Sr., and Carol Lombard, to name a few off a long list. And so, the answer to Hart's question, "Who wants people?" is ... movie actors do.

The Montecito Inn was built in a sturdy Mediterranean style, with three stories following a basic horseshoe shape. Many of the rooms have wrought iron balconies, lined with flowers. In contrast to the earthy hacienda-style of the Biltmore, or the New England lines of the Upham, the Montecito Inn nods toward Europe, with its marble and gilt lobby. The elevator is the original one installed in 1927, but Hart's wishing well was replaced by a swimming pool in the 1950's. That didn't feel right, apparently, because the hotel later built another wishing well, which probably works just about as effectively as the first one.

Amenities: Complimentary continental breakfast and valet parking; room service; Cable television with VCR; pool; spa.

Dining tip: The Montecito Cafe is open for lunch and dinner.

Location notes: Montecito is a swanky suburb on the south edge of Santa Barbara.

UPHAM HOTEL   1871

1404 De La Vina, Santa Barbara 93101. Tel. 805/962-0058; 800/ 727-0876; Fax 805/963-2825. 50 rooms. Rates: $120-360.

"December 21st, 1869, Santa Barbara: ... I cannot describe this funny old Spanish town to you. It is very pretty as you come up the harbor, all green and bright surrounded by smooth hills not covered with trees like our hills... " Abbie Lincoln immediately wrote home to her cousin in Massachusetts when she and her husband, Amasa, arrived in Santa Barbara to buy a ranch. However, after a year of hard work and little reward, they sold their ranch and moved into town in order to build a hotel.

An airy Victorian building, with a cupola on the roof, the new "Lincoln House" was built on a structure made of redwood timber from Northern California; to date, it has survived some jolting earthquakes with only limited damage. It was far in advance of other hotels in town, with private plumbing facilities and complimentary buggy service around town. The Lincoln had lofty airs in the early days, but soon slid into a more comfortable, domestic atmosphere. Renamed the "Upham," the hotel was in continuous use, though it catered to long-term guests for many years. More recently it was fully restored, and re-identified as a hotel. Over the years, cottages and other additions extended the original ten room hotel into 49 rooms, in seven buildings and cottages.

Amenities: Rates include breakfast. Rooms have television, VCR, telephone; many have fireplaces. Complimentary newspaper; wine-and-cheese reception daily for guests.

Dining tip: California cuisine served on the verandah.

Location notes: In a residential neighborhood adjoining downtown Santa Barbara.

Santa Maria
THE SANTA MARIA INN   1917

801 S. Broadway, Santa Maria 93454. Tel. 805/928-7777; 800/ 462-4276. 166 rooms. Rates: rooms, $89-160; suites, $150-340.

The Santa Maria Inn opened in 1917 with two dozen rooms and has continued to expand, a little at a time, through the ensuing years, such that it is now a rambling enclave of new rooms, original rooms and medium-old rooms: take your pick. For all of the growth, however, the inn still pays homage through its atmosphere to the founder, a natural-born hotelier named Frank McCoy.

McCoy arrived in central California in 1904, to work as an executive of a major sugar factory. One of his jobs was arranging housing for other employees. Opportunities for making good money abounded in the area for a man of McCoy's experience, but he eventually realized that giving people a place to stay was exactly the work he wanted to do. He purchased an overgrown property on what was then the south end of Santa Maria, cleared the buildings, left the eucalyptus and magnolia trees, and built a two-story hotel in stucco, with leaded-glass windows. McCoy decorated his new place in antiques and surrounded it with gardens. In fact, he was able to cultivate his three-acre garden so carefully that the rooms in the hotel received up to 1,500 fresh-cut flowers every day of the year. For a man born in Ireland, McCoy seemed to understand the appeal of California.

The Santa Maria Inn grew and thrived during the 1920's, surging again with oil discoveries in the region in 1936, and later with the establishment of Vandenburg Air Force Base 16 miles away. The Tap Room was known in the 1950's and '60's for a pair of bartenders named (Willie) Ginn and (Angel) Bourbon. However, new roads diverted traffic away from the old hotel in the 1970's. It closed and McCoy's former garden grew over with weeds. A development group began an amiable restoration in 1981, including a rather gigantic addition. The little old hotel is a bustling, big place now, but it still has something of the flowers, the antiques and the quiet terraces that Frank McCoy thought should greet the guests at every turn.

A movie buff can make a tour of Hollywood just by stopping at the Santa Maria Inn: Charles Chaplin stayed in room 132; Clark Gable, room 238; Cary Grant, room 144; Marilyn Monroe, room 258; Jimmy Stewart, room 158; Shirley Temple, room 211; Rudolph Valentino, room 221, and John Wayne, room 209. Ronald Reagan was a frequent guest, and Richard Nixon made a detour to stop by in the early 1990's, because he remembered it fondly from much earlier days for both of them.

Amenities: room service, VCR, refrigerator in all rooms, some of which have fireplaces; spa, pool, whirlpool.

Dining tip: The Wine Cellar specializes in wine produced in the vineyards that surround Santa Maria.

Location notes: The town of Santa Maria is located 160 miles north of Los Angeles, about ten miles inland from the Pacific coastline.

Santa Rosa
HOTEL LA ROSE   1907

308 Wilson St., Santa Rosa 95401. Tel. 707/579-3200; 800/527-6738; Fax 707/579-3247. 49 rooms. Rates: rooms, $119; suites, $174.

The city of Santa Rosa is surrounded by vineyards, a rather independent kingdom that never fully understood Prohibition. Few people understood Prohibition in the 1920's, but the Hotel La Rose in Santa Rosa developed its own response, with neither Tommy guns nor fast cars. According to the legend repeated by

Evan Neumann, the manager, the hotel had two bars. After Federal agents closed one, the hotel would open the other, and the patrons would shuffle over to it: all inconvenienced, and to what end? Eventually, the Feds would close the second bar, and the hotel would re-open the first. The fact that the La Rose was located in Railroad Square, then a rough part of town, probably helped to insulate it from any concerted effort.

Today, Railroad Square is a charming part of town, full of old buildings that have come back to life. The hotel was among the first, a three-story building, not so very big: six-windows-wide across the front and five-wide along the side. Yet in the early 1980's, intrepid investors poured $7 million into restoring it.

The hotel had been built by an Italian-born quarryman, whose specialty was cutting and laying the pinky-gray blocks used at the turn-of-the-century to pave streets in California. The walls of his hotel are nearly two feet thick and could no doubt support a trolley-car, should the need ever arise. Even so, by 1980, the masonry had to be repaired in places. The interior woodwork at La Rose was refurbished and even augmented with pieces from the period buildings, including a grand staircase salvaged from the San Francisco Cable Car barn. The guestrooms were brought in line with modern standards of safety, soundproofing, and convenience, while retaining characteristic details and furnishings.

Altogether, though, the cost was too great, in business terms. The hotel went bankrupt and closed for several years in the late 1980's. When it re-opened, under the experienced management of the Neumann family, it awoke to a Railroad Square neighborhood newly discovered as a historic district; there are even plans to once again run passenger train service to the 1907 depot in the square.

Amenities: Free parking; in-room television, telephone, private bathroom.

Dining tip: Lunch and dinner are served in the European-style restaurant, Josef's. The hotel has its own coffee roast and even its own candies, left in the turn-down service.

Location notes: Santa Rosa is north of San Francisco. The Hotel La Rose is adjacent to shops and restaurants in Railroad Square. It is six blocks to the Luther Burbank House and Gardens.

HAWAII

Honolulu
THE SHERATON MOANA SURFRIDER   1901

2365 Kalakaua Ave., Honolulu 96815. Tel. 808/922-3111; 800/ 325-3535; Fax 808/923-0308. 793 rooms, including modern addition: request rooms in original building by asking for the "Moana Section." Rates: rooms, $260-490; suites, $900-975.

In the 1890's, Waikiki Beach was mostly just a marshland, home to bugs and other crawling creatures. There was only a narrow strand of ground between the wetland and the water, just wide enough to hold a few mansions that were owned by Hawaiian royals and other rich people, including Walter C. Peacock. Among the mansions was one small beach hotel, which consisted of a cluster of cabins: a favorite spot for Robert Louis Stevenson in the 1870's. Stevenson wrote about Waikiki in glowing terms, but the man who gave it to the world was Walter Peacock.

Peacock was an adventurer from England, who'd made a fortune in San Francisco, and then another in Australia and then another in Hawaii, selling liquor. Nonetheless, in 1896, when he decided to replace his beachhouse with a first-class hotel, he had to borrow money from his sister. That is often the way of it with adventurers, whose sisters are not and still have some cash. Peacock's hotel, called the Moana, opened in 1901 and was quite mansion-like, with a colonnaded front entrance. It was fairly large, standing four stories tall. In terms of influence, however, the Moana was gargantuan.

You can still sit in the lobby of the Moana Hotel, reading a fresh copy of the Pacific *Commercial Advertiser* for March 12, 1901. The hotel has reprinted the whole thing, including the page on which the Pacific Vehicle Co. advertised "An Immense Assortment of 20th Century Vehicles," all horse-drawn wagons. (Wrong again, Pacific Vehicle.) However, beyond such quaint anomalies, the paper reflects the whole, rounded, cultured and active community into which the Moana was launched, that very day, March 12, 1901. As the paper reported, "O.G. Traphagen, the architect of the building, spent much time in studying the features of Colonial architecture, best adapted to the climate of the Hawaiian Islands." As one impressive result, each floor of the hotel was paneled and furnished in different wood, suited to the tropical climate: white oak (first floor); oak (second floor); mahogany (third floor) and maple (fourth floor). The Moana was a success, both with tourists from Honolulu, arriving on the mule-drawn trolley, and with longterm guests from America and Japan. "Surf-boating" or surfing, was demonstrated and taught by Hawaiian "surf boys" at the hotel. One of them, Duke Kahanamoku, had enormous charisma and did more than anyone to popularize surfing in the 1920's; he was later an Olympic swimmer.

Because the Moana Hotel was a success, two wings were added in 1918, forming the Banyan Court in the back of the hotel, facing the ocean. The huge old Banyan tree growing there has been a celebrity since the hotel opened, a famous and popular tree that has been to more parties than any other living being in the world. Because of the fame of the Moana, the wetlands behind the beach were drained in the mid-1920's, allowing for the construction of more and bigger hotels. They came and the Moana remained, purchased by a Japanese company in 1963. It has been known as the "Moana Surfrider" and operated as a Sheraton ever since.

It was never exactly modernized, but its appearance changed through the years, and in the late 1980's the owners decided that since the Moana was a landmark in Hawaiian history, it should be restored to its original appearance. White verandahs and columns distinguish the hotel exterior, against the light grey of the building itself. Inside, the carpets were woven with period designs; the china pattern is the one used at the hotel in the 1930's, the floors once again feature different woods, respectively, and best of all, the roof garden returned to the simple appearance it had when the hotel opened. The Moana Surfrider has a historical room, and also gives historical tours of the hotel every day.

Amenities: Valet parking; 24-hour room service; concierge; nearby fitness-center; valet service; swimming pool; private beach; in-room safe hair-dryer and sundries.

Dining tip: The Banyan Verandah, overlooking the Pacific, just past the tree, has live music every day and evening. Not all of it, by any means, is that type of Hawaiian music made popular in international radio broadcasts from the Banyan Court, from 1935 to 1975.

Location notes: The Moana Surfrider is on Waikiki Beach, about three miles from downtown Honolulu.

OREGON

Portland
THE BENSON   1912

309 S. Broadway, Portland 97205. Tel. 503/228-2000; 800/426-0670; Fax 503/226-4603; web, http://www.holog.com//benson. 290 rooms: $145-190; $210-700.

Simon Benson traveled around the country in the years around the turn of the century, selling Oregon lumber in other cities, making a fortune – and studying great hotels. By 1910, he was ready to build his own grand hotel: a big-spender's vision of what big-spenders would want. He ordered crystal chandeliers for the lobby from Vienna, and marble for the floors from Italy, signing all the bills without flinching. He ordered Circassian walnut from Russia for the paneling, but he almost fainted when he saw the bill for that. The Benson was a hit after it opened in 1912, but Benson was bored. He liked building it, but not running it, and so he sold out in 1919.

The hotel later expanded into an addition built on the site of a hotel that had once stood next door. The remarkable thing about the addition is that it was built in 1959, a time of outright antagonism toward historic hotels. And yet the Benson's new wing did not apologize for the architecture of the original building with some flagrantly modernistic high-rise: rather, it matched the old style. In 1991, the hotel was restored. The public rooms are still Simon's, but the guestrooms are now utterly contemporary.

Amenities: Concierge; exercise room; 24-hour room service; valet service.

Dining tip: The Lobby Lounge features live jazz every night.

Location notes: The Benson Hotel is in downtown Portland, across the street from O'Bryant Park, and within two blocks of the financial district.

THE GOVERNOR   1909

611 S. W. 10th St., Portland 97205. Tel. 503/224-3400; 800/554-3456; Fax 503/224-9426. 100 rooms. Rates: rooms, $165-195; suites, $200-500.

The Governor Hotel was built in 1909, a tourist hotel that billed itself as the "hotel of quiet elegance." It couldn't have been completely quiet; the only chairs in the lobby were rockers. Still, there may have been a rustic hush about the place, with its fine carpets and wood-beamed ceilings. In 1992, however, when the Governor was refurbished, it really became historical: a mural painter from California, Melinda Morey painted a panoramic mural in the new lobby (formerly the dining room) of the Lewis & Clark Exposition.

The murals and the other pieces brought in for the re-opening actually define a style only glimpsed in the original Governor ... not Idaho style, certainly not California style, but Oregon style. One of the tables in the lobby, for example, has a top sliced like a disc off a piece of timber and lacquered to a shine. In most states, that's the sort of thing they sell at the state fair, but this table is cool. And it's very cool to be cool in Oregon, these days.

Amenities: Concierge, valet parking; 24-hour room service; fitness center with indoor pool; in-room mini-bar, dataport, iron, hair dryer.

Dining tip: Jakes' Grill, the hotel's dining room, is the former lobby, with its original terracotta flooring, and mahogany beams.

Location notes: The Governor is in downtown Portland, one block from the MAX free rail; three blocks from Pioneer Courthouse Square, and four blocks from the Portland Art Museum.

Shaniko
SHANIKO HISTORIC HOTEL   1902

P.O. 86, Shaniko 97057. Tel. 541/489-3441; 800/483-3441. 18 rooms. Rates: rooms, $66; suites, $96.

Shaniko was a wild town at the turn-of-the-century, a trading center where the railroad ended and the frontier began. Wool came in from the sheep farms and cattle came in from the ranches: out on the range, there were fatal wars between the ranchers and the sheepmen, and sometimes Shaniko caught some of the violence, too. Perhaps that is why the Shaniko Historic Hotel has walls two feet thick, built of handmade bricks. It is a two story building, with a balcony running along two sides. A Salem couple bought the hotel in 1985, and has restored it.

Amenities: Complimentary breakfast; free parking, private bathrooms. No telephones or televisions in the rooms.

Dining tip: The hotel restaurant serves American cuisine.

Location notes: Shaniko is in central Oregon.

WASHINGTON

La Conner
HOTEL PLANTER   1907

715 First St., P.O. Box 702, La Conner 98257. Tel. 360/466-4710; 800/488-5409; Fax 360/466-1320. 12 rooms. Rates: $75-120.

La Conner is a tiny old fishing port on the coast of Washington, north of Seattle on the Puget Sound. Just as important, it is at the mouth of the Skagit River and was once the shipping point for produce from the Skagit Valley on steamships bound for Seattle. At the turn-of-the-century, LaConner was a busy town with an eye on the tourist trade, and by 1907, it had a La Conner-sized version of a grand hotel, called the Planter.

The new hotel brought inventions and innovations, which were, according to the hotel's history, "indoor plumbing (one bathroom), electricity and a cement sidewalk." A vintage photograph shows the difference: a wood-plank sidewalk on the other side of First Street. As a matter of fact, the whole Hotel Planter building was built of conrete blocks, a simple but handsome structure of two stories, with three storefronts across the first floor. And at the top, adorned in fanciful scrollwork, is the original sign for the "Hotel Planter."

Donald and Cynthia Hoskins bought the Planter in the late 1980's, bringing the shops to life and then painting the exterior of the building crisp white. They then refurbished the guest floor upstairs to a contemporary standard, while retaining period details including the original doors, railings and moldings. Meanwhile, La Conner needed its grand hotel, having become a busy place again, a picturesque outing for tourists from Seattle.

Amenities: In-room television, telephone, ceiling fan; complimentary coffee; hot tub.

Dining tip: The hotel does not serve food, but a bakery-cafe called the Calico Cupboard is just across the street. It has a statewide following among breakfast-connoisseurs.

Location notes: The Planter is in the midst of La Conner's many galleries and restaurants. The hotel is 15 minutes from the stop for the ferries, which go out to the San Juan Islands and north to Victoria, Canada.

Port Townsend
PALACE HOTEL   1889

1004 Water St., Port Townsend 98368. Tel. 360/385-0773; 800/ 962-0741; Fax 360/385-0780; web, www.olympus.net/palace; e-mail, palace@olympus.net. 15 rooms. Rates: rooms, $45-75; suites, $99-139.

Captain Henry Tibbals was born in 1829, and it seems a shame that he should be best remembered as the man who built a dapper hotel in Port Townsend. Rather, he should be famous for being the first man to use a diving bell developed in the United States: he should be famous as the man who used the bell to fetch a fortune in silver off the bottom of the Caribbean Sea, where it went down with a Spanish ship. He should be famous as a man who transported a load of railroad iron across the Isthmus of Panama – and lived. However, Captain Tibbals was the man who built the Palace Hotel in Port Townsnd in 1889, and at least he is remembered for something.

The Palace is a striking building, with windows rising all the way from the second story to arched tops on the third. A pair of twin columns separates each window: a striking facade that would catch the eye in Chicago, let alone in a small town on the coast of Washington. The building had many uses through the years, but was a cheap brothel by the 1920's and 1930's. It seems an unhappy episode, yet it is one the hotel now recalls rather sentimentally, naming each guestroom for one of the prostitutes in days gone by.

The renovation of the hotel was, according to the hotel's own description, "long and tedious," taking eight years starting in 1976. Grants from the state and national government helped make the structural repairs that saved the building. Some metalwork had to be fabricated to restore the exterior to its original appearance. The ground floor was returned to its original uses (a restaurant and several shops), while the upper floors were furnished almost entirely with antiques, to be part of the newly reopened Palace Hotel. Some of the rooms have arched windows, of course, filled from the inside with the view of the bay.

Amenities: Television, complimentary continental breakfast delivered to the room.

Dining tip: As this book goes to press, the hotel is working out plans for a new restaurant on the premises.

Location notes: The hotel is located in the downtown section of Port Townsend, adjacent to shops and restaurants. The beach is one block away.

Seattle
FOUR SEASONS OLYMPIC   1924

411 University St., Seattle 98101. Tel. 206/621-1700; 800/332-3442; Fax 206/682-9633. 450 rooms. Rates: rooms, $255-365; suites, $625-1,250.

When the Olympic Hotel opened in 1924, it was actually built over and around a popular theatre, the Metropolitan, which had opened in 1911. The land in downtown Seattle was that valuable: since 1861, the large tract around the Olympic has been owned by the University of Washington, which has managed it cleverly, as in encouraging the construction of hotels on top of theatres.

The Olympic has long been the center of Seattle's social life, which has obviously liked the way it looked against a background of antique mirrors, intricate moldings, crystal chandeliers, marble flooring and oak paneling. When the hotel was threatened with destruction in the 1970's, no less a body than the Washington state legislature passed a resolution in its favor. The state strongly suggested that the University of Washington find a way to save the hotel. Four Seasons was contracted to oversee a $60 million restoration and to operate the hotel on a 60-year lease. With its renovation, the Olympic is once again a deluxe background, but for an even bigger and more social city.

Amenities: Concierge; business center; health club with pool; in-room dataport, valet service, 24-hour room service.

Dining tip: The hotel's chef, himself a vegetarian, offers many alternative and low-calorie choices even on the haute cuisine menu.

Location notes: The hotel is in downtown Seattle, within five blocks of Pike Place Market.

Waterville
THE WATERVILLE HISTORICAL HOTEL 1903
Rt. 2, P.O. 692, Waterville 98858. Tel. 509/745-8695. 8 rooms. Rates, $48-64.

Dave Lundgren was visiting Waterville, Washington, from Northern California in 1989 when he became fixated on the defunct Waterville Hotel, a handsome brick and shingle building that had been empty since 1975. He and his girlfriend decided that someone just had to bring the old place to life. "Why not us?" they asked bravely. As a matter of fact, Lundgren was the one to buy the hotel in 1992, and the one to restore it room by room, table by table, in time for a grand reopening in 1996. The first brick hotel in town in 1903, the Waterville Hotel is officially listed as an example of Jacobean architecture, with its steeply pitched roof and the timbered look of the third story. However, in the isolation of the wheatfields of Western Washington, it rose along its own simple, sturdy lines.

Lundgren found that the wood paneling and flooring were still intact – the hotel even had most of its original furniture. He restored all of it in the shop he maintains next to the hotel. He fitted new mattresses on the original beds, and restored the original porcelain fixtures for the bathrooms. Not all of the rooms have private bathrooms, but they all have sinks, a truthful throwback to how hotels really were in days gone by. The original oak trim gleams throughout the building. The Waterville is a rare hotel: uncompromised. "Every effort has been made to keep the building as original as possible. It's a historical hotel, not a B & B," Lundgren says, and he is rightly reluctant to make too many 1990's improvements to his early 1900's find.

Amenities: Television in guest lounge.

Dining tip: The Waterville Hotel is within a block of several restaurants in Waterville.

Location notes: The hotel is located in Waterville, 10 miles from the Columbia River. It is within three blocks of the Douglas County Historical Museum.

5. THE ROCKIES & THE SOUTHWEST

"I loved to watch the young people who looked so grown-up to me in their beautiful clothes and listen to the music of the orchestras. The whole hotel was my home."

– Betty Mark Mincer, daughter of the manager of the Boulderado during the 1920's [quoted by Silvia Pettem]

ARIZONA

Bisbee
COPPER QUEEN HOTEL   1902

P.O. Drawer CO, Bisbee 85603. Tel. 602/432-2216; 800/247-5829; Fax 602/432-4298. 45 rooms. Rates: (seasonal) $70-105.

Bisbee was a copper town, teeming with life at the turn-of-the-century. Workers came from all over the world to help the Copper Queen Mining Co. take ore off the hills. It was a rough town, too, and the company itself decided to foot the bill for a new hotel, in order to introduce decent accommodations, in addition to peace and quiet, to the center of town. Most of the visitors were mining executives, making deals or inspecting output: Bisbee's tourist days were still 80 years ahead of it. In the early days, even the celebrities who stopped at the Bisbee Queen were rugged people – John "Black Jack" Pershing and Theodore Roosevelt among them.

The new hotel was built in the style of a rather massive Mediterranean villa, with a tiled roof and a columned portico on the second floor. The miners and much of the mining activity have long since drained out of Bisbee, but the hotel has remained, built like a grand fortress. In the past ten years, tourist activity based on Bisbee's colorful history has brought a new wave of visitors to the Copper Queen, which is among the best preserved hotel properties in the West.

Amenities: Air conditioning, telephones, television, meeting facilities; swimming pool.

Dining tip: Continental menu.

Location notes: Bisbee is about ninety miles southeast of Tucson. It is 20 minutes by car from the popular town of Tombstone. The hotel itself is across the street from the Mining & Historical Museum, and around the corner from mine tours.

BISBEE GRAND HOTEL   1906

61 Main St., Bisbee 85603. Tel. 520/432-5900; 800/421-1909. 11 rooms. Rates: rooms, $55-78; suites, $95-110.

The Bisbee Grand is something of a fantasy: it certainly was for a businessman who toured it on a lark in 1989. At the time, the property was dark and empty, the last guests having left two years before. Part of a downtown block, the Bisbee Grand building is two stories tall, lined with storefront windows on the ground floor. The businessman didn't see all the dust and cracked paint, however; he saw a colorful old Western hotel, and in his eye, it was already freshened for Bisbee's growing tourist trade. He switched careers, started the freshening for real, and the Bisbee Grand came back to life.

It is probably more charming today than it was when it was built in the midst of Bisbee's copper boom, simply to offer visiting mine executives a respectable place to stay. Some of the rooms are duly plain, as they would have been then, and some are medium-temperature Victorian. Then there is the Oriental suite, with its hundred-year-old Chinese wedding bed and evocative decorations. It is a fantasy of a different kind.

Amenities: Full breakfast included; billiards room; piano for use of the guests.

Dining tip: The Bisbee Grand does not have a restaurant, but a saloon, with a barback that originated in a Tombstone bar in the 1880's.

Location notes: The Bisbee Grand is downtown, on bus and walking tours of Old Bisbee.

Douglas
THE GADSDEN   1929

1046 G Ave, Douglas 85607. Tel. 520/364-4481; Fax 520/364-4005; web, www.theriver.com/gadsdenhotel; e-mail, rgadsden@theriver.com. 160 rooms. Rates: rooms, $38-60; suites, $70-85.

The proprietor of the Gadsden calls her lobby "the town's living room," which is a definitive statement to make about a grand hotel. Only a place with the vanity and generosity of a true grand hotel would want to be, or consent to be, the town's living room. The lobby of the Gadsden draws on a combination of styles, but has a simple design philosophy: no ferns, no rugs, no brasswork, no drapes. A high-ceilinged room painted in light colors, it is bracketed by four marble columns, russet in tone. Up to that point, of course, it could be a room at a municipal library. But the Gadsden lobby centers on a white marble staircase, a slightly oversized and plain white staircase, leading up to a 42-foot-long Tiffany window. The window is a mural depicting the Sonoran Desert. It is a provocative room, at once opulent and spare.

Doris and Hartman Brekhus worked on a ranch in North Dakota for decades, spending their winters in Douglas, often at the Gadsden, from the 1940's until 1988. That was the year they started spending summers in Douglas, as well, as the new owners of the hotel. They've refurbished the rooms and stripped a coat of bilious green paint off the exterior. And they've kept the doors open: Douglas is a border town, struggling to find new industries, and the Brekhuses have worked diligently to bring a new tourist trade to Douglas.

Amenities: Air-conditioning; open-air sun verandah.

Dining tip: The Saddle and Spur Lounge has a collection of 200 cattle brands.

Location notes: Douglas is across the Rio Grande from Agua Prieta, Mexico.

Phoenix
ARIZONA BILTMORE   1929

24th St. and Missouri, Phoenix 85016. Tel. 602/955-6600; 800/ 950-0086; Fax 602/9540469. 500 rooms. Rates: rooms, $380-420; suites, $780.

Frank Lloyd Wright did not design the Arizona Biltmore, but his influence was so strong in drawing the buildings against the hills of Phoenix that his name has been associated with it ever since it opened in 1929. Wright did consult with the hotel's architect, Albert C. McArthur, and they decided to try one of Wright's own ideas, precast concrete blocks in the construction. The concrete, set into a pattern that rises almost looks like a temple from a distance, makes the Arizona Biltmore like no other hotel, up close. In fact, the *art moderne* design constantly works to overcome the very blockiness of concrete blocks, with asymmetrical terraces and rooflines, delicate bas-relief details and airy plantings. Carved into the desert, the new Biltmore was immediately popular as a stop-over for tourists headed west, and for those looking for the restorative of the desert air, which was still clear in 1929. However, the bold hotel was too isolated and certainly too new, in financial terms, to stave off the effects of the Stock Market Crash.

Unfortunately, it was an immediate casualty of the Depression.

Fortunately, one of its first guests had been William Wrigley Jr., who purchased the whole property at the end of 1929. Wrigley, scion of the chewing-gum fortune, believed in the concept of a glamorous, high-design hotel in the midst of the American West, and he supported it through the worst of the Depression. In fact, he personally designed and supervised the Catalina swimming pool (named after one of his other holdings, much of Catalina Island off of California). The Arizona Biltmore was located within the city limits of Phoenix, but with over 1,000 acres, it was more of a resort than a city hotel through the 1930's.

As Phoenix grew to embrace the hotel, it has crossed into a city address, while retaining resort diversions such as golf and tennis. To publicize Phoenix, and the Biltmore, the management encouraged Hollywood stars to visit and many of them did. Ronald and Nancy Reagan honeymooned there and, according to a brochure, "Spencer Tracy's memory lives on ... as a great tipper and a man who made a point of remembering the names of waitresses and bellboys."

The Wrigley family owned the Arizona Biltmore until the 1970's. Subsequent proprietors, of which there have been a series over the past 20 years, completed several expansion projects, in addition to a program of renovation (under the auspices of the Frank Lloyd Wright Foundation). Today, the Arizona Biltmore is a mammoth hotel, with over 500 rooms.

Amenities: two golf courses, tennis courts, gym, swimming pools, spa, concierge, tours of the architecture and history of the hotel.

Dining tip: The hotel has five restaurants.

Location notes: The Arizona Biltmore is on the outskirts of Phoenix, next to the Phoenix Mountain Reserve.

HOTEL ST. MICHAEL   1901

205 W. Gurley St, Prescott 86301. Tel. 520/776-1999; 800/678-3757; Fax 520/776-7318. 72 rooms. Rates: rooms, $42-63; suites, $63-78.

In 1900, the Hotel Burke was calling itself "the only absolutely fireproof building in Prescott" ... when Prescott went and burned down. It was the Great Fire of 1900, and it took the Hotel Burke with it. Mr. Burke made some changes with his next hotel, which opened in 1901. First of all, he made sure there was space between it and other buildings. Second, the new building was brick, with a terra-cotta roof. After Burke sold his hotel in 1907, the new owners added one more safety measure: they renamed it after a saint. The Hotel St. Michael is not a typical small town hotel. It is an unusually spacious, three story building, almost institutional in proportion, but graced by arched windows across the top story. Shops line the street level. No one knows anymore why there are gargoyles glaring down from the exterior of the hotel.

"Go upee, Go downee." In 1925, the local newspaper made headline news out of the St. Michael's new elevator, the first one seen in Prescott. The elevator, which has worked ever since, still goes up and down, making it the oldest elevator in the region.

Amenities: Complimentary continental breakfast; air conditioning; private bathroom; cable television; telephone.

Dining tip: The hotel's cafe makes all of its own baked goods, including brownies 4-inches square and one-inch high, and equally plump scones, croissants and cookies.

Location notes: The St. Michael is on Prescott's colorful Whiskey Row. It is across from Courthouse Plaza.

COLORADO

Aspen
HOTEL JEROME   1889
330 E. Main St., Aspen 81611. Tel. 970/920-1000; 800/331-7213; Fax 970/925-2784; e-mail, hjerome@aol.com. 93 rooms. Rates: (seasonal) rooms, $160-725; suites, $395-1,790.

Jerome Wheeler founded Aspen. Other people discovered the silver underneath the mountains and settled the town in 1880, but Wheeler was the founding father of the town's supercharged social atmosphere, starting in 1882, when he visited Colorado for the benefit of his wife's health. Mrs. Harriet Jerome was the niece of

R.H. Macy, the New York department store magnate and her husband made a great success as president of Macy's. However, after he saw Aspen, New York City seemed a dull and trifling place to him (not an uncommon train of thought, as it has occurred to many other visitors to the town). Within six years, the Wheelers had a second home in Aspen and by 1889, Jerome was building a hotel for the scrappy mountain town. It was honestly supposed to offer competition to the best hotels in Paris.

Guests had to lurch their own way up to the town's 10,000-foot elevation, but once there, the new Hotel Jerome had an elevator to carry them the last three stories, up to the ballroom or down to the drawing rooms. A red-brick building with arching windows facing the front, the hotel looks something like a school from the outside, but on the inside it was built to be opulent in an era that understood the word, with oak paneling cut in the Eastlake style, a tinted-glass ceiling in the lobby rotunda, and a hothouse in the back to supply fresh-cut flowers, year-round.

According to the book, *The Historical Hotel Jerome* by Martie Sterling, the chef was imported from France, the horticulturalist was imported from Germany and the guests came by train from all over the east and west to celebrate the grand opening in November 1889. Because of that train service, Aspen became a popular Rocky Mountain destination for tourists, as well as a thriving silver mining community. The Hotel Jerome and the lively Wheelers were at the center of an intense social life in Aspen. However, mining camps are full of sad stories, and one of them was Jerome Wheeler's. He slowly but surely lost his fortune and, in 1909, his hotel as well. By then, Aspen was dispirited, anyway. Just as in the heyday, the Hotel Jerome was the center of all activity: unfortunately the activity in the first half of the century was more often charitable than sociable. The Jerome offered a place to be, to anyone still looking for a fortune in Aspen.

After World War Two, soldiers who had been stationed in Aspen for training exercises returned to develop a winter sports industry. At the same time, the town became the center for several different arts festivals. The Hotel Jerome tried to join in the new glimmer of prosperity, but it finally creaked to a halt and closed in 1956. In the mid-1970's a new wave of very rich pioneers discovered that Aspen could be a nouveau resort, a place of trends rather than traditions. They remade Aspen.

In 1984, the restoration of the Hotel Jerome became financially plausible and meticulous work began. Fittings were refurbished rather than replaced wherever possible. Building materials were commissioned to match the era, and a whole Victorian mansion in Missouri was purchased and dismantled in order to augment the renovation of the Jerome. The hotel reopened in 1985, up-to-date in technology and services, and true to its original Victorian mission of helping to define the town around it.

Amenities: airport and ski-slope transfers, swimming pool, spa and fitness room, concierge, room-service, business services, newly renovated bathrooms.

Dining tip: The impressive cherrywood bar and bar-back in the "J-Bar," is the real thing, dating back to the hotel's opening in 1889.

Location notes: downtown Aspen, adjacent to shopping and restaurants; two to three blocks to Aspen Art Museum and Wheeler Opera House; six blocks to Aspen Mt.; four miles to Aspen airport.

Boulder
THE BOULDERADO   1909
2115 13th St., Boulder 80302. Tel. 303/442-4344; 800/433-4344; Fax 303/442-4378. 160 rooms and suites. Rates: $134-275.

The city of Boulder had matured in the last years of the 19th century. No mere mining boomtown, it had grown steadily and permanently as a farming center, and as a college town, the home of the University of Colorado. However, the city wanted a hotel. In fact, the hotel became the hot topic of conversation in Boulder long before the first stone was laid. To reflect the community zeal – and because no big investors came forward – the financing was to be based on a subscription of stock investment from 500 citizens. The money was raised easily. "The new hotel," everyone kept calling it through 1908. Finally, a contest was staged to present the entity with a proper title. Most of the first people to pipe up suggested naming it after the president of the biggest bank in town. They probably wanted loans. Eventually, a local businessman noodled around with a combination of the words, "Boulder" and "Colorado," and came up with "Boulderado." Most Boulderans hated it.

The businessman defended the suggestion very accurately, however, asserting in the local newspaper that, "It will be the only hotel of that name in all of the world." That has proved to be the case.

According to the 1986 book, *The Legend of a Landmark* by Silvia Pettem, the Boulderado's architecture was intended to improve on the Brown Palace in Denver. The Brown Palace (see below) is famous for its six story atrium lobby – but according to engineers in the know, it was supposed to have a stained-glass ceiling over the second story. As things turned out, it didn't. The Boulderado did, and still does: a pale golden-yellow canopy of light.

The Boulderado Hotel takes up a full city block, a villa in design, red brick in construction, with wide balconies on the first four of its five stories. Inside, cherrywood was used throughout the staircase, mezzanine and mouldings. Even in 1909 most of the rooms had private telephones, and the technology throughout was well in advance of the standard expected in most small town hotels. Boulder did not think of itself as a small town, but perhaps it should have: by 1911, the hotel was losing money, and most of the original investors lost their money, as the lease to manage the hotel changed hands, and concessions to new lessors piled up, in order make the property viable.

It was a frustrating business. A cool summer would keep tourists away. Business setbacks on Wall Street seemed to hit the Boulderado first. And one aspect of life in Boulder life that didn't help was that Boulder maintained its own Prohibition of alcohol even after the nation repealed the 19th amendment in 1933. Not until the end of the 1960's was liquor legal in Boulder, or at the Boulderado. In 1940, a rich man from Denver bought the Boulderado and gave it as a wedding present to his son and his new wife. They and their family continued to run the hotel for over 20 years. The wife's parents moved into the hotel and her mother, Rosa May Harmon, took the job as head housekeeper, since her own husband was a traveling salesman, away most of the time. She must have been a remarkable personality, and a phenomenal manager, because she almost never left her own room. "I started as a summer job right out of high school, but liked Mrs. Harmon so much I stayed three years," recalled Mary Pickrell in *Legend of a Landmark*, "We often socialized in her room, as she wasn't well and couldn't get around too much." Mary Pickrell also remembered that Louis Armstrong stayed in a suite at the Boulderado while on tour, and left her a magnanimous tip for the 1940's of one dollar. She kept it all her life.

By the 1960's, the Boulderado depended mainly on elderly residents, living out their years in the downtown ambiance of the hotel. Fluorescent lights had replaced the chandeliers in the lobby in the 1940's. As gratingly, plexiglass replaced the stained-glass ceiling over the lobby in 1960, because snow damage through the years had broken so many of the original panes. New owners restored both the chandeliers and the stained-glass ceiling in the 1970's, and in 1980 the hotel was completely renovated into the first-class, Edwardian era hotel that it had once been. The original purpose of the property was to help the city grow, and it certainly had done that job through the years, as Boulder became one of the most prosperous and stable communities in the state. With occupancy rising over 90 percent, the hotel added a brand new wing in 1985.

Amenities: Free parking; shuttles (with fee) to or from Denver airport; health club passes; dual-port phones; room service.

Dining tip: The Catacombs, downstairs barroom features live jazz or blues, nightly.

Location notes: The hotel is one block from the Pearl St. Mall. The University of Colorado campus is three-quarters of a mile away.

Cripple Creek
THE IMPERIAL HOTEL   1884

123 N. 3rd St., Cripple Creek 80813. Tel. 719/689-7777; 800/235-2922; Fax 719/689-1020. 29 rooms. Rates: rooms, $25-85; suites, $100-125.

The Imperial Hotel was built in the days when Cripple Creek, Colorado, was nationally known as a rugged place to live, and not because the only approach was on a train that went practically straight up through the cliffs and canyons. About $800 million in gold passed through its streets from 1880 to 1920, but apparently every karat of it just kept going. "Its buildings run from shabbiness to downright ruin," the writer Julian Street observed in 1916, "its streets are ill paved, and its outlying districts are a horror of smokestacks, ore-dumps, shaft-houses, reduction plants, gallows-frams and squalid shanties, situated in the mud." In gratitude for such publicity, the town board renamed its most disreputable thoroughfare "Julian St."

George and Ursula Long, the couple who bought the Imperial in 1907, were not typical of the town; they were English of the upper class, and why they chose to live in a tapped-out mining town is not known. Cripple Creek was in transition, though. The mines were closing, but at about 10,000 feet above sea level, the scenery was beautiful. The Longs operated the hotel themselves, even while sending their son back to England for his education. After graduating from Cripple Creek High School, their daughter, Esther, was presented to the King and Queen of England at the Court of St. James; she was later Lady Esther. Back in Cripple Creek, the Longs proved themselves to be dedicated hoteliers, and they improved the Imperial enough so that the hotel became the destination for the many wildflower excursion trains that ferried sightseers back and forth from Colorado Springs. At a time when Pierce-Arrow automobiles were at the top of the market, the Imperial owned seven of them just to greet the trains.

The Pierce-Arrows were gone by the mid-1940's, though, when the Imperial was tired and so was Mrs. Long, by then a widow. The Longs had made a good business of the hotel, but perhaps Cripple

Creek wasn't really ready for their little breath of Mayfair; as one local observed, "No wonder they didn't make it. Those people charged $2 and $3 a night for a room and who is going to pay them prices?"

The Mackins, a young couple scouting for a business while on their honeymoon, bought the Imperial Hotel in 1946. They restored it themselves while raising a large family, a plot line that seems as though it should have been made into a Disney movie, circa 1966. They even started a theater on the basement level and had yet more good times, according to Mrs. Mackin's book of memoirs.

Today, the Imperial is under new ownership, and has been restored as part of the new tourist boom surrounding Cripple Creek's legalized gambling. In fact, the hotel has a small casino. The lobby of the hotel has vintage light fixtures and furniture, but the most intriguing feature is the wallpaper. Dating from the turn-of-the-century, it was discovered on the site a few years ago. The guestrooms at the Imperial are furnished with antiques.

Amenities: Free valet parking; in-room telephone, television.

Dining tip: The theater in the basement now offers cabaret performances, and often books nationally known acts, such as the Coasters and Dan Seals.

Location notes: Cripple Creek is a drive of about 90 minutes from Colorado Springs. The hotel is in the middle of town, four blocks from the District Museum.

Denver
THE BROWN PALACE 1892

321 Seventeenth St., Denver 80202. Tel. 303/297-3111; 800/678-8946; Fax 303/293-9204; web, http://www.brownpalace.com. 230 rooms. Rates: rooms, $195-245; suites, $275-775.

The Palmer House in Chicago opened in 1873, setting a new hotel standard for size, ostentation and amenities. One of those who were most impressed with the Palmer House was Henry C. Brown, who determined that Denver must also have a grand hotel, on a par or better. Brown worked as a builder in Denver even before the massive gold and silver strikes in the region. When they hit, tempting others up to the mountains, Brown made a business decision to stay put and wait for the mountains to come to him, so to speak, in the pockets of successful miners. The hotel he would build, the Brown Palace, had to be so spectacular that new millionaires would not have to strut any further east, if what they wanted to do was strut.

The only way to ensure such quality in Denver in 1892 was to build an oasis of self-sufficiency. The Brown Palace served meat, vegetables, and cream from its own farms. It made its own ice, because it generated its own electricity, and in fact, whenever Denver had a blackout, the hotel serviced parts of the city. It also had an incineration system for garbage and – taking self-sufficiency to an extreme even for 1892 – a crematorium for guests who died. No one ever partook of that feature, and it was dismantled in the 1920's. The hotel still has its original artesian well, with startlingly good drinking water because of it.

Surrounded now by shiny skyscrapers, from the outside the Brown Palace is a dowdy triangle of red-brown stone. Inside, the lobby itself offers a surprising commodity: air, rising seven stories to a stained-glass ceiling. From below, each floor is a continuous balcony behind a green and gold rail; it means to be gorgeous and it is. As one looks across from the door of a guest room, the balconies and the broad stair threaded through them could be the set of an opera. Mr. Brown's Palace is not palatial; it is not like an Austrian castle, an old English mansion, a gentleman's club or any of the other fantasies commonly perpetrated by vintage hotels. If anything, it is a theatre in a grand way: stage and boxes turning around each other, depending upon who is gazing down, up, or across at whom.

If you're interested, the hotel sells a very good history of its first 90 years, written by Corinne Hunt.

Amenities: The best water in the country; valet parking; 24-hour room service; business center; exercise room; in-room dataport.

Dining tip: Afternoon tea in the atrium lobby is grand, truly. The cream comes all the way from England and the jazzy music comes all the way from a piano across the room.

Location notes: The Brown Palace is in downtown Denver, within four blocks of the Sixteenth Street Mall.

OXFORD HOTEL   1891

1600 Seventeenth St., Denver 80202. Tel. 303/628-5400; 800/228-5838; Fax 303/628-5413. 81 rooms. Rates: $129-199; suites, $199-349.

It is not often that one can hail the re-emergence of an original art deco hotel from 1891. However, in the 1930's the old Victorian Oxford Hotel was modernized in a way still appealing today. When the current owners restored it in the 1980's, they chose to retain the blend: most of the hotel has been returned to its Victorian comfort, while the Cruise Room Bar is a true art deco showstopper.

The Oxford was designed in 1890 by Frank Edelbrooke, the architect who would start work on the Brown Palace (see above) the following year. A five-story building in reddish hues of terra cotta and stone, it was a grand hotel by any standard, with marble floors, sterling silver chandeliers, one of the early elevators seen in Denver, and an interior atrium. The hotel was close to Union Station, and it thrived, as something of an adjunct to it. According to a historical sketch by Thomas J. Noel, "Oldtimers still remember the Oxford lobby filled with reporters, lounging their feet on the window sill, watching traffic come and go from Union Station." The remodelling in 1933 was as well-considered as the initial design of the hotel. Later refurbishments, though, only meant laying new carpet over old, painting the chandeliers (even the sterling silver ones) or tacking up a false wall or ceiling as a temporary measure. The Oxford lived by the sword and nearly died by it: as train traffic fell away, the neighborhood became something less than fashionable. It survived for awhile by becoming rather funky, staging music and plays. "Hundreds jammed the hotel at night," Noel wrote, "to see The Oxford Players stumble through 'Ten Nights in a Barroom!"

When the neighborhood fell apart completely, the hotel very nearly did, too. And when the neighborhood began to spring back to life as a Victorian historic district, so, too, did the Oxford. New owners in the 1980's stripped away the patches of the more recent past and found the 1891 hotel underneath. It is a disciplined renovation: very true to the hotel's Western Victorian origins (as opposed to a more sentimental and plush version of the style). And the Cruise bar, along with 11 of the guestrooms, were restored to their own art deco origins, which are just as truthful.

Amenities: Complimentary limousine to downtown locations, morning coffee and newspaper, sherry hour, shoeshine; 24-hour room service; business services; triple-sheeted beds; valet parking.

Dining tip: McCormick's Fish House is famous for seafood.

Location notes: The Oxford is in lower downtown Denver. It is six blocks from the middle of downtown and three blocks from the Sixteenth Street Mall shuttle bus. The Denver Center for the Performing Arts is eight blocks away.

Durango
THE STRATER HOTEL   1887

699 Main St., Durango 81301. Tel. 970/247-4431; 800/247-4431; Fax 970/259-2208. 93 rooms. Rates (seasonal): rooms, $89-169; suites, $119-179.

The Strater was built in 1887, a cheerful, high-Victorian hotel that takes up quite a large chunk of downtown Durango. Painted red with white trim on the outside, it claims to have the largest collection anywhere of American Victorian walnut antiques.

Amenities: Complimentary airport transportation, full breakfast; free parking; room service; valet service.

Dining tip: The Diamond Belle Saloon features live ragtime piano music.

Location notes: The Strater Hotel is two blocks from the Durango/Silverton narrow gauge railroad and 30 minutes from the Purgatory ski resort.

Leadville
THE DELAWARE HOTEL   1886

700 Harrison Ave., Leadville 80461. Tel. 719/486-1418; 800/748-2004; Fax 719/486-2214. 36 rooms. Rates: $68-$130.

Let it be a lesson to all that the first miners to arrive in Leadville tore through the black sand of the area looking for fortunes in gold. They called the sand "lead," because it did contain that element, and expended little imagination in naming their new town after it. They should have called the course sand, "silver," though, because it also contained that element and only later were large – very large – fortunes made by extracting it from the heaps around Leadville, Colorado.

Three brothers from the state of Delaware, by way of a successful business in Denver, opened a fine hotel in the middle of town in 1886, only eight years after the railroad reached Leadville. Their Delaware Hotel constituted a solid red-brick corner facing a busy intersection, and many of the more prosperous miners used it as a headquarters. One of the most famous of them was Horace Tabor, who ran the general store down the street and made his fortune by gaining control of the "Matchless Mine." He later rose to prominence as a U.S. Senator. And, later still, sank into scandal by divorcing his wife for a teenager known as "Baby Doe" Tabor. Even after her husband died in 1899, and the fortune petered out, Baby Doe lived in a shack at the mine and walked with her feet wrapped in rags to the Delaware Hotel, to avail herself of the warmth of the lobby. She froze to death at her mine in 1935. One of the region's other colorful celebrities, Butch Cassidy, was known to have stayed at the Delaware.

Restored in 1992, the Delaware Hotel is at home with its Western atmosphere. It is neat and simple in the public spaces and plush in the guestrooms, which feature brass beds and the lace-curtain elegance of the earlier era.

Amenities: Complimentary breakfast; private bathrooms, telephones and television.

Dining Tip: Callaway's, the hotel's main dining room, serves local dishes.

Location notes: Leadville is 60 miles west of Denver. The hotel is within a short drive of ski mountains.

Ouray
ST. ELMO HOTEL   1898
426 Main St., Ouray 81427. Tel. 970/325-4951; Fax, 970/325-0348. Nine rooms. Rates: rooms, $65-92; suites, $72-102.

The St. Elmo is a well-proportioned two-story brick building, with a comfortable lobby on the first floor, most of the guestrooms on the second floor, and a good restaurant on the lower level. It does not want to be a castle or a gentleman's club, the way some vintage hotels obviously do. It wants to be nice and it is.

However, according to a history of the St. Elmo written by Doris Gregory, the hotel has seen sad and scandalous days. It was built in 1898 by Kittie Heit, who had arrived in Ouray in 1886, with her son Freddie in tow. Like everyone else in the silver-mining town, Kittie was out to make a fortune, but she was willing to earn it and got off to a good start by managing the best restaurant in town. Eventually, she saved enough money to build her own hotel, the St. Elmo.

Kittie was classy, and so was her establishment. But Freddie – Freddie was a lawless, womanizing, dandified rogue. He would have been an excellent character in a book or movie, but as a son, he was rather less winning. Kittie adopted another boy when Freddie was 21, as though she meant to start over, but she died not long after and the St. Elmo passed to Freddie. He married, but he didn't settle down. In 1917, on the verge of losing the hotel to gambling debts, he shot himself. As it turned out, the hotel wasn't lost, and Freddie's widow, to her credit, turned it over to the adopted son, just back from service in World War One. He later sold it to a judge. The hotel remained in fairly good condition until 1984, when the current owners, Dan and Sandy Lingenfelter, purchased it and freshened it up considerably. The little hotel stares a mountain in the eye – or in the belly button, more accurately, because the mountain goes up quite a bit from the streets of Ouray.

Amenities: All rooms with private bath; television in the front parlour.

Dining tip: The BonTon, named after Kittie Heit's original restaurant, serves continental cuisine.

Location notes: Ouray is located about 30 miles south of Montrose, where there is an airport.

MONTANA

Essex
IZAAK WALTON INN   1939

U.S. Hwy 2, Essex 59916. Tel. 406/888-5700; Fax 406/888-5200. 31 rooms, 4 cabooses. Rates: rooms, $98-150; suites, $155-160; cabooses, minimum three nights, approximately $100 per night after that.

August 10, 1935 was the date of the disastrous fire in Essex. It didn't burn down the whole town, but it didn't have to, to be a disaster. It burned down the town's only restaurant. Fifty years later, locals still remembered where they were and what they were doing when the Red Beanery caught fire. Essex was a new town at the time, founded for the sake of employees of the Great Northern Railway, which operated service along a rugged route in Montana (part of its longer line from St. Paul to Seattle). The loss of the Red Beanery left an issue to be discussed at the highest levels of G.N.R. management back in Minnesota. The company finally authorized a private company to build a whole hotel (and beanery) on company land. It was to be named the Izaak Walton Hotel, after the renowned fishing expert of the 17th century. That, it was felt, would give potential guests an idea of what there was to do in Essex. (First, they had to know who Izaak Walton was, of course.)

Built in a bulky Tudor style, the new hotel was spacious inside, with pine-paneling throughout. In proportion and style, it fit Montana, but it didn't make any money. Its most dependable customer base began to fade as railroad crews were replaced by mechanization. However, Glacier National Park was established next to Essex after World War Two and tourism began to grow.

Today, fishing, cross-country skiing and railroad lore are the three diversions associated with the hotel. Amtrak trains still stop at Essex, and, in fact, the hotel has four sidelined cabooses, which have been renovated into suites. The rooms in the main building are rustic, with pine furniture and handmade comforters – emblazoned with the Great Northern Railway's mountain goat logo, of course.

The Izaak Walton Inn by Gail Shay Atkinson and Jim Atkinson is a scrapbook sort of history of the towns around Essex and the men who put the rails there, somehow.

Amenities: Cross-country ski trails, ice rink, snowshoes to borrow. Rooms do not have TV or telephones, though there is a pay phone near the lobby.

Dining tip: Local ingredients are used as much as possible for dishes in the "Dining Car," the hotel's dining room. A favorite dish is huckleberry chicken breast.

Location notes: The hotel is the only business in Essex, and is thirty miles from either entrance to Glacier National Park.

Kalispell
THE KALISPELL GRAND HOTEL   1912
100 Main St., Kalispell 59901. Tel. 406/755-8100; 800/858-7422, Fax, 406/755-8100; e-mail, grand@vtown.com; online, www.vtown.com/ grand/history.htm. Forty rooms. Rates: rooms, $44-84; suites, $91-115.

For a small hotel in a tiny town to name itself a "grand hotel" may seem delusionary. However, in 1912, Kalispell, Montana had eight hotels, and so some differentiation was necessary. The Grand immediately took its place as the swankiest of the whole lot, offering such amenities as locks on the doors, while charging twice as much as the other hotels.

Kalispell was a prosperous town in the Flathead Valley of northwest Montana and the new, three-story red-brick hotel had an appealing dignity about it. The lobby was well-designed, with a pressed-tin ceiling, tile floor and an oak stairway. According to the hotel's own history, the cowboy artist Charles Russell and humorist Irvin S. Cobb both liked to sink into comfortable chairs and relax in the lobby of an afternoon, chatting with another writer, Frank Bird Linderman, who leased the property and ran it for a time in the mid-1920's. The hotel sank just about as far as it could in the 1960's – but it didn't go out of business. It was still a grand hotel underneath its indignities, and it survived long enough to undergo a complete renovation in 1991. The rooms were reconfigured slightly to provide private bathrooms in all of them, and they recouped their Victorian style, with cherrywood furniture.

Amenities: Complimentary continental breakfast; fitness room; in-room cable television, dataport, telephones.

Dining tip: Oriental restaurant on the premises.

Location notes: The Grand is in downtown Kalispell, near shops and restaurants, and within one block of two theaters.

NEW MEXICO

Albuquerque
LA POSADA DE ALBUQUERQUE 1939

125 Second St. NW, Albuquerque 87102. Tel. 505/242-9090; 800/777-5732; Fax 505/242-8664. 113 rooms. Rates: $69-115; suites, $195-275.

When you learn the hospitality business in a place like San Antonio, New Mexico, you have to master it. You have to give people a reason to stop in a town of a few hundred in the middle of the desert. Or else they won't. Conrad Hilton learned the hotel business at his family's boarding house/restaurant in San Antonio and then went to Texas (see the Aristocrat, listed with Dallas hotels) in the 1920's, to start his own chain of hotels.

After fighting his way through the Depression, he was ready to return home and give New Mexico a hotel worthy of any city in the world. And yet, the Hilton Hotel that he opened in Albuquerque in 1939 could only have been in New Mexico. Hilton hired native craftsmen to reflect his state's unique cultural blend in the decor of the hotel, with tile floors, carved beams, and arched ceilings. All of that remained even when the Hilton chain divested itself of the property in the late 1960's. And it remained even when the hotel started on a long slide in quality over the next fifteen years.

New owners set about to restore the hotel, renamed the Posada de Albuquerque, starting in 1983. But what didn't remain were the hundreds of artifacts and individual pieces of artwork that had set the tone in the hotel's opening years. In one of the most painstaking of all hotel restorations, preservation architects and decorators worked with as many of the original craftsmen as possible. They studied old photos and even interviewed former employees and guests, in order to resurrect the hotel, with every single detail in its place. The tinwork and carved furniture could be reproduced, but the original artwork was lost, and could only be replaced by work with similar purpose, if not the exact same style.

Amenities: Television with VCR available; business services.

Dining tip: A Flamenco guitarist plays in the hotel's dining room at dinner.

Location notes: The Posada is next door to the Convention Center and one block away from Rt. 66, a shopping district. It is 1 1/4 miles from Old Town.

Santa Fe
LA FONDA   1920

100 E. San Francisco St., Santa Fe 87501. Tel. 505/982-5511; 800/523-5002; Fax 505/988-2952; e-mail, la-fonda@travelbase.com. 152 rooms. Rates: rooms, $179-189; suites, $200-500.

The La Fonda likes to think that it began in 1607, since an inn did open at approximately its address in Santa Fe that year. The location, the very end of the vaunted Santa Fe Trail, became more and more important with continuing settlement of the area, and another hotel was built on the spot in 1813. Eventually, it took the name "La Fonda," which means "the hotel" in Spanish.

It is not too well known that there were important battles in New Mexico fairly early in the Civil War and, for a time, the Confederates used La Fonda as a headquarters. That was its heyday. By the time of World War One, the hotel was a burned-out hulk and it served one further military purpose, as the target in a demonstration of tank warfare. After the rubble was cleared away, a new hotel was planned: a new La Fonda for Santa Fe. An architect best known for designing museums was given the assignment to give the city a pueblo-style building, one that would wear well for one year or a hundred. The hotel, which was completed in 1922, does have a timeless quality about it. Albeit, real adobes don't have paned-glass windows, but still, the soft-edged stucco of the exterior does not smack of 1922 or 1952 or 1992: it is true to the style, not the date.

The new hotel had civic-minded investors who made sure that the hotel had integrity. However, like many civic hotel projects, La Fonda was a failure from the start. Fortunately, the Harvey Hotel chain saw possibilities for a charming hotel, like the La Fonda, located on a major railroad line and surrounded by fabulous scenery. As matter of fact, for almost 70 years, the Harvey chain had made its reputation finding just such properties all through the West. The chain was also famous for the good food it served in its restaurants and even more famous for the charm of the waitresses it hired to work in those restaurants. More surprising, though, was that the Harvey management cared as much about the artistic potential of the hotel as had the original owners. The company hired a curator, Mary Colter, to refurnish the interiors with Native American arts and furniture produced in the Southwestern style.

The columnist Ernie Pyle once wrote of Santa Fe in the 1930's: "Life among the upper crust centered by daytime in the La Fonda Hotel ... You could go there any time of the day and see a few artists in the bar or an Indian that some white woman loved, or a goateed nobleman from Austria, or a maharajah from India or a New York broker, or an archeologist, some local light in overalls and cowboys boots. You never met anybody anywhere except at the La Fonda." Nonetheless, by 1969, La Fonda was in decay and the Harvey chain sold it. The new owner was a local businessman named Sam Bellan, who had a characteristic necessary for any historic-hotel owner. He loved the place.

The hotel has been restored and upgraded, polished and expanded without losing its original Southwestern atmosphere, its art or hand-carved furniture. Since 1959, a local folk artist named Ernesto Martinez has had a wide-ranging commission: to decorate the hotel's walls with paintings, simple or intricate. Martinez' original art is unexpected. So is a hotel in which the general manager once told a newspaper, "The hotel is definitely not for everyone. Sometimes guests do think it's pretty strange."

Amenities: Room service; concierge; swimming pool; in-room dataports.

Dining tip: New Mexican cuisine in the hotel's main dining room.

Location notes: Downtown location two blocks from the State Capitol.

HOTEL ST. FRANCIS   1923

210 Don Gaspar Ave., Santa Fe 87501. Tel. 505/983-5700; 800/ 529-5700; Fax 505/989-7690. 82 rooms. Rates (seasonal): rooms, $78- 208; suites, $178-353.

When the St. Francis was built in 1923, it was either the most formal hotel in Santa Fe, or the set for a passing Cole Porter musical. As recalled by a longtime patron, it was "a first-class hotel with a wonderful dining room – waitresses and bellhops in uniform ... in the lobby, men in top hats and coats and women in full-length dresses."

"Hotel guests had to show a marriage license just to get a room with their wives," he added.

The hotel was called the De Vargas then and it was known around town for a big blackboard placed so that everyone in the bar could see it. Each year, during the World Series and on Election night, the bar was jammed with Santa Feans craning to see the latest results, which were posted on the board just as they came in from wire reports. Obviously, there must be something to be said for sitting at home, in stony silence, watching a baseball game via satellite, or in knowing the projections of an election winner even before the sun goes down. However, neither is as appealing as seeing a blurry scrawl go up on a blackboard in the bar of the most respectable hotel in Santa Fe, and hearing the groans and cheers that are the real news, anyway.

The St. Francis, renamed after its 1986 renovation, retains antiques from the original hotel, including many pieces of furniture; the switchboard that was installed in the 1930's and a vintage telephone saved from one of the guestrooms. It is now used in the lobby as the house phone. The St. Francis Hotel is in a three story building, situated so that many of the guestrooms take in views of the city and the foothills beyond.

Amenities: Concierge; free parking; room-service; in-room refrigerator and safe, cable television.

Dining tip: Afternoon tea, served on the verandah in fair weather, has been a popular tradition since the hotel re-opened in 1986.

Location notes: The St. Francis is one block from the Plaza, and two blocks from the State Capitol.

TEXAS

Austin
THE DRISKILL   1886

604 Brazos, Austin 78701. Tel. 512/474-5911; 800/252-9367; Fax 512/474-2214; e-mail, Driskhotel@aol.com. 179 rooms. Rates: rooms, $155-180; suites, $425-1,500.

For most hotels, closing day is a depressing event. Even a favorite old hotel becomes a sad derelict, when it is longer wanted. The lights go out and the front door is locked, usually for the first time ever – and perhaps for the last, before the wrecking ball makes all locks moot. For the Driskill Hotel, however, closing days were rather routine. Its first closing came only five months after its grand opening, December 20, 1886. It closed fairly regularly after that, usually about six to eight months after some new manager took over, pronouncing a new era of lower prices. Or higher ones. It didn't matter, because the Driskill Hotel in its first 20 years was a veritable financial bucking bronco.

No owner could stay put for long. The only person who could stay, and did, was a businessman named Peter J. Lawless, who resided at the hotel from its opening in 1886 until 1928. When the lights stopped working, he got candles, and when the front door was locked, he used his own key.

No matter who was the manager, the Driskill was simply too grand a hotel for Austin in the 1880's. The town may have been the state capital, but sessions were short and the population otherwise was only a few thousand. Meanwhile, the Driskill had cost $400,000, top dollar for a large hotel, but the Driskill had only 60 guest rooms when it opened. At over $6,500 per room, it may have been the costliest hotel of its era. Not all of the investment was devoted to the architecture, which was a detailed rendition of Romanesque style in light-colored bricks and limestone trim. Some of the money was hidden in construction techniques that made the hotel a fortress, and "as nearly fire-proof as is possible."

Every wall within the building was made of bricks, the ceilings were made of corrugated iron and as to the floors, they were double-framed around three inches of cement. Each room was thoroughly insulated by masonry and metal. The decoration inside the Driskill generally used carved wood in repeating the design of the outside of the building. Some of the interiors were lost in a 1952 remodelling, but even so, the Driskill's ambitions remain in the grand staircase with its delicate bulk and the lobby, with its 20-foot ceiling and forest of limestone pillars.

A good hotel is responsible for its guests, in more than just providing a pillow and a place to sleep. An anecdotal history of the Driskill by Joe Frantz recalls that during the earliest days of the Franklin Roosevelt administration, all banks were closed tight for about a month, leaving most people, including travelers on the road, without any cash. W.L. Stark, the manager of the Driskill, responded by clearing out the hotel's safe and simply handing money to any guest who was in need. No notes were signed, but he received all of it back, when the bank crisis was over. The Driskill was long considered the unofficial capitol building of Texas, being across the street from the old one and not far from the current one. Lyndon Johnson not only ran most of his campaigns, state or national, from the Driskill, he made sure to have his hair cut there whenever he was in town.

Several of the Driskill's closings have inspired lush farewell parties, including one in 1966, at which a patron named Walter Long gave a speech that ended ... "Once more, I listen for that tantalizing sound that comes to me over eight decades – Head Waiter Old Sam is calling, `Dinnah is now served in the Crystal Ball Room, Roast Ham, Fried Chicken, O'Possum an' Sweet Potatoes Virginia style, thirty-five cents ...' and the sounds from the old walls fade away."

They came back, they always do, at the Driskill.

Amenities: Concierge; complimentary peanut butter and jelly sandwiches in the evening; 24-hour room-service; business services.

Dining tip: The hotel has live entertainment almost every night in a city known for good music of all types.

Location notes: The Driskill is four blocks from the State Capitol, the convention center, and the campus of the University of Texas.

Dallas
THE ADOLPHUS   1912

1321 Commerce St., Dallas 75202. Tel. 214/742-8200; 800/221-9083; Fax 214/651-3561. 435 rooms. Rates: rooms, $295-395; suites, $425-2,000.

Most people who spend a fortune building a hotel name it after themselves. Mr. Brown did in Louisville. Mr. Bullock did in Deadwood. So did Mr. Busch in Dallas, but he was one of the few to specify his first name, not his last, and his hotel has been known ever since as the Adolphus. Perhaps he always thought of himself only as "Adolphus," being the youngest of 21 children. Perhaps he didn't want to confuse the new hotel with his famous brewing business, Anheuser-Busch. More likely, he never gave it as much thought as any of the foregoing.

Busch only built the hotel because a group of Dallas civic leaders came to him in St. Louis in 1910 and asked, very politely, if they could please have a grand hotel. According to a report prepared by Elise Mitchell for the Dallas County Historical Commission, he looked into the matter and went ahead, at a cost of $1.7 million. The Adolphus Hotel is odd looking from the outside: a fairly standard brick block as it rises for its first 15 floors, it is capped by an elaborate mansard roof five stories high at the top. It looks a plainly-dressed woman, wearing an outrageous hat. Inside, the Adolphus was detailed in Beaux Arts style, and was profuse with European antiques. The Adolphus and the Baker Hotel (now gone) competed as the centers of social life in the highly social city of Dallas.

The list of celebrities who stayed at the hotel or entertained there goes on in two rows for five pages. A former busboy named Foster Prather remembered a couple of them, including Rudolph Valentino, who was engaged to make an appearance in the Junior Ballroom: "That room was packed with ladies, and we were supposed to serve tea at $5 a plate. But once he started to dance, we all just watched. Caruso came once, but not to sing. He ordered spaghetti and had me bring everything to the table for him to mix himself." On one evening in the Century Room, Maria Callas sang at a dinner honoring Grace Kelly.

Through the years, the Adolphus may have presented the most dignified atmosphere in town, but behind the scenes, the hotel had a mad habit of constructing additions and making changes, without rhyme or reason. In fact, when Vice President Hubert Humphrey visited in the mid-1960's, his Secret Service staff couldn't even find out how many rooms were in the hotel. No one knew for sure. According to a historical sketch in *The Adolphus Cookbook*, "The supervisory staff organized teams to count doors, stairway open-ings, and the smallest apertures to get an inventory of what the hotel had. They found some unusual features. On the 9th floor, for instance, two 2-room suites seemed to be connected by a door, but the doors on each side opened to a blank wall ..." The only thing about the patched-over building that wasn't surprising was that it was pronounced impractical to save by engineers who examined it in the 1970's.

Nonetheless, new owners made the commitment to rescue the Adolphus in 1980, an $80-million effort that sorted out the guestrooms, reduced their number by half and rebuilt them with contemporary conveniences and traditional, English country style. The restoration also mixed new restaurants and meeting rooms into the hotel, without compromising the grandeur of the newly buffed public rooms and lobbies.

Amenities: Concierge; fitness room; in-room mini-bar, fax, dataports, walk-in closets.

Dining tip: The hotel serves Afternoon Tea every afternoon, Wednesday to Saturday, serving finger sandwiches, scones, and pastries, including cream puff swans.

Location notes: The Adolphus is in the financial district of downtown Dallas. It is one block to Neiman-Marcus; three blocks to the Dallas Convention Center; and six blocks to either Union Station or the Dallas Museum of Art.

THE ARISTOCRAT   1925

1933 Main St. Dallas 75201. Tel. 214/741-7700; 800/231-4235; Fax 214/939-3639. 172 rooms. Rates: rooms, $149; suites, $189. The Aristocrat is a Holiday Inn hotel.

Conrad Hilton was just another hotelier in the early 1920's, with a gaggle of generally run-of-the-mill properties in Texas. He managed to turn profits, though, and saw the potential for even more. In 1925, he took a breathtaking chance, building his own hotel from scratch at a cost of over one million dollars. The first Hilton Hotel was anything but run-of-the-mill: a 14-story skyscraper (for Texas at the time), with the most impressive architectural statement that Conrad could commission.

Built on a horseshoe pattern, the proportions are supposed to be those of a pair of Corinthian columns, with the strongest effect at the top and bottom. Hilton had strong ideas about certain aspects of his hotel, and yet, the overall standard that it set for the many Hilton Hotels that followed was narrowly defined by the hotel market in Dallas at the time. Hilton didn't want to compete with the Aldolphus (see above) for the highest end of the market, nor did he see much room for medium-priced accommodations in town. Hilton opened his hotel for the middle-class tourist, and the mid-level business traveler, neither of whom was likely to put up the premium for a room at the Adolphus. And yet both of whom wanted to be pampered, a bit.

All of the guestrooms at the new Hilton Hotel had private bathrooms and air conditioning. Hilton rented out shopspace in the lobby on a scale rarely seen before, in order to make money, of course, but also to cater to the myriad needs of the guests. Except for the initial architecture, his Hilton did not carry itself with much imagination, and that, too, was a selling point for people who wanted no surprises, good, bad or otherwise. Conrad's million-dollar gamble was a success, and led directly to the chain that bears his name.

Another of his innovations, however, involved the lease structure that financed his hotels, an arrangement that allowed him to squiggle out of the Dallas Hilton in 1938. The new lessor was a man named White, who named it the White Plaza – a point of confusion, no doubt, for all the travelers who found instead a brownish plaza at the hotel address. In 1985, the hotel received landmark status in Dallas. It was refurbished the same year and named The Aristocrat, a place that has probably made the most of its vintage architecture, with enlarged and redecorated guestrooms, to become an even more interesting hotel that it was when it opened.

Amenities: Complimentary transportation to Dallas Love Field and downtown Dallas; discounted parking in garage; in-room mini-bar, multiple phones; separate dressing room and executive work-desk, ironing needs, hair dryer, and coffee-maker.

Dining tip: The specialties of the dinner menu are off the mesquite-grill.

Location notes: The Aristocrat is in the Harwood Historical District. It is eight blocks from the Dallas Convention Center, five blocks from the Dallas Museum of Art, and one block from the original Neiman-Marcus store.

THE STONELEIGH   1923

2927 Maple Ave., Dallas 75201. Tel. 214/871-7111; 800/255-9299; Fax 214/871-9379; e-mail stonehot@flash.net; web http://www.netpp.com/stoneleigh. 153 rooms. Rates: rooms, $195-250; suites, $250-400.

The Stoneleigh was a swank hotel, the tallest building in Dallas throughout its first 20 years. Perhaps that is why Colonel William Stewart built the hotel in 1938: perhaps he really just wanted the top floor, and took the rest of hotel just to hold it up. Stewart took the 11th floor, all 7,000 square feet of it, for his Penthouse. According to the hotel, his suite "is honeycombed with hidden passageways and boasts a rooftop terrace. Tradition has it that these passages were used as escape routes to late night poker parties and even as access to other parts of the hotel." Today, the 11th floor is used for meetings and parties.

The Stoneleigh has Federal decor, styled in a way modern for 1923. It is a well-maintained hotel, and in a recent freshening, the guestrooms received new bedspreads, draperies, carpets, and televisions.

Amenities: complimentary parking and valet, transportation within a 5-mile radius, and morning newspaper; room-service; concierge; dual phone-lines in room.

Dining tip: One of the hotel's two restaurants serves a sushi menu.

Location notes: The Stoneleigh in the Turtle Creek neighborhood of Dallas. It is one mile to the Convention Center and a half-mile to the West End.

El Paso
CAMINO REAL HOTEL   1912

101 S. El Paso St., El Paso 79901. Tel. 915/534-3000; 800/722-6466; Fax 915/534-3024; e-mail, elp@caminoreal.com; web, http://www.caminoreal.com. 359 rooms. Rates: rooms, $69-114; suites, $155-990.

Pancho Villa stayed at the Camino Real, known in his day as the Paso del Norte Hotel. But that was in 1914, when he was a dapper and welcome guest, not only of the hotel, but of the United States. Two years later he became a desperado, a targeted enemy of the U.S. Army, and he certainly never stayed at El Paso's best hotel again. At least not so that anyone noticed: Clark Gable stopped in the del Norte for a meal in 1943 and no one even recognized him. He was sitting in the coffee shop with some friends from the Army. A judge, having heard a rumor that the movie star was around, stopped by the table and asked if any of them had seen Clark Gable in the hotel. They all shrugged and the judge left.

Among the guests who made sure they were noticed, however, were Dr. and Mrs. G. Jorgeson, authors of *The Hunchback of Valentine Swamp,* a murder novel about a "Mexican hunchback who knows the secret of making synthetic morphine." The story took place in the lobby of the Paso del Norte Hotel. The Jorgesons stopped at the hotel in the early 1930's on their way to Hollywood, to see about movie rights.

The Paso del Norte, on the border with Mexico in reality and spirit, was intended to be one of the most European hotels this side of Deauville. The original 1912 building consists of two 10-story wings. In between, the former lobby rises two stories to a stained-glass rotunda ceiling. Now known as the Dome Bar, it is a magnificent room, lined with arched windows and doorframes. In 1986, when public-minded citizens restored the old Paso del Norte, they enlarged it by building a 17 story tower, which doubled the number of guestrooms and provided new lobbies and meeting spaces. The Edwardian public rooms of the old hotel were turned into restaurants, as the lobby was made into the Dome Bar.

Today, the hotel is the only American property in the Camino Real chain, which is based in Mexico. The emphasis has moved to the modern part of the hotel, the old rooms being today a gracious afterthought that some guests never even see, rushing from the lobby to rooms in the tower. If El Paso felt it needed a new hotel, at least it didn't destroy an old one to build it, and now you have your choice, even while staying on the same property.

Amenities: Complimentary airport shuttle; business center; swimming pool.

Dining tip: The hotel has a number of restaurants; the Dome Restaurant is in the historic part of the hotel.

Location notes: The Camino Real is in downtown El Paso, across the street from the El Paso Convention Center and Performing Arts Center, four blocks from Union Station and six blocks from the Mexican border.

Fort Davis
THE HOTEL LIMPIA   1912

Main St. on the Square, Fort Davis 79734. Tel. 915/426-3237; 800/662-5517. 20 rooms. Rates: rooms, $68.

There was an invention in Texas even before air conditioning and it was called the Hotel Limpia, which opened in 1912 to entice refugees from San Antonio and Galveston to "sleep under blankets all summer." Such a thought, in the midst of a hot, sticky summer, would make the Limpia seem the grandest of hotels. In fact, the Limpia has devoted much of its long life to educating people in and out of Texas, who might think of the state as uniformly flat and seasonally hot. "One mile high –" states the original letterhead, still used by the hotel, "Ideal climate – cannot be surpassed ... apples raised here cannot be beat ... the finest place anywhere for children and run down mothers," it goes on, toward the bottom of a long list of selling points.

The Limpia Hotel was built on land originally granted to a veteran of the Army of the Republic of Texas. Constructed of pink limestone, it has a wrap-around porch on the ground floor and another across the front on the upper story. In the early days, the hotel catered mainly to ranch families in west Texas, who would visit Ft. Davis for supplies and stay on at the hotel to catch the breezes. From 1921 to 1936, the hotel was owned by Mr. and Mrs. W.S. Miller. A relative of the Millers recalled, "Salesmen always made it a point to stay here. They knew Dad Miller would always have a good domino game going." Eventually, the hotel's chirpy public-relations campaign took hold and city dwellers planned vacations to the Davis Mountains, a part of the Rocky Mountain chain.

In the 1950's, the Limpia was used as office space for the Harvard University Astronomy Department. In the 1970's, a high school teacher challenged his students to find out what the Limpia and other buildings originally looked like. Their efforts actually spurred restoration efforts throughout the town. The teacher, J.C. Duncan, purchased the Limpia and restored it as a hotel. It has since absorbed other buildings in downtown Ft. Davis, to house more guestrooms, a dining room, and a giftshop.

Amenities: Business services; complimentary tea and coffee; televisions, but no room phones.

Dining tip: There are no restaurants at the Limpia, but the neighborhood offers many options.

Location: The main Hotel Limpia is a mile from the Fort Davis National Historic Site.

Fort Worth
THE STOCKYARDS HOTEL   1907

109 E. Exchange Ave., Fort Worth 76106. Tel. 817/625-6427; 800/423-8471; 817/624-2571. 52 rooms. Rates: rooms, $125-135; suites, $160-350.

The Stockyards Hotel was cowboy before cowboy was cool. It was built in 1907 in the part of Fort Worth known as Cowtown, where ranchers brought cattle to sell and companies such as Swift Premium and Armour turned it into meat for table. The Stockyards were more than miles and miles of fencing: they constituted the market, the reward for a year of ranching.

A former Confederate Army officer, Col. Thomas Thannisch, decided that Cowtown needed a fine hotel, and he must have been right, because his Stockyards Hotel took up a whole city block, and still needed to expand just a few years after opening. A tawny brick building, with a gothic version of gingerbread at the top, it stands three stories. Real cowboys sold cows, they didn't have shoot-outs, as in the movies. Shoot-outs were for outlaws – and the Stockyards accommodated a couple of those in 1933, when Bonnie and Clyde used room 305 as a hideout. Bonnie's very own gun is today sentimentally displayed in the room.

The history of the Stockyards is little more than the history of Cowtown: when the packing houses moved away in the 1960's, the hotel became something of a fleabag, but when a very different kind of packing house returned – bigtime saloons where urban cowboys packed themselves in – the Stockyards Hotel regained its rightful mantle again. The hotel was refurbished in 1984, to a purified style fitting a place that lists its address as the Republic of Texas. Cowhide wall-hangings and furniture carved with a lone star help to carry the patriotic theme. In fact, the guestrooms offer a choice of decor, including Victorian, Rustic Western, or Native American.

In 1907, the Stockyards Hotel succeeded by catering to the ranchers' sentiment: "Now that the work is done, let's have fun." In a wider sense, it is still doing the same thing, because in Cowtown, the work is done.

Amenities: Complimentary cocktail; satellite television; in-room coffee-maker, hair-dryer, iron, ceiling fan; valet parking; room service.

Dining tip: Perhaps it is needless to say, but in the hotel's restaurant/bar, Booger Red's Saloon, the bar-seats are saddles.

Location notes: The hotel is located in the heart of the revitalized entertainment district of Fort Worth. It is next door to the Cowtown Coliseum, home of cowboy shows. Downtown Fort Worth and the Tarrant County Convention Center are two miles away.

Galveston
THE HOTEL GALVEZ   1911

2024 Seawall Blvd., Galveston Island 77550. Tel. 409/765-7721; 800/392-4285; Fax 409/765-5780, ext. 197. 228 rooms. Rates: $111-173; suites, $175-350.

The Great Storm of 1900 was very nearly devastating, meaning that the city of Galveston almost didn't rebuild itself. Six thousand people were killed and practically every building was wiped out by the ferocity of an ocean storm with winds of 120 mph. In the days before hurricanes received human names, it was "the Great Storm," and always would be. In the uncertainty that followed, a forceful group of Galveston residents publicized building plans for a variety of buildings: not *rebuilding* plans, but designs with even more ambition than anything seen in the city before. One of the buildings they proposed, or insisted upon, was a grand hotel looking straight into the beach, as though to proclaim that Galveston was not afraid.

In 1911, the Hotel Galvez opened for business, just as promised: "a richly furnished seaside hotel," in the words of a 1912 issue of *Hotel Monthly*. The hotel was sturdy, built of concrete and stucco in Spanish Colonial style, and it was a success from the start. It thrived during the city's Little Las Vegas phase after World War Two, when gambling was legal, but started to waiver in the 1960's, passing through the hands of various owners who either restored it or modernized it, by turns. Dr. Denton Cooley, the heart surgeon, was one of those who purchased the hotel and made an effort to restore it. Today, it is the gleaming beach hotel that it always was (usually was), and the guestrooms are contemporary. However, the current owners are historic preservationists and they have launched a three-year project to reclaim the public rooms and gardens as they were in 1911.

Amenities: Valet parking, free parking; swimming pool; golf privileges; business services; in-room dataport.

Dining tip: Bernardo's, open all day, overlooks the Gulf.

Location notes: The Galvez is across a boulevard from the beach. A trolley that stops at the hotel takes passengers to the Strand Historic District.

Houston
THE LANCASTER   1926

701 Texas Ave., Houston 77002. Tel. 713/228-9500; 800/231-0036; Fax 713/223-4528; web, www.slh.com; e-mail, lancastersales@compuserve.com. 93 rooms. Rates: rooms, $175-225; suites, $325-825.

With its richly appointed walls, its oil paintings of dogs and horses, its brass lamps and generous armchairs, the Lancaster Hotel could be nowhere else but the rolling hills of Suffolk – or downtown Houston. It opened as the Auditorium Hotel in 1926, a fine hotel catering to the theater-folk and theater-goers. In fact, during World War Two, it turned its basement into a special sort of theatrical nightclub: a U.S.O. Canteen modeled on those in New York and Hollywood.

As Houston's theatre district sagged, though, so did the hotel. A bedraggled cabbage leaf by 1983, the old Auditorium was renovated into the right-proper Lancaster in 1983, a transformation worthy of Professor Higgins. The theater district has also come back, with seven major venues in proximity of the Lancaster Hotel, which has become popular once again with visiting actors and actresses.

Amenities: Twenty-four hour room service; exercise room, valet service; in-room mini-bars, CD and VCR systems, dataport, fax machine.

Dining tip: The *haute cuisine* Bistro Lancaster has learned to cater to the pre-theater crowd, serving a civilized dinner beginning to end in about an hour: "refined, creative, great-tasting, but fast," in the words of the head chef.

Location notes: The hotel is across the street from the Houston Symphony, Grand Opera and Alley Theater. It is within five blocks of the financial district.

Port Aransas
THE TARPON INN 1920
P.O. Box 8, Port Aransas 78373. Tel. 512/749-5555; 800/365-6784. 24 rooms. Rates: $45-85.

Duncan Hines was a real person, not just a box of cake flour. He must have been a real person, he got married – that proves something, surely – and the wedding took place at the Tarpon Inn on the Texas coast. An eminent food critic, Mr. Hines wandered the country from the 1930's to the 1950's exploring worthy restaurants, fighting standardization all the way. And Mr. Hines was wild about the Tarpon Inn.

The original Inn was built in 1886 out of wood left over from an old Civil War barracks, but a fire took care of it about fifteen years later. It was replaced by a larger building, a true hotel. But a hurricane took care of *it* in 1919 and the following year, J.M. Ellis and his family rebuilt on the basis of all of the inn's various experience. The new hotel was supposed to resemble the Civil War barracks building, but it was as strong as a battleship underneath. Many coastal buildings are secured by pilings driven into the earth and extending as high as the first floor, typically. Ellis set pilings to be as tall as the whole building, two-and-a-half stories. Needless to say, pilings that long are apt to be slightly askew by the time they reach a point 40 or 50 feet above ground. But Ellis' were not and are not, to this day. Hurricanes come and they go, but not those pilings. The Inn will happily give interested parties a tour of the attic to see the structure.

But pretty pilings were not what Duncan Hines liked about the Tarpon Inn. He liked the seafood. Many famous people came to the Inn to fish for their own dinners. The lobby walls are lined with over 7,000 fish scales – each an individual trophy taken by almost that number of guests, Hedy Lamar, Billy Mitchell, and Franklin Roosevelt, among them. The guestrooms are simply furnished with antiques and individual mementos. None has a telephone, but each has access to a porch, equipped with a technological device at the other end of the spectrum from the telephone: a rocking chair. Maybe even two or three.

Amenities: Free transportation from any dock in town, or from the airstrip; rental of beach equipment.

Dining tip: The hotel dining room is in a surviving section of the 1904 inn, and often has locally caught seafood, such as ling fish.

Location notes: The Inn is near the wharf, where fishing charters are available; it is three blocks to bay fishing areas.

San Antonio
THE FAIRMOUNT   1906

401 S. Alamo, San Antonio 78205. Tel. 210/224-8800; 800/642-3363; Fax 210/224-2767. 37 rooms. Rates: $195-550.

One day in 1986, residents of San Antonio looked out their windows and saw something unusual. The Fairmount Hotel was rolling down the street. It was well within the speed limit for cars, but at a block per day. it was close to the land-speed record for a building. Being stubborn in San Antonio has been something of a civic obligation ever since the Battle of the Alamo – and when the residents there were faced with the prospect of seeing the Fairmount torn down, they simply refused to allow it. If the fine, old hotel had to be separated from its land, it would go in one piece, not as rubble. And so, the move of the Fairmount was accomplished during one very well-planned week: an engineering marvel. The hotel is listed in record books as the heaviest building ever transported on wheels.

When the Fairmount was built in 1906, it was a highly respectable hotel for railroad passengers. Today, it is quite a bit more than that, plushly decorated with a mixture of antique furniture and modern art. Architectural details remain from the original hotel – in moldings and chandeliers, wood paneling and stonework – but the interior is more an expression of first-class Southern style than Edwardian style. Already a historic hotel, the Fairmount became an archaeological one to boot: artifacts from the Battle of the Alamo were found during preparation of the hotel's current site. They are displayed now at the Fairmount.

Amenities: Twenty-four hour room service in-room marble bathrooms, terry robes, three phones, television with VCR, hair dryers.

Dining tip: Polo's is a well-respected contemporary restaurant.

Location notes: The Fairmount is two blocks from the Hemisfair Plaza Convention Center or the RiverWalk, and about three blocks from the Alamo.

THE MENGER   1859

204 Alamo Plaza, San Antonio 78205. Tel. 210/223-4361; 800/ 345-9285; Fax 210/228-0022. 330 rooms. Rates: rooms, $112-132; suites, $182-364.

In 1836, the Mexican Army marched into Texas: "Full seven thousand, in pomp and parade; The chivalry, flower of Mexico; And a gaunt two hundred in the Alamo," according to a poem of the day. The lines forfeited strict numerical accuracy to the meter, but indicated the basic inequity. Having secured the fort, the Mexicans executed the handful of prisoners that they took. To Texans ever since, it seemed a reprehensible way to win a battle and a glorious way to lose one.

Eventually, the battle site became a major tourist attraction. In the 1890's, an Army officer stopping at San Antonio's Menger Hotel walked outside and asked a cabby to take him to the Alamo; three hours later they arrived, and the officer paid the fare, which was considerable. A few minutes after that, he noticed that the Menger is across the street from the Alamo.

The Menger opened as a luxury hotel in 1859, when Alamo Plaza was still lined with mud huts. The Menger was square and solid, reflecting the German immigrants who founded it, with accents of the region in its delicate ironwork railings and red tile – and the lone star in the gable. It has expanded numerous times, though the oldest section and the patio garden have remained in remarkable original shape, perhaps because the hotel has had only three owners in 135 years.

In May 1898, at the outset of the Spanish-American War, the Menger was the unofficial headquarters for high-society members of the 1st Volunteer Cavalry, which was better known as the Rough Riders and best known for its second-in-command, Theodore Roosevelt. The Rough Riders camped in San Antonio. The "Fifth Avenue Crowd," according to the dailies, made a tradition of having a big breakfast at the Menger before acceding to the regimental allowance of 18 cents a day for food. Even Colonel Roosevelt couldn't resist a last stop at the Menger for breakfast, on his way to join the regiment. He stayed at the Menger on other occasions, but then, Roosevelt is to historic hotels what George Washington was to inns; it's hard to find the place that existed before 1920 at which he did not stay.

For years, just before lunch was served in the Menger dining room, the waiters and busboys had to walk in a line from one end of the room to the other, fanning the flies toward the windows and shooing them out. The men sang as they performed this chore, a treat for the guests to hear, according to Aaron Townsend, who started at the Menger in 1894 and retired as headwaiter more than 50 years later. "These boys here now can sing too," he told a reporter in 1946, "but now we get no flies."

Amenities: Concierge; business services; 24-hour room service; exercise room.

Dining tip: The Menger Bar, an exact reproduction of a bar in the House of Lords, has some memorabilia related to Theodore Roosevelt.

Location notes: The Menger is across the street from the Alamo. It is also adjacent to Rivercenter Mall and within three blocks of the River Walk.

UTAH

Ogden
THE RADISSON SUITE HOTEL   1891/1927

*2510 Washington Blvd., Ogden 84401. Tel. 801/627-1900; 800/
333-3333; Fax 801/394-5342. 122 rooms. Rates: $59-225.*

Ogden was a railroad town, growing fast in the 1880's, and its
citizens literally clamored for a grand hotel. A developer named
A.E. Reed was the most likely man to create something suitable, but
he held out for a sweetheart deal. And he received one: the city gave
him the first $10,000 he would need to build a grand hotel. Reed
added $90,000 more and in 1891, he opened a substantial six story
hotel, Romanesque in architecture. As long as he'd used the
Ogdenians' money, old A.E. decided that it would be appropriate
to name the hotel after himself.

However, a family named Bigelow soon purchased the Reed
Hotel, and operated it for years. By 1926, Ogden's citizens were
once again roused to open displeasure with the hotel situation in
their town, feeling that the Reed Hotel looked old. Well, it was
supposed to look old, but was beginning to look ... old-fashioned,
as well. Once again the citizens were compelled to prime the pump,
investing enough money to induce the Bigelows to remodel and
expand the hotel. As a result, all but the first four floors of the
original building were removed, and an L-shaped tower was built
just behind, as though embracing the older building. The new
tower was much plainer than the original building, but generally
continued its Italian-Renaissance influence, inside and out.

Having used the Ogdenians' money, the Bigelows decided that
it was about time they named the hotel after themselves. However,
they were forced to sell it in 1931. By the 1960's, a corporation
owned the hotel, and no one knew what to with it. In the early
1980's, new owners realigned the guestfloors into an all-suite hotel,
while respectfully restoring the public rooms in each part of the
hotel to their respective heydays. The interiors revealed beautiful
details and furnishings, many of which had been long hidden:

polished wood-paneling; marble inlaid floors; coffered ceilings ornate in the Florentine style; and carved stone masonry.

Amenities: Free covered parking; complimentary breakfast buffet; room-service; fitness center; in-suite wet-bar, refrigerator, cable television; hair-dryer.

Dining tip: The dining room on the 11th floor offers spectacular views of Ogden and the mountains beyond.

Location notes: The Radisson Suite Hotel is in Ogden, 35 miles from Salt Lake City's airport and 10 miles from Great Salt Lake. In downtown Ogden, it is within four blocks of the Peery Egyptian Theatre and David Eccles Conference Center, and the 25th Street historic district.

Salt Lake City
THE PEERY   1910

11 W. Broadway, Salt Lake City 84101. Tel. 801/521-4300; 800/331-0073; Fax 801/575-5014. 77 rooms. Rates: $99-149.

The Peery was built as a monument to the success of Utah's mining industry. It is a three story brick building, designed on an "E." Family owned since it was built, the Peery has been very well-maintained through all of its years, and still has its profuse, original wood-paneling.

Amenities: Complimentary airport shuttle, continental breakfast; sauna and exercise room.

Dining tip: The hotel has a bistro.

Location notes: The Peery is in downtown Salt Lake City, within a block of the Salt Palace, Bank One Tower and the Capital Theater.

WYOMING

Cody
THE IRMA   1902

1192 Sheridan Ave., Cody 82414. Tel. 307/587-4221; Res. 800/ 745-4762; Fax 307/587-4221, ex. 21. 40 Rooms, 15 with period furnishings. Rates: historic rooms, $91.50-112; modern rooms, $64.50- 84.40.

The Irma Hotel was built, owned and operated by one of the most famous men of the 19th century, Buffalo Bill Cody. A person of his own invention, Cody started out as a run-of-the-mill scout and buffalo hunter, and aggrandized his life, packaged it and presented it, until he became a one-man antidote to the urbanization of America. By the 1880's, Cody had likewise capsulized the entire frontier and brought it to one city after another in his Wild West Show.

But Cody was not a crass showman. He did love the West, and fell hardest of all for a certain corner of Wyoming. It was a wide-open space in dire need of two things, water and Buffalo Bill. Using his profits from the shows, and investment from four men in Buffalo (coincidentally enough), he founded the city of Cody and built the Irma Hotel within it. The hotel, which opened in 1902, was constructed of stone, a two story building meant to anchor the new town. The hotel, named after his daughter, was also to be a repository for all of the various stuff that people gave him in his travels. Among the more impressive examples of his booty is an ornate bar, carved in cherry and given by Queen Victoria.

The 15 guestrooms in the original hotel, each named after a town pioneer, have been renovated to match their original decor. One of the suites is the one used by Buffalo Bill himself when he was home. The hotel also has a modern addition with standard rooms. Every evening, the Irma stages a shootout between Old West gunfighters on its side portico – if you are not sure that hotels should be in the show-business, remember that this is the Irma, Buffalo Bill's hotel.

Amenities: Air conditioning, television.

Dining tip: The dining room specialty is prime rib.

Location notes: Located in downtown Cody, the hotel is walking distance to the Buffalo Bill Historical Center.

6. THE MIDWEST

"Louis Armstrong sent down his handkerchiefs with a note telling us how to fold them. We couldn't figure out how to fold them, so we flipped the note over, and told him we couldn't figure out how to fold them ... he wanted the squares folded so he could use his thumb and forefinger to flip them down. It made you feel important to help someone that was important. To do something for him made you feel important."
    – Josephine Lee, former laundress of the Hotel Patee, Perry, Iowa.

IOWA

Des Moines
HOTEL FORT DES MOINES   1919
1000 Walnut St., Des Moines 50309. Tel. 515/243-1161; 800/532-1466; 515/243-4317. 240 rooms. Rates: $89-129.

"One hotel seems to be uppermost in the minds of most hotel men at the present time," the *Hotel News* reported in August of 1919, "It is called the Hotel Fort Des Moines." That may sound like the hyperbole of an over-excited reporter, yet it was almost certainly true. "The reasons for the unusual interest attaching to the Hotel Fort Des Moines are twofold," the writer explained, counting first its "up-to-the-minute ideas in modern American hotel construction and equipment" and second, the personal popularity of the proprietor, Bill Miller. Those two things contributed, but the fact was that the Hotel Fort Des Moines had thrown a three day grand opening party in July that attracted hoteliers from all over the country. The contingent of Chicago hotelmen, for example, chartered a special train on the Rock Island Line – when they arrived in town, they paraded in a line through the streets to the new hotel. There were parties, there were acts, there were speeches, there were "Princess Paudhi's Tropical Maids."

Of *course* the Hotel Fort Des Moines was uppermost in the minds of most hotelmen.

The new hotel was 11 stories high, built in an "H" pattern on a corner lot. It was an unusually spacious hotel, especially in the size of its guestrooms, which were apt to be outrageously small at other newly built hotels of the era. Marble was used throughout, most strikingly in the main staircase in the lobby, which also featured glossy wood-paneling on the walls and columns. Among the up-to-the-minute ideas the hotel featured was the Ultra Violet Ray Sterilizer System for the water. It killed water-borne diseases – just hearing that name would kill most healthy lifeforms – but according to the manufacturer, the machine was also "practically the only known method of water sterilization which did not remove the exhilarating properties of the water."

It is hard to think of water as exhilarating, one way or the other. However, in Iowa it may have been: Iowa was a "dry" state for a long time before and after Prohibition on the national level. In fact, one night in 1945, the Gotham Club at the Hotel Fort Des Moines was raided. The managers of the club had been rather smug, having hidden their slot machines just before the police arrived. Nonetheless, the club was locked, at least temporarily.

Thirteen U.S. Presidents have stopped at the Hotel Fort Des Moines, including Woodrow Wilson, who visited only two months after it opened. One night in 1960, John Kennedy, Lyndon Johnson and Hubert Humphrey attended the same dinner at the hotel, plotting out, perhaps, what they should make of the decade to come.

Amenities: Complimentary airport shuttle; exercise room; swimming pool. Pets are allowed.

Dining tip: The original hotel dining room has always been known for steaks.

Location notes: The Hotel Fort Des Moines is downtown, near businesses and shopping. The Governor's Mansion is about 12 blocks away.

THE SAVERY HOTEL   1919

401 Locust St., Des Moines 50309. Tel. 515/244-1228; 800/798-2151; Fax 515/244-2151. 221 rooms. Rates: rooms, $79-99; suites, $225-1,200.

Even while the Hotel Des Moines was throwing itself a grand opening in July 1919, workmen were putting the finishing touches on the new Savery Hotel, due to open in September. And yet, the Savery was much the older hotel – a Des Moines institution.

The Hotel Fort Des Moines had named itself after the old army installation, established in 1843 (at the request of the Sac and Fox Indian tribes, who were afraid of trouble with other tribes following the disruption of U.S. settlement). Built in 1862, the original Savery House was practically an adjunct to the fort. During the Civil War, regiments on leave were cheered at formal dinners there; women met regularly at the Savery to sew uniforms. The hotel undoubtedly profited during the war, and then, on the news of the capture of Richmond, it shook to the timbers when the governor ordered a 100-gun salute, outside its doors. A week later, the governor returned with another 100-gun salute, to celebrate Lee's surrender. One more Northern victory, and the hotel might not have survived. It didn't last forever, and was replaced in 1888 by a new Savery, which gave way in 1919 to the third and current version of the hotel.

During World War Two, Fort Des Moines was re-established as the training ground for the Women's Army Auxiliary Corps, and the Savery was commandeered as their billet. The hotel recently collected the memories of some of the former soldiers, which show the hotel from a different perspective. "There was a wide, winding marble stairs in the lobby that lead to the balcony and second floor," one began, "A roommate and I scrubbed those steps as part of the Housekeeping duties of our Company."

"Since our company was on the 6th floor," the same veteran added, "We could not use the elevators during training. We marched in a fashion up and down the six flights daily to all of our activities. Column of two up and down the stairs! No wonder I'm in good shape."

As a matter of fact, the Savery is now presenting itself as a "hotel and spa," though its six flights of stairs are not on the list of spa equipment.

Amenities: Indoor pool, exercise equipment, masseur and tanning beds;

Dining tip: The hotel has several restaurants.

Location notes: The Savery is connected via Skywalk to 34 blocks in downtown Des Moines. The Civic Center is one block away, the State Capitol is eight blocks away, and Drake University is two miles away.

Keosauqua
HOTEL MANNING   1899

100 Van Buren St., Keosauqua Tel. 319/293-3232; 800/728-2718. 19 rooms. Rates: $35-72.

Schubert's Mandolin Orchestra of Ottumwa played at the grand opening of the Manning Hotel. It seems redundant to add the date: April 27, 1899. When else would a mandolin orchestra give a performance? The Manning is a well-preserved Victorian hotel, with many of its original furnishings and fixtures. The clock in the lobby was specially made for the hotel, and the pine woodwork used profusely in the room was also installed for the opening. From the outside, the hotel has been described as "appearing to be an old riverboat beached on the banks of the lazy Des Moines River."

It is a long, fairly low building, with a verandah, like a ship's deck, running the length of the second story. The style is actually known as "Steamboat Gothic." The guestrooms in the Manning Hotel are filled with pine or oak antiques, and remain very true to turn-of-the-century country style. People who want modern amenities, such as television, can book a room in the hotel's modern adjunct, the Riverview Inn. The Manning itself is for people who can listen hard and hear the mandolin orchestra – Schubert's Mandolin Orchestra of Ottumwa – pink-pank-pinking a symphony into the river air.

Amenities: Complimentary breakfast. There are no telephones or televisions in the rooms.

Dining tip: Breakfast is the only meal served at the hotel.

Location notes: Keosauqua is 125 southeast of Des Moines. The hotel is within four blocks of local attractions such as the Van Buren Country Courthouse and the Pearson House (former Underground Railroad stop.)

Perry
HOTEL PATTEE   1913
1112 Ave., Perry. Tel. 515/465-3511; 888/424-4268. 40 rooms. Rates: rooms, $70-125; suites, $145-165.

In 1994, Roberta Green Ahmanson purchased the derelict Hotel Pattee in her hometown of Perry, Iowa for $60,000. It was a three story red-brick building, lying ignored along a main street with empty storefronts on the ground floor: hardly a landmark of world architecture. But it is part of Perry's past and that past was part of Mrs. Ahmanson, who invested over $12,000,000 – *$12 million* – to restore the old Pattee. If the economy stays the same, she might see a return on her investment by the year 3000. Those figures and her motivations speak more about the history of the grand hotel in America than does the hotel itself. It is certainly a unique case.

Mrs. Ahmanson grew up in Perry, where the two major industries were the slaughterhouse and the railroad depot, but she left at the usual age to go to college. Eventually, she moved to Orange County, California and worked as the religion writer for the newspaper there. Assigned to interview a philanthropist named Howard Ahmanson, young heir to a real estate fortune, her life changed, as she later termed it. The two were married and they now live in Newport Beach, California. Meanwhile, Mrs. Ahmanson found herself with the two ingredients necessary to every grand hotel builder: overt pride in her hometown and a great deal of money.

In the restoration, the new Hotel Pattee was rebuilt throughout; the public rooms are now in Arts & Crafts style. Each of the guestrooms was named for someone or something from Perry's past, and custom-decorated by way of tribute. For example, the Alton School Room is explained this way: "For nearly a century young Iowans learned to read and write in one-room schools like Alton School on the outskirts of Perry. This room celebrates all who learn and all who teach." Many of the others honor various immigrant groups, while a few are more self-indulgent, honoring Mrs. Ahmanson's parents, for example, or her son. The vintage two-lane bowling alley is named for her grandfather. Even the boiler in the basement honors someone, Harvey Siglin, the plumber who installed it in 1946.

"I wanted to honor and remember a lot of people who are so important in our small towns but don't usually get remembered," she said. A grand hotel is a showcase: it's all about the town, and it's always about the builder, as well.

Amenities: Complimentary shuttle; business services; computer rental; menu of pillow choices.

Dining tip: The hotel's chef was previously the executive chef at the four-star Grand Hotel in Boras, Sweden.

Location notes: Perry is in central Iowa, about 40 miles north of Des Moines.

KANSAS

Lawrence
THE ELDRIDGE HOTEL   1925

7th & Massachusetts, Lawrence 66044. Tel. 785/749-5011; 800/ 527-0909. 48 suites. Rates: $78-235.

Amos Lawrence of Massachusetts donated $10,000 in cash to found an Abolitionist town in Kansas in the 1850's. The town was called, of course, "Lawrence." At the time, Kansas was considered crucial to the balance of Pro- and Anti-Slavery states among the not especially united states of America. The new town's hotel helped express Lawrence's point-of-view: it was called the Free State Hotel. Not that it was the "State Hotel" and it was free to stay there, but that the proprietors felt that Kansas should become a state free of Slavery. Sheriff Tom Jones did not share that view. He burned the hotel down in 1856.

Up went another hotel, built by Colonel Shalor Eldridge. Down it burned in the middle of the Civil War, when William Quantrill, a murderer in a soldier's uniform, led a slaughter of 150 civilians in Lawrence. Col. Eldridge survived that attack and rebuilt the hotel once more. After the war, Lawrence settled down as a peaceful college town, home to the University of Kansas, and to the Eldridge Hotel, still a symbol but no longer a target. In 1925, the hotel was deemed too deteriorated to save, yet the citizens wanted to perpetuate the hotel, as a symbol of Lawrence's endurance through its violent past. People from the community invested in a new hotel, a new Eldridge Hotel.

Opened in 1927, it was a five story building, with brick on the upper floors and stone on the lower. It was an elegant hotel, but by 1970 it had to close. Even in its last moment, the Eldridge proved the type of hotel it was; there was no key for the front door. It had never before been locked. In 1985, new owners arrived with new respect – and a total of $3 million – for the Eldridge Hotel. The public rooms were restored or recreated, and furnished with hand-carved mahogany, while the guestfloors were turned over to two-room suites. The lobby has a fish pond, with two catfish and a goldfish.

Amenities: Valet parking; exercise room; business services; in-room mini-bars, complimentary morning coffee.

Dining tip: The hotel dining room serves good steaks, in a state known for good steaks.

Location notes: The Eldridge is located in downtown Lawrence, one mile from the U. of K. campus and close to outlet malls. There is also shopping adjacent to the hotel.

MISSOURI

Branson
THE BRANSON HOTEL   1903

214 W. Main St., Branson 65616. Tel. 417/335-6104. 9 rooms. Rates: rooms, $95; suites, $105.

The Branson Hotel looks like a swell old clapboard house, a manse, even. But it was built as a hotel by the Branson Town Co. in 1903, in order to serve passengers and crews who came through on the new railroad. Not just any railroad, but one with a name like a chant, the St. Louis Iron Mountain and Southern. A hotel is more than an accommodation, it is a public place for its town, and so it was that Branson's first lending library was installed at the hotel, by the Maids and Matrons Study Group. The Branson was a working hotel until the 1970's, when the town stalled. Of course, it fired up again in the 1980's, transformed into an entertainment capital.

In 1990, Jim and Terry Murguia bought the empty hotel and refurbished it, a souvenir of Branson's homey past, with two verandahs fit for lazing away an afternoon in an Adirondack chair. But it is within wailing distance of that new Branson, of mega-theaters and bright lights and it thrives by catering to people come to Branson for a spree.

Amenities: All rooms with private bath, telephone, cable television; complimentary sherry and full breakfast. Suites include bottle of champagne.

Dining tip: Hotel only serves breakfast, buffet-style in a glass-enclosed nook.

Location notes: Within five minutes' drive of four theaters, including those of Wayne Newton and Tony Orlando.

St. Louis
THE MAYFAIR   1925

806 St. Charles Street, St. Louis 63101-1507. Tel. 314/421-2500; 800/437-4824; 314/421-6254. 184 rooms. Rates: rooms, $130-185.

Charles Heiss had been working in the hotel business since he started as a busboy in a German hotel. While manager of the Statler Hotel in St. Louis in the early 1920's, he took the opportunity to build his own hotel, the Mayfair, which opened in 1925. He or his heirs continued to own it for the following 35 years. The Mayfair is an 18 story building in brick and stone, with a certain Teutonic tint to its wood-paneled lobby.

It hosted many celebrities, especially in the days when famous actors toured the country after a run on Broadway in New York. The hotel is still chortling over the fact that when John Barrymore ran up a rather gigantic bill of $434 (in the days when a room was $4), he paid with a check that bounced. The only thing funny about that story is that an otherwise sane hotel of the day would accept a check from a Barrymore, and expect it to clear.

Amenities: Complimentary transportation to downtown locations, coffee in the lobby, shoeshine, and newspaper; in-room dataport, iron, and hairdryer.

Dining tip: The Mayfair Grill features stained-glass artwork on the walls.

Location notes: The hotel is across the street from the Executive Conference Center; 12 blocks from Union Station; eight blocks from the Gateway Arch; two blocks from St. Louis Centre Shopping Mall, and one block from Transworld.

SOUTH DAKOTA

Deadwood
HISTORIC FRANKLIN HOTEL   1903

700 Main St., Deadwood 57732. Tel. 605/578-2241; 800/688-1876; Fax 605/578-3452. 91 rooms. Rates: $49-155.

The town of Deadwood was made by the discovery of gold in 1876, but it considered itself much more than a boomtown. In 1892, a local cattle baron named Harris Franklin sold everything that he owned – or at least every cow – and started construction on a hotel, something that would reflect the town's admiration for itself. When Harris ran out of money, however, the hotel was only half-finished and so he sold out to his own son, who gathered the capital to complete the building in 1903. When it finally opened, the new Franklin Hotel had nothing of the small town attitude about it.

It was a grandiose hotel, no less than a grand one, with a handsome exterior in brick and stone, and interior decoration inspired by classical Greek or Roman villas. The lobby is a large room with Corinthian pillars and a patterned mosaic-tile floor. The main stairwell ends in a rotunda on the top (fourth) floor. Needless to say, the Franklin was putting on airs: it considered itself an outpost of civilization in the West and indeed, before its first decade was up, it had already entertained two presidents, Theodore Roosevelt and William Taft.

The town of Deadwood generally slept during the decades after World War Two, but it has enjoyed a second boom with the legalization of gambling in 1991. Even the Franklin has its own casino. The hotel is now owned by a group headed by Bill Walsh, a television personality in South Dakota. His group has spent years restoring the hotel, such that it is not easy to tell current photographs of the public rooms from vintage shots. The Otis Elevator is original and it requires one of the other great innovations of the past century: an elevator operator. Guestrooms are individually decorated in Victorian style, and the hotel makes a point of naming each room or suite after someone famous who stayed at the hotel, from Fredric March to Mary Hart (former co-anchor with Bill Walsh).

Amenities: Free parking, television, telephone.

Dining tip: By way of either warning or suggestion: the hotel does have a sports lounge with a big-screen TV, which was not in place in 1903, but the main dining room is plain and pretty, and true to the hotel's first days.

Location notes: The hotel is in the very center of town.

THE BULLOCK HOTEL   1895

633 Main St., Deadwood 57732. Tel. 605/578-1745; 800/336-1876. 36 rooms. Rates (seasonal): rooms, $65-85; suites, $155.

Seth Bullock was the first sheriff of Deadwood, a town founded on an epidemic of gold fever. By 1895, the town had settled down a little bit, and so had Bullock, opening a solidly respectable hotel. The Bullock is three stories built of stone blocks, with a Victorian atmosphere within. Revitalized during Deadwood's epidemic of gambling fever in the late 1980's, it is a lively place today, with its own round-the-clock betting.

Amenities: Air conditioning; room service; bell-service; free parking; television; private bathrooms.

Dining tip: The Bullock has a restaurant, with live entertainment in its own theatre.

Location notes: The Bullock is in Deadwood's gambling neighborhood.

Dell Rapids
ROSE STONE INN   1908

504 East 4th St., Dell Rapids 57022. Tel. 605/428-3698. Eight rooms. Rates: $45-55.

The rose stone that gives the Rose Stone not only its name, but also its walls, was quarried right outside of the town of Dell Rapids. The hotel sits on a corner downtown, a cute little two story box, thus proving that a box can be cute, especially if it has a front porch. Just south of Dell Rapids, the Big Sioux River divides into two channels for a span of about 2 1/2 miles. One is a slow, meandering route, popular for canoeing. The other channel moves in a rush through the steep walls of the dells; it is popular only for looking, and from a safe distance. The Rose Stone Inn is about a half-mile from the picturesque dells, a fine walk in fair weather.

In use continuously since 1908, the hotel was purchased in 1991 by Rick and Sharon Skinner, who have tried to treat it with integrity. The rooms are freshly decorated, but incorporate original features as much as possible. "We maintain it as a historic hotel," said Rick Skinner, "leaving as much as possible unchanged. For example, we updated the plumbing, but used original fixtures where we could. The rooms don't have televisions, but we do have a common TV parlor, with a fireplace, for the guests."

Amenities: Complimentary continental breakfast. All rooms have queen-sized brass or four-poster beds. Rooms do not have telephones, but the proprietors will loan guests a mobile phone upon request.

Dining notes: The hotel only serves breakfast, but two steakhouses are within a block or two.

Location: Dell Rapids is 13 miles from Sioux City. The Rose Stone Inn is located in downtown Dell Rapids, a designated historic district.

Rapid City
ALEX JOHNSON HOTEL   1928

523 6th St., Rapid City 57701. Tel. 605/342-1210; 800/888/2539; Fax 605/342-1210. 142 rooms. Rates: $98-110.

Alex Johnson was a railroad executive – that was his living, but he was a student of Lakota Sioux culture, and that became his life. He collected pieces of Native art, and finally opened a hotel in Rapid City, in large part as a museum, or tribute, to the beauty of the artifacts produced by native craftspeople.

The Alex Johnson Hotel is six stories tall, with Bavarian architecture inside and out. Some of Johnson's original collection is still in place, including hand-painted floor tiles depicting the "Sacred Four Directions," a travelers' motif.

Amenities: Free parking; exercise room; room-, bell-, valet-service; business services.

Dining tip: The restaurant makes an effort to serve local recipes, including buffalo and pheasant dishes.

Location notes: The Alex Johnson Hotel is in downtown Rapid City.

7. THE SOUTH

"Friend Flagler," Henry Plant reportedly asked, "Where is that place you call Palm Beach?"
"Friend Plant," Henry Flagler replied, "Just follow the crowd."
– quoted in *The Breakers,* by Charles Lockwood

ARKANSAS

Eureka Springs
BASIN PARK HOTEL   1905

12 Spring St., Eureka Springs 72632. Tel. 501/253-7837; 800/643-4972; Fax 501/253-6985. 61 rooms. Rates: $66-81; suites, $90-175.

There must have been something in the water: Joseph Perry came to Eureka Springs in 1879 and ended up building a hotel. William Duncan arrived a few years later and he ended up building a hotel, right on the site of Perry's Hotel, which had burned in 1890. Actually, little Eureka Springs had 50 hotels at the turn-of-the-century, catering to people who visited the town for its mineral waters. Duncan made a fortune in Eureka Springs, bottling the water as "Ozarka" and shipping it to other cities.

The hotel that he built looked a little like the old Perry, except that it was made of stone. That may have fireproofed the building to some extent, but Duncan wanted to fireproof the people inside, too, so he had his masons construct "bridge-walks" leading from each of the eight floors of the hotel to the steep mountain just behind it. Ripley's Believe It Or Not described it in a newspaper feature as "an eight-story hotel with every floor a ground floor." The Basin Park Hotel was used as a museum for a while in the 1970's, but it is completely restored today as a hotel, with large, homelike rooms.

Amenities: Business services; pets allowed; in-room television.

Dining tip: The Ballroom was long the town's party hall – "you could hear the music from the Ballroom even up on the mountain" – and is coming back in that role, with seasonal events that are open to the public.

Location notes: The Basin Park Hotel is the heart of Eureka Springs, overlooking its namesake park.

NEW ORLEANS HOTEL   1892

63 Spring St., Eureka Springs 72632. Tel. 501/253-8630; 800/243-8630. Eighteen suites. Rates: Sunday-Thursday, $79; weekends and holidays, $90-125; $5 extra in October.

The story of the New Orleans Hotel begins with Miss Jennie Loftus, a bareback rider in the circus. A man named Wadsworth, who was known to have a few dollars, fell in love with Jennie and, after they were married, they moved to Eureka Springs. It was a resort, where, one might conjecture, former experience as a bareback rider would not keep a person out of the best dinner parties.

Whatever the reason for the move, the Wadsworths built a hotel in 1892, and Jennie operated it after her husband died. It earned its own way through the years, but closed for six years starting in 1981. New owners invested $1,000,000 in a restoration that changed the guest floors into an all-suite configuration. Some are contemporary, but a few remain true to Victorian decor, with antique furniture and lace curtains.

Amenities: Free parking; in-room refrigerator, and coolers of mineral water.

Dining tip: Fat Tuesday's, on the lower level, serves Cajun cuisine.

Location notes: The hotel is in the middle of the shopping district, and is less than a block from Basin Park.

Little Rock
CAPITAL HOTEL   1876

111 W. Markham St., Little Rock 72201. Tel. 501/374-7474; 800/766-7666; Fax 501/370-7091. 123 rooms. Rates: rooms, $127-168; suites, $290-385.

In 1880, Ulysses S. Grant, the immortal Northerner, visited Little Rock. Some un-Reconstructed Southerners went to elaborate lengths to pay him no attention whatsoever: a gaggle of women sat out in the sun all afternoon, just to make sure that when old Mr. Grant passed by, he could take note that their backs were turned to him. The vast majority of local citizens, however, formed a line outside the Capital Hotel in order to shake the hand of General Grant, perchance to say a word or two to him. According to a hotel brochure, Grant was "bone weary from travel and obliged to stand endless hours in the lobby." Finally, according to the legend, a substitute was found, a former prison warden who looked exactly like Grant (quite a few people do, actually). It was a ruse that worked until a former prisoner came through the line.

The lobby of the Capital is an extraordinary backdrop for any such masquerade: with its delicately patterned mosaic floor, a colonnaded mezzanine, and best of all, the original stained-glass ceiling, two stories up. That lobby is the masterpiece of the Capital, restored about ten years ago under the supervision of a research architect named Edwin Cromwell. Stained glass ceilings were fairly common to grand hotels in the late 19th century, but the vast majority were "upgraded" in the 1950's and 1960's to plexiglass or hung-ceilings. The Capital was no exception – but it was an exception in that its stained-glass plates were carefully stored in the cellar, stored and forgotten until the renovation was underway.

As a matter of fact, the Capital Hotel was *not* built as a hotel originally – it was an office block, built in 1872 and detailed in Beaux Arts style. Four stories high, it is a rather delicate looking building, considering it takes up a full block, painted white and graced by arched windows on the second and third stories. In 1876, however, Little Rock's leading hotel burned, leaving the ambitious city with an emergency. "Wanted – A First Class Hotel!" was the newspaper's reaction, in headline type. And so the office building was quickly transformed into a hotel, open for business by the end of the year. Considering the state of emergency, it still counts as a true hotel. The guestrooms in the hotel are completely refurbished, and decorated with reproduction antiques. And the Capital Hotel is still home to Presidents: it was Bill Clinton's campaign headquarters in 1992.

Amenities: Twenty-four hour room service; complimentary buffet breakfast; in-room safe, two-line phone; 100% Egyptian cotton bedding.

Dining tip: The Capital has always been a hang-out for Little Rock politicians, who now favor the Bar & Grill room at the hotel.

Location notes: The hotel is across the street from the Statehouse Convention Center. It is located downtown, within walking distance of the River Market.

FLORIDA

Amelia Island
FLORIDA HOUSE INN   1857
20-22 South 3rd St., Amelia Island 32034. Tel. 904/261-3300; 800/258-3301. 11 rooms. Rates: rooms, $70-125; suite, $135.

Before the Civil War, Fernandina Beach was a bustling commercial center on Amelia Island, off Florida's Atlantic coast. In 1857, the Florida Railroad tried to generate interest in the area by opening a hotel to accommodate business people and some of

Florida's earliest tourists. Later in the 19th century, Amelia Island became the favorite resort island for Northern millionaires, including John D. Rockefeller and Andrew Carnegie. A clapboard building in the Greek Revival style, with tall windows decked by shutters, Florida House would be at equally at home in New England. Now calling itself an "inn," the Florida House is still anchoring Fernandina Beach, an elegant historic district, made for strolling.

Amenities: Air conditioning; complimentary breakfast; laundry facilities; business services.

Dining tip: The hotel restaurant serves Southern food, boarding-house style.

Location notes: The Florida House is in a historic district, with blocks of the shrimp docks and marina. Atlantic beaches are two miles away.

Cedar Key
ISLAND HOTEL   1859

P.O. Box 460, Cedar Key 32625. Tel. 352/543-5111; Fax 352/543-6949; e-mail ishotel@gnv.fdt.net. 10 rooms. Rates: $85-95.

Located on the Gulf of Mexico, the Island Hotel is a two story building in very original condition, with full, wrap-around verandahs and a gently pitched roof. The construction material is seashell tabby (a type of stucco) with oak members, and so it can be said that the hotel is literally part of the Florida coast. Decorated with murals painted in the state's fashionable heyday in the 1940's, the public rooms have changed little through the years, except that the floors have started to slope, from footfall.

Amenities: Air conditioning, ceiling fans, complimentary breakfast; original handcut wooden walls and floors. No televisions.

Dining tip: The restaurant specializes in very local seafood, accompanied by homemade poppy seed bread.

Location notes: The hotel is near two museums of local history.

Coral Gables
BILTMORE   1926

1200 Anastasia Ave., Coral Gables 33134. Tel. 305/445-1926; Fax 305/448-9976. 273 rooms. Rates (seasonal): rooms, $209-359; suites, $379-449.

The Biltmore Hotel is built in a Mediterranean style – but of course it is, it's in Coral Gables. The town has regulated architecture ever since it was founded by a young promoter named George Merrick in 1925. He insisted that Coral Gables would not be just another Florida landboom town, but a beautiful, controlled community. Yet in most ways, it was a quintessential boomtown: the idea was to sell lots and Merrick enlisted no less than William Jennings Bryan and the chorus of "Earl Carroll's Vanities," to help close deals in Coral Gables. At first, all buildings had to have generally the same Mediterranean style (later on, exceptions were planned into the look of the town). Within a year of incorporating Coral Gables, Merrick had founded the University of Florida there; opened the new Biltmore Hotel; and welcomed thousands of new residents.

The Biltmore is a large, long building, with something like the silhouette of a ship from a far distance. Each section steps higher toward the tallest one in the center, which adjoins a bell-tower (almost like a funnel, from a far distance). The building is a faithful rendition of a Southern European palazzo, with arched doorways and vaulted ceilings, stone columns and marble floors. It also has the biggest swimming pool in the continental United States, and one of the first swimming teachers to work in it was Johnny Weissmuller – before he won his Olympic medals and became "Tarzan" in the movies. The Biltmore was host to many movie stars and members of royalty, according to the hotel's own history, but only for a short time.

By World War Two, it was just barely in business and was requisitioned for use as a regional hospital by the Army Air Forces. Historic preservation was not a priority with the military in 1942 – unless you count preserving old things such as the Constitution – and the Biltmore was soon redecorated in vinyl and high-gloss paint, its windows cemented over. The building remained a hospital until the 1970's, when it became a haunted house, as far as the neighborhood children were concerned. They dared each other to go near the empty hulk on Halloween – no one else dared go near it, either, least of all developers and hoteliers. Finally, however, it drew considerable respect and received an ambitious restoration in 1983. It faltered once more, but underwent an even more meticulous refurbishment in 1992.

Even beyond the architecture, the Biltmore has resumed its original polish and its place in the life of the area. On the occasion of the Biltmore's 70th birthday in 1996, President Bill Clinton remarked on its "splendor and serenity" and said it was "a wonderful public asset for the benefit of the people of Coral Gables and Dade County."

Amenities: Complimentary airport or train shuttle; exercise room; tennis courts; concierge; 24-hour room service.

Dining tip: Once a month, the hotel's Palme d'Or restaurant hosts a Michelin-rated chef from France, with a demonstration and luncheon. On Tuesdays, the hotel features an operatic performance during dinner.

Location notes: Coral Gables is four miles from Miami International Airport and five miles from downtown Miami. Tours of the Biltmore are given every Sunday afternoon.

Indiantown
SEMINOLE COUNTRY INN   1926

15885 S.W. Warfield Blvd., Indiantown 34956. Tel. 561/597-3777; Fax 561/597-4691. 25 rooms. Rates: $65-85.

Some hotels have a roster of famous guests – the Seminole Country Inn had one very famous employee. Wallis Warfield, the future Duchess of Windsor, sometimes worked there as a hostess. It was her uncle, S. Davies Warfield, who opened the hotel in 1926 as the centerpiece of a model town he had planned. Founding towns in Florida was something of an upper-class pastime in the 1920's, and Mr. Warfield tried to set a standard for his new town by appointing its first hotel with cypress paneling and bronze chandeliers, specially commissioned for the place.

His involvement in the town did not last nearly as long as the hotel, however. And that is likely to be a very long time: the architecture of the Seminole Country Inn is graceful, looking something like a Spanish mission. The outer walls are 20 inches thick, an early means of keeping the heat out.

Amenities: Air conditioning, telephones, cable television, swimming pool.

Dining tip: The hotel serves a Sunday buffet, including Southern dishes.

Location notes: Indiantown is 30 miles northwest of West Palm Beach. The hotel is near to Owens Grove (orange trees) and 30 miles from Lake Okeechobee.

Palm Beach
THE BREAKERS   1925
One S. County Rd., Palm Beach 33480. Tel. 561/655-6611; 888-273-2537; web, http://www.thebreakers.com. 622 rooms. Rates (seasonal): $160-575; suites, $475-2,200.

Even John Rockefeller thought that Henry Flagler was overly interested in making money. They worked together to build the Standard Oil Co. in the 1860's and 1870's, and they made some money, it can be said with accuracy. Rockefeller, however, was careful to balance his life with pursuits outside of business. Henry Flagler's job, hobby and sole interest in life was making money, both in and out of the Standard. It worried Rockefeller, a bit.

In the 1880's, however, Flagler discovered Florida as though that state had never been seen by man before. Basically, it hadn't: it was a scruffy terrain with a few ranches, an army post or two and no big cities whatsoever. To Henry M. Flagler, Florida was a money-making opportunity – that's obvious, to him everything was – yet at the same time, it was also a philanthropy. In other words, Florida not only needed his money, it needed *him*. It got both.

First, Flagler improved railroad service on the peninsula. In 1896, his Florida East Coast Line reached Miami, which then barely existed as a community. During the 1880's, Flagler had retired from his duties at the Standard to devote himself to his principality in Florida. During the 1890's, he built a string of fantastic hotels along the coast, another step in the development plan. It was not a tepid effort: the Ponce de Leon in St. Augustine was the largest concrete building in the world when it opened in 1888. However, Rockefeller was especially interested to see how Florida was changing his old partner, as Allan Nevins related in his book on Rockefeller: "Flagler found a new zest in life, and evinced a new concern for humanity. Every section boss on his East Coast Line became a personal friend; every man who set out an orange grove was cordially advised and aided. All along the railroad he provided schools, churches, and hospitals, insisting that strict secrecy surround his gifts."

Even so, Flagler made money every time he looked around, and in 1896, he looked around the back of his gargantuan Royal Poinciana Hotel in Palm Beach and decided to build an annex even nearer to the ocean. It was called the Palm Beach Inn, and it had colonial architecture that would have been at home on Block Island or Cape Cod. From the first, people loved to be at the Inn, "down by the breakers." The original Inn burned in 1903, but it had been a patchwork of additions, anyway. Having almost stumbled on the magic of the location and its allure, Flagler built a major hotel to replace it. Nothing as accidental as a nickname: by then, it was called, officially, "The Breakers." A snobby and silly place, it was a phenomenally popular place, with rich Northerners looking for each other in the Florida sun.

In 1913, Henry Flagler died and his civilization had to continue without him. However, a dozen years later, the Breakers burned. The heirs to the Flagler fortune rebuilt it and, just as in 1903, the new Breakers made the old one look like a shack. It is a fairly long, seven-story building made distinctive even from a distance by the two bell towers that brace the center section. The exterior is not overbearing in architectural style, it is rather plain, except for the fact that it is surrounded by gardens in the ocean air. However, inside, the Breakers is ornately decorated in Florentine style. It was built as a resort, and still qualifies as one, with two golf courses (including the oldest one in the state), 21 tennis courts, and a swimming pool. But that is not what makes a resort: *croquet* makes it a resort. Hotels don't offer croquet, or shuffleboard or horseshoes, either, all of which the Breakers does offer. However, the Breakers practically gave birth to Palm Beach, which is today a city in its own right, of course, and the Breakers has always been its hotel.

The Breakers has never been sold. Flagler left it to his wife, who left it to her family, which still actively manages it today. Among American hotels, only the Wittmond (see Illinois) has been in its original family longer.

Amenities: Free parking (if available); valet parking; business services; exercise room (and many other recreational options); in-room mini-bar, safe, radio, hair dryer, two telephones, individual climate control.

Dining tip: The original clubhouse for the Ocean Course, Florida's oldest golf links (1897) is now the Centennial dining room, serving a prix fixe gourmet dinner every night at 8pm.

Location notes: The Breakers is 65 miles north of Miami. It is six miles from Palm Beach's airport.

St. Petersburg
THE HERITAGE   1920

234 Third Ave., St. Petersburg 33701. Tel. 813/822-4814; 800/283-7829. 71 rooms. Rates: rooms, $79-89; suites, $129. The Heritage is a Holiday Inn hotel.

Originally known as the Martha Washington Hotel, the Heritage is a Mediterranean-style, pink stucco hotel. That doesn't sound very Martha-ish; however, the interior was intended in the 1920's to have a colonial atmosphere and it still does today. The guestrooms were recently refurbished, but still feature cherrywood furniture in the Queen Anne style.

Amenities: Free parking; swimming pool; room service; laundry and valet services.

Dining tip: The hotel's dining room, which doubles as a serious art gallery, specializes in local seafood, including snapper. The bar in the restaurant was once installed in the home of Jefferson Davis, the president of the Confederate States.

Location notes: The Heritage is in the Museum District of St. Petersburg, within eight blocks of the Bayview Center, and within three blocks of the waterfront marina. The Gulf of Mexico is 15 minutes away by car.

GEORGIA

Americus
THE WINDSOR 1892
125 W Lamar St., Americus 31709. Tel. 912/924-1555; 800/678-8946; Fax 912/924-1555, ext. 113. 53 rooms. Rates: rooms, $68-78; suites, $129-189.

The Windsor Hotel's story begins in a picturesque way on the afternoon of August 22, 1888, when two young men were discovered taking measurements of the Courthouse Square in Americus, Georgia. A passing reporter couldn't resist asking them why they were surveying the town center. "Because Major Moses Speer and Papa told me to," one of the boys responded. The reporter searched out Major Moses Speer, the president of a local bank, and then heard for the first time that a grand hotel was to be built on the square. The major was already gathering investors, on the three theories that the new hotel would attract rich Northern tourists; reflect Americus' best qualities to itself and others; and generally stir things up in town.

The planning process, alone, stirred things up, even before the first brick was laid. Two architects submitted designs. The first depicted a plain wooden box of a hotel. The second depicted a fantastic Moorish castle. The investors' selection committee chose the box. But unexpectedly, at the full meeting of all the investors, the selection committee's decision was tossed aside in favor of the castle. Things had undoubtedly stirred in Americus in the interim. Just as the hotel was about to open, the name was changed from the "Alhambra," to the "Windsor," which so happened to be the name of one of the investors, the one with the most money. More specifically, the one with the wife whose uncle had left the most money. Something stirred in Americus.

The Windsor Hotel was a unique building, a design both solid and fanciful, with a turret on the corner and arched balconies recessed into two main wings. Expenses for furnishings had undoubtedly raced out of control – the hotel was the first one in the South with its own specially engraved silverware, for example – and sadly enough, the Windsor was bankrupt only six years after it opened. As a matter of record, the man who stepped forward with enough money to buy it was the very jeweler who had sold the first load of specially engraved silverware ever seen in a hotel in the South.

The Windsor declined a bit. It was a good hotel, but not the grand one it had been at the start. Charles Lindbergh once stayed at the Windsor – and wasn't mobbed there, not in the least. The year was 1923 and he was in Americus awaiting delivery of his first airplane. Nor did it necessarily say much for the hotel that it was the choice of an itinerant flyer. Franklin Roosevelt also stayed at the hotel before he was a household name: in 1928, as Governor of New York, he gave a speech from the verandah of the hotel. Roosevelt could afford to stay anywhere he liked, but the place he liked most in the country may well have been Warm Springs, a town only a few miles from Americus.

In 1978, the last owner wearied of the aging Windsor Hotel and donated it to the city of Americus: a dubious gift, by that point. The mayor was faced with the decision to either tear it down for a parking lot or to refurbish it. Lots of towns have too many parking lots, but precious few have a grand hotel. Saving the hotel would be a monumental task, but the mayor and his constituents decided overwhelmingly to try, and in doing so to save downtown Americus. Government agencies, to their credit, initiated the effort, providing seed money for planning; the state even brought inmate labor to begin the actual restoration. As hope began to grow, hundreds of local residents purchased shares in a new corporation responsible for the hotel's future. All of the $5.8 million for the restoration was raised locally.

The lobby at the Windsor is detailed in golden oak, with a marble floor and a mezzanine level. The public rooms and most of the guestrooms are furnished with antiques, though only one item, a clock, is known to have survived from the hotel's first opening day, well over a hundred years ago.

Amenities: Room-service; bell-service; free parking; each room has television, telephone, coffee-maker.

Dining tip: The hotel restaurant is known for fresh seafood dishes.

Location notes: Americus is 130 miles south of Atlanta. The Windsor Hotel is 11 miles from the Andersonville Historic Site and the National P.O.W. Museum, and nine miles from the Little White House, F.D.R.'s Southern home.

Atlanta
THE GEORGIAN TERRACE   1911

659 Peachtree St., Atlanta 30308. Tel. 404/897-1991; 800/437-4824; Fax 404/724-9116. 320 rooms. Rates: rooms, $175; suites, $175-650.

It is much more than entertainment history to relate that the grand premiere of *Gone With the Wind* was in Atlanta, December 15, 1939, and doesn't Clark Gable always look handsome, even in newsreels? That day in December was also the exact date of the close of Reconstruction, an era that started as a slow millenium in the South right after the Civil War. It started bleakly, but ended with floodlights, on the night that Vivian Leigh and Clark Gable came to celebrate the South's side of the story. The epicenter of the great gala was the Georgian Terrace Hotel, which hosted the stars and hundreds of others following the premiere showing of the movie at Loew's Theatre on Peachtree Street. The party in the Grand Ballroom lasted long into the night, and so perhaps the history books, in order to be perfectly accurate, ought to state that Reconstruction ended on December 15th *and* 16th, 1939.

The Georgian Terrace Hotel had been built in 1911, a light-colored, 10 story brick building on one of the most important corners in Atlanta, Peachtree at Ponce de Leon Avenue. In fact, the building is wedge-shaped and rounded at the vortex, with a gentle Georgian appearance that would indeed be at home in Maida Vale or Mayfair. The interiors were fashionably sumptuous, with marble columns by the score (fifty in all), mosaic floors, and crystal chandeliers set amid intricate plasterwork in the ceilings. The grand staircase in the lobby leads to a mezzanine.

In the 1980's, the Georgian Terrace was saved from destruction, but converted into an apartment building. It underwent a restoration of the public rooms, but the apartment scheme didn't last. In 1997, it re-opened as a hotel, and is appreciated now as Atlanta's only historic hotel.

Amenities: Swimming pool; exercise room.

Dining tip: The hotel has three restaurants.

Location notes: The Georgian Terrace is in midtown Atlanta, across from the Fox Theatre. It is about three miles to either the convention center or Turner Field.

LOUISIANA

New Orleans
THE FAIRMONT   1908

123 Baronne St., New Orleans 70112. Tel. 504/522-7111; 800/527-4727; 504/522-2303. 700 rooms. Rates: rooms, $199-289; suites, $250 and up.

Eight presidents have stayed at the Fairmont, which was long known as the Roosevelt Hotel. Eight presidents and one kingfish:

Huey Long was devoted to the place from the late 1920's until his death in 1935. He used a room at the hotel as his campaign headquarters; he used a suite as his home; and, according to lore, he used the Main Bar as his office. The Fairmont would appeal to the ambitions of a man like Long (who was Louisiana's governor and later a Senator), because it was bold and big, a dramatic proclamation of luxury in New Orleans.

The public rooms are large, even over-sized – the main lobby is a block long – but nonetheless, they are lined in exotic, imported marbles of vivid colors. Gold columns, eagle decorations, plush red carpeting, the Fairmont is splendid, but it isn't subtle. Perhaps that is why Arthur Hailey used it as the model for his novel, *Hotel*. Employees still remember him standing around the public rooms, looking, listening and scribbling into a notebook. That isn't very subtle, either.

The progenitor of the Fairmont, the Grunewald Hotel, was built in 1893. It was a popular place, augmented by a huge addition in 1908. In 1925, the original, old Grunewald was replaced by a 16 story building that merged into the 1908 annex. Since the hotel has remained in continuous operation, despite the leap-frogging building dates, the Fairmont can say that it opened for business in 1893, if not in the current buildings. The hotel is a bustling giant, with plenty of room for recreation facilities on the rooftop.

Amenities: Valet parking; concierge; 24-hour room service; valet service; swimming pool; rooftop tennis courts; business center; exercise room; in-room dataport, two phones, hair dryer, down pillows, complimentary postcard and postage.

Dining tip: The Sazerac, supposed to be the first cocktail, was invented in New Orleans and popularized at the bar of the same name now at the Fairmont. Apparently, the bartender mixed the drink in a cup called a "coquetier," which the patrons soon pronounced, "cocktail." You can still order one at the hotel's Sazerac Bar.

Location notes: The hotel is next to the French Quarter.

THE LAFAYETTE   1916

600 St. Charles Ave., New Orleans 70130. Tel. 504/524-4441, 800/ 733-4754; Fax 504/523-7327. 44 rooms. Rates: rooms, $155-350; suites, $285-650.

Businesses cannot defy gravity, anymore than apples can. The Wirth family proved that in 1916 when they built a small, exquisite hotel in a New Orleans neighborhood best known for its boarding houses. The new Lafayette Hotel had beautiful, neo-classic rooms and modern conveniences, including a new type of plumbing that offered the choice of a needle-bath (shower). The hotel was gorgeous, but the neighborhood was nonetheless frumpy, and guests couldn't seem to push through it to the Lafayette, which closed only about four years after it opened. Empty much of the time since, it was used during World War Two as a barracks for WAVES, female Navy personnel.

Rediscovered in the 1980's, the Lafayette Hotel was perfectly suited to the new appetite for smaller, boutique hotels. After 75 years, it was finally the right hotel in the right place, on a Lafayette Square grown natty in the intervening years. The Lafayette re-opened in 1991, a restored Edwardian building with an atmosphere and furnishings that could easily be at home in London.

Amenities: Valet, mini-bar, twice-daily maid service.

Dining tip: Mike's on the Avenue, the hotel's dining room, serves super-chic Southwestern cuisine.

Location notes: The Lafayette Hotel is about three blocks from either the business district or the courts, four blocks from the Convention Center, and six blocks from the French Quarter.

THE PAVILLON   1907

833 Poydras St., New Orleans 70112. Tel. 504/581-3111; 800/535-9095; Fax 504/523-7434. 227 rooms. Rates: rooms, $250-270; suites, $595-1,495.

During the first half of the 19th century, the site of the present Pavillon Hotel was unworldly. A passage from the hotel's earliest history of itself could just as well be the first paragraph of a gothic novel: "The area was a forbidding outward fringe of the city, described by a writer of the time as a place of `foul deeds and midnight murders ... the dismal willows could be heard uttering plaintive sounds with every gust of wind.' Cypress thickets and cemeteries; treacherous bogs inhabited by mosquitoes, bats, hoot owls and runaway slaves, the land was a place where 'no ordinary courage was required to venture alone.' The night was filled with the sounds of wild men and beasts, the air thick with intrigue and desperate plots."

And then what happened was even worse. First a theater was built on it, but the air became really thick with intrigue and desperate plots when ownership of the land fell into a monstrous legal dispute between several private parties and the city of New Orleans. The case actually went to the Supreme Court before it was through, twenty-five years after it began. Overall, the 19th century was not good to the property, but as the 20th century began, the deed was finally in firm hands and civilization was about to arrive in a big way.

By the early 1900's, the neighborhood was considered the finest in town and the lot became the site of the New Denechaud Hotel. (There had been an old Denechaud Hotel elsewhere in New Orleans.) All hotels try to implement the latest technology: the New Denechaud had hydraulic elevators, for example, but even more impressive as an engineering achievement in the delta: it had a basement! It was first one ever seen in New Orleans. Italianate in decor, the New Denechaud was a true grand hotel, and was well-known throughout the South.

The hotel was renamed the Pavillon after a 1970 restoration that incorporated details from several defunct European hotels, including marble railings from the Grand Hotel in Paris. They are not original, certainly, but they are in keeping with the original style.

Amenities: Concierge; rooftop pool and deck; valet parking; complimentary newspapers, peanut butter-and-jelly sandwiches served nightly in the lobby; shoeshine; in-room safes; 24-hour room service fitness center; business services.

Dining tip: The Gallery Lounge serves a special sushi menu every afternoon.

Location: The French Quarter is four blocks from the Hotel Pavillon; the Superdome is three blocks away, and the Lake Charles streetcar line is one block away.

MISSISSIPPI

Natchez
NATCHEZ EOLA   1927

110 N. Pearl St., Natchez 39120. Tel. 601/445-6000; 800/888-9140; Fax 601/446-5310. 125 rooms. Rates: rooms, $80-95; suites, $120.

Not much – at all – was happening in downtown Natchez as the Depression settled in, in the early 1930's. All that the town really had was a bunch of old mansions and a bankrupt hotel called the Natchez Eola. The mansions dated from before the Civil War and they were surprisingly fanciful; the one called Longwood was an octagon, built on the very eve of the war by a local doctor. The hotel, on the other hand, only dated from 1927, when it had been built in a swell of civic pride: a skyscraper for a river town, at seven stories tall.

In 1932, the town took stock of what it had, added a little imagination, and made itself the destination of what it called the "Natchez Spring Pilgrimage." With marching orders in hand, tourists became pilgrims and flocked to the town to look at the old mansions and their gardens, and also to stay at the Natchez Eola Hotel, which began to boom. In the 1970's, the town needed another boost, and received it as the hotel became the centerpiece of a designated historic district in downtown Natchez. The whole town has the gentle sway of a prosperous old town, and several of the ante-bellum mansions are now open year round.

Amenities: Valet parking; free parking, cable television.

Dining tip: The Mon Flower restaurant takes in the Mississippi River and other views from the 7th floor.

Location notes: The hotel is within three blocks of the riverfront and two old mansions, open to the public, Stanton Hall and Rosalie.

Starkville
STATEHOUSE HOTEL 1925

215 E. Main St., Starkville 39759. Tel. 601/323-2000; 800/722-1903; Fax 601/323-4948. 43 rooms. Rates: $45-109 ($69-129 during special events).

Starkville started out as "Boardtown" in 1831, but tired of that, understandably, after six years and renamed itself after John Stark, the Revolutionary War general from New Hampshire. In 1925, a new hotel opened in Starkville: it was called the Chester, but it also felt compelled early on to rename itself after John Stark, a man who seemed to have quite a following in eastern Mississippi. The Stark was a three story building on a corner downtown: a small town hotel with its own barbershop.

In 1985, it was extensively refurbished and expanded, enveloping the theater nextdoor, which had also been built in the 1920's. It recently took the name "Statehouse Hotel." Most notably, the front desk and some of the artwork are from the original hotel, though the guestrooms were completely redecorated to a modern standard.

Amenities: Air conditioning; television with HBO; telephone; individual climate control; valet service.

Dining tip: The Waverly dining room serves steaks and seafood.

Location: The hotel is in downtown Starkville, the home of Mississippi State University.

NORTH CAROLINA

Charlotte
THE DUNHILL   1929

237 N. Tryon St., Charlotte 28202. Tel. 704/332-4141; 800/354-4141; Fax 704/376-4117. 60 rooms. Rates: rooms, $89-165; suites, $300.

When Paul and Linda McCartney stayed at the Dunhill Hotel, they booked 40 rooms. According to an article in *Our State* magazine, the entourage included 10 security agents, who covered every approach to the McCartney suite during the entire stay. The McCartneys, who are vegetarians, not only refrain from eating dead animals, they refuse to sit on them, and so Linda requested that all leather furniture and other animal products be removed from their rooms. Fab Four Fan Alert: they also faxed ahead to specify that the suite's kitchenette be stocked with juice, mineral water, and crumpets.

That is the type of special service that any hotel in the world will give Paul McCartney, and gladly, but a grand hotel is supposed to be flexible to most special requests. The Dunhill was born into that tradition, opening in 1929. A 10 story brick building, it was supposed to be Georgian in style, with the general feel of an English townhouse of the 18th century. It sagged through the years, until the 1960's, when the owners tried in vain to compete with suburban chain hotels by calling it a "Motor Inn" – the James Lee Motor Inn. But hotels like The Dunhill could never pretend to be motor inns: they're grand hotels. After closing in 1981, it reopened in 1983, polished once again to its old style, as The Dunhill ... *Hotel*. The guestrooms have four-poster beds, with original art on the walls.

Amenities: Free parking, valet service, airport shuttle; concierge; complimentary beverages in room; exercise room, business services.

Dining tip: The main dining room specializes in original variations on continental cuisine.

Location notes: The Dunhill is nextdoor to Discovery Place (science museum), and one block away from the Blumenthal Center of Performing Arts.

Fayetteville
RADISSON PRINCE CHARLES HOTEL   1925
450 Hay St., Fayetteville 28301. Tel. 910/433-4444; 800/277-4623; Fax 910/485-8269. 83 rooms. Rates: $55-87.

In its earliest days, Fayetteville was a Scottish colony: not officially, perhaps, but it was settled in the 1740's by Scots fleeing the defeat of their hero Charles Edward Stuart, better known by his catchy nickname, "Bonnie Prince Charlie." Among other resources, the Scots found a freshwater spring in their new land, and it functioned as a colonial water cooler, around which they liked to gather to just talk and no doubt gripe about the English, and Bonnie Prince Charlie, and the English some more. It was important in Fayetteville's early days, but after about 1860, no one even knew where it was anymore.

In 1925, a grand hotel opened on Hay Street in the oldest section of Fayetteville; it was a neo-colonial building named after Prince Charles. The interiors were elegantly decorated with marble floors, crystal chandeliers and arched Palladian windows. The hotel guestrooms have since been realigned, and now consist largely of two-room suites.

In the 1980's, archaeologists started looking for the Scotch Spring, out of use for over a century. They found it in the parking lot of the Prince Charles, under the pavement. The hotel was rather honored and cooperated with excavation efforts. In fact, the hotel is owned by local investors, and the city undoubtedly appreciates its historic hotel. "We have no secrets around here," an employee said, "the hotel's business is the town's, it seems. They care about it, around here."

Amenities: Free parking; room-service; complimentary coffee; exercise room.

Dining tip: The lounge is a tribute to Babe Ruth, who was in Fayetteville when he hit his first professional homer; he must have liked how it felt.

Location: The hotel is in the historic district of Fayetteville, and the Markethouse is one block away.

Black Mountain
MONTE VISTA HOTEL   1935

308 W. State St. Black Mountain 28711. Tel. 704/669-2119; 800/ 441-5400. 49 rooms. Rates: $57-90.

"The Monte Vista is not a cute imitation of a bygone era," the brochure states briskly, "We just have not made a lot of changes."

Rosalie and Lucien Phillips borrowed $70,000 in the midst of the Depression to build their new hotel, a three story brick building with 30 rooms and a domestic tone throughout. They catered to vacationers, greeting them with a thoroughly Southern form of hospitality, and the Monte Vista prospered through times that took a toll on most other hotels. The hotel is much the same today: pristine, but utterly true to the original concept, as it was launched in 1935. The wide front porch is an outdoor lounge, full of white wicker furniture; the lobby is a spacious, mellow living room. The guestrooms, neither fussy nor standardized, are typical of bedrooms in a very good home.

The hotel brochure doesn't try to make the Monte Vista sound like the perfect hotel for everyone in the world, as do most such brochures; it describes a hotel that is perfect for itself. To quote at length: "We have a library-television room instead of TV's in the rooms, one payphone and a front message board instead of room phones, old oak trees instead of air conditioning ... The Monte Vista is furnished with our collection of a few antiques and a lot of old furniture. The main updates are paint, cheery fabrics and new mattresses." At its best, a historic hotel is nothing more than an idea that doesn't need improvement.

Amenities: Free parking, swimming pool.

Dining tip: The Monte Vista serves homemade country cooking, buffet style. The baked trout is a specialty.

Location notes: The Monte Vista is eight miles from the Blue Ridge Highway and about 15 miles to the Biltmore House in Asheville.

SOUTH CAROLINA

Aiken
THE WILLCOX INN   1900

100 Colleton Ave., Aiken 29801. Tel. 803/649-1377; 800/368-1047; Fax 803/643-0971. 36 rooms. Rates (seasonal): $95-135.

The popular activities in Aiken, South Carolina, are thoroughbred horse training, fox hunting, and polo. Needless to say, it is at the other end of the state, and the planet, from Myrtle Beach. Swanky little Aiken became a popular winter destination among rich Northerners after the Civil War, in part because it was one Southern town that had not suffered any war damage. That, after all, might be dreary to look at. And inconvenient to live with. Aiken, on the other hand, was the same as ever: a cheerful, breezy town, still sturdy in its Federal roots.

In 1898, its greatest problem was that it didn't have a hotel, because the Highland Park Hotel had burned to the ground that year. Horsemen were in need of a place to stay between morning workouts. In addition, hostesses were in dire need of a place to send extra guests; and they were the ones who encouraged a young caterer from the Highland Park, Frederick Willcox, to open a new hotel in town. His Willcox Inn was a neo-colonial building, with pillars all the way across the front, and a set of paned double-doors between each of them. All white, it has three stories.

According to the hotel's own history, the doormen at the Willcox Inn were trained not to admit men "unless their shoes were of the right quality and shined to a high luster." But that smacks of a tale ... because no one would be admitted to the city of Aiken in the first place, unless they had good shoes and a great shine. Not during the winter season. Among those who were let in – to both the town and the hotel – were Winston Churchill, Averill Harriman, and Elizabeth Arden.

Aiken is about 15 miles from Augusta, Georgia, the home of the Masters Golf Tournament. During Masters Week, there is a scramble for rooms: one year, the hotel told the Duke of Windsor he couldn't get a room during the tournament. When the hotel says that not even the King of England could even get a room at the last minute, they have at least come close to proving it.

Amenities: Free parking; room service; in-room television, telephone, coffee maker.

Dining tip: The Inn's specialty dish is the Carpetbagger, filet mignon stuffed with crab meat and covered with Bearnaise sauce.

Location notes: The Willcox is in the heart of Aiken's historic district, three to four blocks from a choice of three horseracing tracks, or Hopeland Gardens.

TENNESSEE

Chattanooga
RADISSON READ HOUSE   1926

827 Broad St., Chattanooga 37402. Tel. 423/266-4121; 800/333-3333; Fax 423/267-6193. 237 rooms. Rates: standard room, $108; 2-room suite, $118.

The Radisson Read House is the third grand hotel on the same site. The first, called the Crutchfield House, was the scene of a frightening moment on the eve of the Civil War, when the proprietor drew gun and threatened the life of Jefferson Davis, a guest at the hotel. Davis had just made some remarks in the lobby regarding the prospect of a divided Union – a duel seemed imminent, but Mr. Crutchfield's own brother dragged him away.

Davis went on to become president of the Confederacy and the Crutchfields sold their hotel. It was a Union hospital late in the war.

A doctor named John Read and his son, Samuel, opened a new hotel on the spot in 1872. Amazingly, Samuel would own and manage the hotel, called the Read House, for the next 70 years. In fact, the building wore out long before he did: he built its replacement, the current Read House, in 1926. It is a 13 story brick building on a tree-lined street; the decor in the lobby is English Georgian, warm with walnut paneling. However, the hotel also recalls its own history and that of the Crutchfield House by honoring a different Civil War battle on each of the guestfloors. They are soberly treated, in tribute to the soldiers of both sides. The guestrooms have all been refurbished in mid-19th century style, with fine reproduction furniture, textiles, artwork and wallpaper.

Amenities: Free airport shuttle; health club pass; swimming pool; in-room mini-bar.

Dining tip: The main dining room is a steakhouse.

Location notes: The Radisson Read House is on the edge of downtown Chattanooga, near the convention center and the Tennessee Aquarium.

Memphis
THE PEABODY   1925

149 Union Ave., Memphis 38103. Tel. 901/529-4000; 800/732-2639; Fax 901/529-3600; web, www.peabodymemphis.com; e-mail, peabody@wspice.com. 468 rooms. Rates: rooms, $140 and up; suites, $250 and up.

In the 1980's, restoration was the trend in historic hotels, but in the 1920's the trend was replacement. The Shoreham Hotel in Washington, the Palmer House in Chicago and the Parker House in Boston were built in direct succession to legendary hotels of the 19th century. The Peabody was built in the 1920's as a replacement for the original 1869 hotel of the same name.

The original Peabody was more than a business, it was a symbol of the rebuilding South after the Civil War. In fact, it was built by a wealthy Memphis resident named Colonel Robert Brinkley, but he named it for the philanthropist George Peabody, a Northerner (resident in London) who had donated large sums to help the South rebound after the war. The Brinkleys would be associated with the Peabody Hotel until 1965. Of the three replacement hotels mentioned above, the Peabody is probably the only one more impressive than the original. Built in 1925 by Col. Brinkley's great-grandson, it was lavishly decorated inside in Italian Renaissance style, profuse with imported marble. The lobby was built around a fountain, ornamented with cherubs.

For all of the millions (5 of them) spent on the hotel in 1925, and all the millions (7.5 of them) that polished it to a new gleam on its reopening in 1981, the hotel has been most famous through the years for about $3 worth of baby ducks. Five extremely lucky ducks live in a "penthouse" coop on the roof at the Peabody and spend afternoons in the lobby fountain, marching in by themselves at exactly 11 am and marching out again when they are called at 5 pm. It is more than cute, it is deeply satisfying to see the ostentatious hotel brought to its knees by five little birds. (When the ducks are old enough, they go back to their duck farm to be released into the wild.)

The Peabody's first restoration, the one completed in 1981, was a phenomenon. It brought a derelict building back to a beautiful state. It sparked a much broader revitalization of downtown Memphis. And it became a symbol of Memphis' spirit, a rallying point for immense pride in the city. While a few other historic hotels had been meticulously restored before 1981 – see, for example, the Pfister in Milwaukee – it was the Peabody Hotel that became a model for dozens of others around the country. It was indeed a phenomenon, one that every city looked at. Those that could, repeated it.

Amenities: Concierge; 24-hour room service; business center; exercise club with pool.

Dining tip: The old "Plantation Roof," now known as the "Skyway," is the hotel's rooftop dining room, open for Sunday brunch.

Location notes: The Peabody is in downtown Memphis, four blocks from the Hunt Phelan House and two blocks from Beale Street.

Rogersville
HALE SPRINGS INN   1824
110 W Main St. Rogersville 37857. Tel. 423/272-5171. 9 rooms. Rates: rooms, $45-70; suites, $65-90.

Rogersville is currently in the State of Tennessee. From 1784 to 1789, though, it was in the great state of Franklin.

The pioneers who settled the Smokey foothills around Rogersville were feisty from the start, bickering with the local Indians almost constantly. They were just as noisy facing in the other direction. Less than a year after America was even recognized as a nation, the residents of that certain pocket up in the Smoky Mountains were already fed up. They felt they were being ignored by their state officials way east in North Carolina, and so they declared themselves a state and called it Franklin. The truly sad thing is that even though they declared themselves a state called Franklin, they were still ignored. As though swatting a fly, the government in Washington eventually remarked that no entity could be a state without the permission of the other states, and in 1796 George Washington overlooked Franklin altogether and recognized all of Tennessee as a new state. Even Rogersville. So it is that the University of Tennessee gets to go to bowl games, while the Franklin State uniforms never even got ordered.

Getting over the disappointment somehow, Rogersville became a bustling town, prospering with the extension of the Wilderness Road in the early 1800's. In 1820, John McKinney, an Irishman practicing law in Philadelphia, visited Rogersville to settle a case and never left. Whatever his stature had been in Philadelphia, he was soon considered Tennessee's best attorney. McKinney was a highly social man, in an egalitarian way, and he used some of his new wealth to build a fabulous hotel for Rogersville. It was not to be some quaint stagecoach stop, but a sophisticated hotel worthy of any city in the country (Philadelphia, for example). Even under construction, the historian Carol Ross surmised, the sight of the new hotel must have been breathtaking, "as the building rose to its full three stories. At about sixty feet square, it was one of the largest buildings in Rogersville as well as the most beautiful. There were four lofty chimneys and four fancy dormers on the roof. The building was Federal in style, with Georgian embellishments such as the very fine cornice at the roofline. Porches extended across the front and back of the building, and were referred to as the 'galleries.'"

People who know enough to call the porch a gallery know exactly what they are doing. McKinney did. The slaves who worked for him built the hotel. As can be seen today, they matched the best workmanship to be found anywhere.

Tennessee had some potent politicians in the first decades of the McKinney Tavern House, including Andrew Jackson, who managed to stop there often. A man named H. Clay Crawford long remembered a banquet Jackson attended at the McKinney House in 1832: "In company with other boys, who were curious to see the general at close quarters, I had taken my position near one of the ground floor windows that opened right into the dining room. Near this window stood the table at which General Jackson was eating, and at the head of which my father sat. Seeing me at the window, my father lifted me in and said he would present me to Old Hickory. The General received me with great kindness and had a chair placed for me between himself and my father. He inquired kindly my given name, age, etc."

During the Civil War, Rogersville was traded back and forth several times between the North and South. The only battle actually fought in the town lasted a long time after the war. The McKinney House had a great rival across the street: the Kyle House. Whenever the town was in Southern hands, the Kyle House was used as Confederate headquarters. Meanwhile, whenever the North held the town, the McKinney House became an infirmary for Union troops. Officially a Confederate state, Tennessee was never of one mind on the war – individuals chose sides. And stayed on them: until long into the century, one would see residents of Rogersville purposefully crossing the street, rather than be on the same "side" as the Kyle House, if they were proud of the Union, or the McKinney House, if they were still loyal to the Confederate "Cause."

McKinney's hotel was renamed the Hale Springs Inn after the Civil War. In the 1930's, it belonged to a man with an obvious antipathy toward history. He then chopped the fireplace chimneys off at the roofline. He put fake marble over the mellow red-brick exterior. He tore out fireplace mantles and tacked up walls to make the rooms good and cramped, without the welcome ventilation so carefully engineered by McKinney's builders. Worst of all, perhaps, he sold the Inn's pretty side garden to someone who built a movie theater in its place.

In 1982, Carl and Janet Netherland-Brown bought the old misery that the Inn had become. Carl was a boat pilot, with roots in the area going all the way back to the state of Franklin; the couple devoted themselves to reclaiming the Inn in its heyday. In all, 170 tons of the 1930's, 1940's and 1950's was carted away as rubbish, leaving a gratifying amount of the 1820's. Among the original features are the fireplace mantles (found in the attic), the wainscoting and the pine floors. The guestrooms have been returned to their original spaciousness and furnished with antiques, some of which are believed to have been original to the Inn.

If you really want to read a fine article about the life of a hotel, ask the Inn or the Tennessee Tourist Board how to get a copy of Carol Ross' "History of Hale Springs Inn."

Amenities: Free parking, television; complimentary continental breakfast. There are no phones in the room, but there is one in the parlor.

Dining room: Carriage House Restaurant serves a varied menu that always includes some dishes contemporary with the hotel: wild mushroom bisque, for example, and game such as quail, pheasant, wild turkey, and even wild black bear.

Location notes: The Hale Springs Inn is in the middle of the historic town of Rogersville. It is an hour-and-a-half by car to Dollywood; 30 miles to Kingsport or Greeneville, and 65 miles from Knoxville.

8. THE MID-ATLANTIC

"Upon arriving in his room, Jackie Gleason called Room Service for ice cream. When an employee asked him how many scoops, Gleason cheerfully roared, 'Scoops? Send the whole bucket!'"

– Marianne Lee, writing of the William Penn Hotel, Pittsburgh

DELAWARE

Lewes
NEW DEVON INN   1926
142 2nd St., Lewes 19958. Tel. 302/645-6466; 800/824-8754; Fax 302/645-7196. 26 rooms. Rates: $50-170.

The New Devon Inn sits at a quiet corner in the seaside town of Lewes, at the head of Delaware Bay. The most exciting thing ever to happen on the site was the day the British Navy bombarded Lewes during the War of 1812. The door of the building at the corner took a nick: somebody saved the door, which is now in the local museum. However, the second most exciting thing to happen on the site was the opening of the Cesar Rodney Hotel in 1926. It was a dapper three story building, red brick with white trim: respectable and rather humble. The historian Hazel Brittingham noted that during World War Two, the inter-city bus-stop was in front of the hotel, and the so the place had enormous meaning for soldiers: "Many can recall their excitement as they stood at the Cesar Rodney Hotel, awaiting the bus – pass in one hand and bus ticket in the other." It makes for a snapshot of the Rodney, or any small town hotel.

Now called the New Devon Inn, the hotel recently underwent a three year restoration that was itself the talk of Lewes: it emerged as a grander place than ever, or, as the proprietors express it, "a blend of history and elegance." The guestrooms feature antiques and Oriental rugs, for example, while breakfast is served on antique china and crystal.

Amenities: Air conditioning; private bathrooms; telephones; complimentary continental breakfast; business services.

Dining tip: The Buttery is a small, well-regarded restaurant.

Location notes: Lewes (pronounced "Loo-iss") is about two blocks square. The New Devon Inn right is in the center.

Wilmington
THE HOTEL DU PONT   1913

11th Street and Market Streets, Wilmington 19801. Tel. 302/594-3100; 800/441-9019; Fax 302/594-3108. 216 rooms. Rates: rooms $149-289; suites $350-550.

In the years around 1910, Wilmington, Delaware was sorely in need of a hotel. Many of those who traveled there on business had to bunk with the very people with whom they were meeting. It takes fortitude to make mincemeat out of somebody in negotiations and then go home to play with the mincemeat's tots on the carpet. That sort of thing hadn't been necessary anywhere else since the days of the castles on the Rhine, but as Wilmington had only one outdated hotel, and hundreds of visitors a day, the choice for most was to either stay in a private home or to hang on a rope. Or to stay in Philadelphia.

Promoters approached Pierre du Pont, head of Delaware's giant chemical company and explained that a new hotel in Wilmington was a sure-fire business opportunity. Du Pont seemed to pause long enough to wonder why, if it was such a sure-fire idea, he had to put up all the money, but in 1912 he set up a subsidiary of the Du Pont Co. to build a hotel. The company has owned the place ever since.

The new Hotel du Pont was to be as grand as an embassy, but as comfortable as a cottage: that was Pierre's general edict. The result obviously mattered to him, since he lived with his wife in a suite at the hotel from 1913 until he died in 1954. In fact, in one of the funny anecdotes related in former manager Harry Ayres' book on the Hotel du Pont, Pierre even called to complain when rents were raised for the hotel's small number of permanent residents. "I think you are trying to push me out through the roof!" he exclaimed.

The Hotel du Pont was a success, in a singular case of a small city requiring a rather large and very grand hotel. Twelve stories in white stone, the hotel expanded over most of a full block, looking like a button-down version of Italian Renaissance architecture. Actually, the hotel is part of the greater DuPont headquarters. The public rooms inside reflect a variety of styles, connected by a Beaux Arts sensibility that no room should be too big, no decor overwhelming. The hotel's art collection is a serious asset, with one room, the Brandywine, devoted to work by the Wyeths.

Amenities: Valet parking; 24-hour room service; concierge; fitness center; in-room mini-bar; business center; television, VCR, dataport.

Dining tip: A harpist plays from the musicians' gallery in the Green Room.

Location notes: The du Pont is in the same building as the DuPont headquarters. The Delaware History Museum is six blocks away.

DISTRICT OF COLUMBIA

THE RENAISSANCE MAYFLOWER   1925

1127 Connecticut Ave. NW, Washington 20036. Tel. 202/347-3000; 800/468-3571; Fax 202/466-9083. 660 rooms. Rates: rooms, $250-300; suites, rooms, $450-2,500.

The Mayflower has been on a gallop ever since it opened in 1925. For a long time, it was the biggest hotel in Washington – the guestfloor hallways are so long, they show the curving of the earth, or at least a pronounced narrowing, like train tracks – yet the Mayflower was overbooked through most of World War II. The mezzanine overlooking the lobby was commonly converted into a dormitory for desperate travelers.

A man named John Dasch arrived in Washington on a Thursday in 1942 and managed to get a room at the Mayflower, but only after he promised to check out by Monday. Dasch was certain he would. He was a Nazi saboteur, in charge of a group that had disembarked from submarines in Long Island and Florida about a week before. Abandoning the master plan, Dasch went to Washington to give himself up and to turn in the others. He had to spend more than a day in his room, calling various agencies, before anyone arrived to arrest him. All seven of his fellow saboteurs were captured and six of them were electrocuted two months later.

J. Edgar Hoover was well known to have lunch at the Mayflower every day when he was the F.B.I. director. One day he looked up and happened to notice Public Enemy No. 3 dining five tables away. Hoover calmly called his office and had the man arrested, leaving everyone to wonder how a criminal could rank number three and not know enough to stay away from the Mayflower at lunchtime.

Amenities: Valet parking; concierge; business center; fitness center; complimentary limousine within three miles, if available; 24-hour room service; multilingual staff; free line-access for calling-card, collect calls.

Dining tip: The Cafe Promenade offers a popular Mediterranean menu.

Location notes: The hotel is four blocks from the White House; a half-mile from the Smithsonian, and a mile from the Capitol.

OMNI SHOREHAM   1930

2500 Calvert St. NW, Washington 20008; Tel. 202/234-0700; 800/843-6664; Fax 202/332-1373. 836 rooms. Rates: rooms, $159-229; suites, $279-1,200.

The Shoreham was built in 1930 to replace a fashionable old hotel of the same name. The idea was to make it a city hotel in a country setting, right in the middle of Washington. Surrounded by 16 acres of its own and adjoining Rock Creek Park, the new Shoreham offered country sounds and peaceful views, along with recreation options such as horseback riding. However, the previous Shoreham and its famous cafe had always attracted social butterflies, not real ones; eventually the new Shoreham did, too.

Its Blue Room dinner club was one of the most sophisticated venues in the region, bringing bigtime acts to the capital at a time when "nationally known" acts weren't necessarily known in Washington. Probably Washingtonians were their own favorite entertainers: they didn't need others. At the Shoreham, the Capital finally learned to nightclub (verb) with help from Maurice Chevalier, Judy Garland, Marlene Dietrich, Frank Sinatra and Lena Horne: all played the Blue Room.

The Shoreham has been a hard-working convention hotel for many decades, but a recent $70 million restoration has reclaimed its art deco glamour, even while its rooms are being refurbished, one wing at a time, in a major, three-year project.

Amenities: Concierge; business center; swimming pool; tennis courts; room service.

Dining tip: Monique's Cafe et Brasserie serves hearty dishes, such as roasted peppercorn pork tenderloin.

Location notes: The Shoreham is one block from Connecticut Avenue and its many ethnic restaurants, and four blocks from the National Zoo.

THE CARLTON   1926

923 16th and K Streets, Washington 20006. Tel. 202/638-2626; 800/879-6911; 202/638-4231. 206 rooms. Rates: rooms, $320; suites, $700-2,500.

The Carlton is a small hotel, built with the idea that what most people want when they visit Washington is to feel at home ... in an Italian palazzo. Franklin Roosevelt stayed at the Carlton in the years before he found permanent lodgings in town, and he said that "the setting was more like a gracious residence, than a hotel." A gracious palazzo, he should have said, because the Carlton is heavy with its gilded, gorgeous Renaissance atmosphere. Although it is a spacious hotel, it is small in the number of rooms it has, and so it is a perfect combination for a power trip in Washington: it's both exclusive and a showcase.

Amenities: Twenty-four hour room service; in-room stereo television, remote control clock-radio, fax machine, dual phone line, dataport, safe large enough for a laptop.

Dining tip: The hotel's restaurant, Lespinasse, is the Washington version of the restaurant of the same name, at the St. Regis Hotel (see New York City below).

Location notes: The Carlton is two blocks from the White House, not far from the Smithsonian, and near shopping in downtown Washington. National Airport is seven miles away.

HOTEL WASHINGTON   1918

15th and Pennsylvania Ave N.W., Washington 20004. Tel. 202/638-5900; 800/424-9540; Fax 202/638-1594. 350 rooms. Rates: rooms, $135-250; suites, $300-750.

There was a time when the average Congressmen lived at home and only traveled to Washington for the odd month here and there in the year, when Congress was in session. The ones who kept homes in the city were suspect: either very rich, or worse, very ambitious. The Hotel Washington – which is named for the President and not the city, though it is admittedly hard to tell that by the spelling – was one of the more popular places for Congressmen to stay after it opened in 1918. As many as 50 Representatives and five Senators were known to stay at the hotel at one time. The elevator-operator could probably recognize a quorum, most days.

In location, the Washington Hotel is a more likely adjunct to the Executive branch, as it is across the street from the White House, and overlooks it. The hotel is light in color and European in appearance, with arched windows lining the street level. The Washington proudly calls itself the oldest continuously operating hotel in the capital: a fine distinction, since the Willard, which is older, took a break for a while and stood empty. The Washington has persevered and deserves credit for it.

But more than being the oldest in town, it is the most Southern in aura. In its heart, Washington is a Southern city, after all, and its oldest (continuously operating) hotel has a soft hum, a graciousness, that just couldn't be found one yard further to the north. It probably can't be found too often in the South, anymore, either, but the Hotel Washington has it, even to its high-ceilinged lobby: approximately one mile long, but still an unhurried parlor. In 1997, the Hotel Washington underwent a restoration of its guestfloors.

Amenities: Concierge, exercise room, in-room mini-bar, hair dryer.

Dining tip: The Sky Terrace, the hotel's open-air rooftop restaurant, is probably the best thing about Washington: a comfortable jumble of wicker chairs, the cool air, and terrific hamburgers, among other items on the menu. As to the views, the city never seems as close as it does from the roof of the Washington.

Location notes: The hotel is five blocks from the convention center, two blocks from the Mall and about one mile from the Capitol.

THE WILLARD INTER-CONTINENTAL 1902

1401 Pennsylvania Ave. NW, Washington 20004. Tel. 202/628-9100; 800/327-0200; Fax 202/637-7326. 341 rooms. Rates: rooms, $395-455; suites, $800-3,500.

Throughout most of the 19th century, Washington was a terrible hotel city, known more for its overgrown boarding houses than for real hotels. Willard's, however, made a great impression when it opened under the management of the Willard brothers in the 1850's.

In 1861, the Lincoln family made plans to stay at Willard's during the presidential inauguration. To evade an assassination plot, Abraham Lincoln stole into the hotel before dawn, in total secrecy. Hotels being what they are – where total secrets are concerned – a large crowd had gathered by mid-morning under his window. In the indexes of history books covering the Civil War, the listings for the Willard Hotel are often longer than those for the White House. The Willard itself likes to quote Nathaniel Hawthorne on the subject. "The hotel," he wrote in *The Atlantic Monthly* in 1862, "in fact, may be much more justly called the centre of Washington and Union than either the Capitol, the White House or the State Department." Men who spent their days in the Willard lobby looking for the government or just waiting around for it, came to be known as lobbyists.

The new Willard Hotel, which replaced the original one in 1902, slipped from the top rank by the 1930's, surpassed by the stylish places that had opened the decade before: the Hay-Adams, the Carlton, the Madison. By the early 1960's, the Willard had become a "dilapidated old firetrap," according to someone who stayed there often. "The reason it stayed open," he added, "was that it was about the only hotel in Washington that charged less than the government's per diem for lodging." After it closed in 1968, the owner requested a permit to raze it. After that was denied, the building sat empty for nearly 20 years. In 1986, the old hotel reopened as the Willard Inter-Continental, having been brought back from the very brink with a meticulous restoration. The guestfloors were renovated to a modern standard, with reproduction Queen Anne furnishings, while the lobby, in particular, was returned to its late-Victorian formality.

Where most hotels have help from decorators, the Willard had help from the Secret Service in designing three suites on the 6th floor for visiting heads of state and high-security guests. It seems to work, because, where most hotels issue a list of actors and other celebrities who have visited, the Willard only deigns to brag about kings, queens, presidents and, in special cases, crown princes.

Amenities: exercise room; business center; 24-hour room-service and valet; in-room mini-bar, dataport.

Dining tip: The Round Robin Bar is ... round. It is also wood-paneled and very cozy, fitting concentrically in a rounded turret on the corner of the hotel.

Location notes: The Willard is one block from the White House, three blocks from the mall and about one mile from the Capitol Building.

KENTUCKY

Louisville
THE CAMBERLEY BROWN HOTEL   1923

335 W. Broadway, Louisville 40202. Tel;. 502/583-1234; 800/555-8000; Fax 502/587-7006. 292 rooms. Rates: rooms, $189-239; suites $425-700.

Most hotels have a grand-opening dinner. The Brown Hotel had five of them in October 1923. First, for the workers who had built the $4 million hotel in jig time. They deserved to see their accomplishment first, and besides, in case of a debacle, they didn't know any columnists. The next night, the politicians came through, for a tour and dinner. The next night, dinner was laid out for the city's socialites and reporters, 1,200 in all. Louisville being a cosmopolitan city, it could spare another 1,200 socialites and reporters, who arrived hungry the next night. Finally, on the fifth night, the Brown Hotel threw its doors open and 10,000 people came through just to look at all the marble and gilt, the polished floors and Palladian windows.

Long associated with the festivities surrounding the Kentucky Derby, the Brown became one of the nation's most famous hotels, but it was also a neighborhood place in Louisville. "Between 11:30

and 1:30 you could see every other businessman in Louisville – everyone you would want to see for business or social reasons," a banker named Dick Haas recalled in 1984, "If you were clever, you would have a drink in the English Grill and then go downstairs and have lunch in the Coffee Shop. That way, you would cover everyone." In the English Grill, according to a waiter, 200 people would be seated for lunch and 190 of them would be having a "Hot Brown," the hotel's signature sandwich, invented as a midnight snack (open-face turkey with bacon, pimentos and Mornay sauce). Doctors would have a table, where they could come and go; paint-company executives would have their own. The Brown Hotel offered Louisville a club, but a public one.

The Brown Hotel was not related to any other hotel of the same name, such as Denver's Brown Palace. It was named for J. Graham Brown, who built his hotel on a corner of 4th Street in the midst of the Brown Building, the Brown Theater, and the Martin Brown Building (named for his brother). Brown was a bachelor devoted to business, especially the lumber business: as he said, that's where the "real jack" was, and it supported the hotel which was his home. Even so, during the Depression, he nearly lost control of the hotel. According to lore, he gathered the bankers and told them "to go to hell." But then he gathered the employees and had to ask them to work without pay for a few weeks. The crisis passed and the employees received a bonus. "Back during the Depression, the Derby would pull the hotel out," according to one of those employees, who had also helped pull the hotel out.

"The big time was Sunday after breakfast," recalled Fred Caldwell, a head waiter, of Derby Week" (the race itself being run on Saturday). "The hotel would empty up and the help really made the money then. We were all dog-tired because most of us had been in the hotel since the Wednesday before, or at least it seemed like that."

In 1969, Graham Brown died, leaving an estate of $100 million that included a very historic hotel. However, historic hotels were out of fashion at the time and so was downtown Louisville. Without Graham and his "jack," the hotel closed in 1971. By 1979, there was a glimmer of hope, as downtown Louisville was taking on more and ever more ambitious reclamation projects. The next year, a plan was in place. No one person saved the Brown Hotel; the restoration was part of a three block development that also included new buildings reflecting the architecture of the hotel. The hotel had its second grand reopening in 1985. The restoration was magnificent, but some bit of style must have been lost. There was only one great dinner party, not five.

Amenities: Airport transportation; overnight shoeshine; complimentary newspaper; exercise room.

Dining tip: Yes, you can still have a Hot Brown.

Location notes: The Camberley Brown Hotel is in the Theater District of Louisville's downtown. It is five blocks away from either the Louisville Slugger Museum or the Science Center. Churchill Downs is five miles away.

THE SEELBACH   1905

500 Fourth Ave., Louisville 40202. Tel. 502/585-3200; 800/333-3399; Fax 502/585-9240. 321 rooms. Rates: rooms, $179 and up; suites, $229 and up. The Seelbach is a Hilton Hotel.

Did you think you were an ambitious kid? Louis Seelbach was 17 when he arrived in America from Germany ... and 22 when he opened his restaurant and cafe, which was immediately a favorite place for gentlemen to eat in Louisville. Women weren't allowed, a rule which was not uncommon in restaurants of the 1870's. Since the restaurant grew into something of a club anyway, Louis opened a hotel in 1886 and offered accommodations. As a building, it sufficed. But in 1904, Louis and his brother, Otto, opened a hotel that would overwhelm.

The new Seelbach was so popular that the brothers had to start work on an addition the very first year. At the Seelbach, the linen was from Ireland, the rugs from Persia, the oak furniture from Belgium, the tapestries from France, and so on: the brothers did not so much build their hotel, as gather it from all over the world. One of the most effective rooms, however, originated in Ohio. The

Rookwood Pottery Co., a leading force in the Arts and Crafts Movement, supplied tiles and ceramic decorations that were fitted like wallpaper in the Rathskeller dining room. With its vaulted ceilings and the warm, orange glow of the tiles, it is either a cloister for a very fashionable order of 12th century clerics or one of the most beautiful dining rooms in the country.

Heaven only knows what goes on in the mind of a novelist: certainly, no one ever knew what went on in the mind of F. Scott Fitzgerald, but the hotel claims that the "Muhlbach Hotel," mentioned in *The Great Gatsy*, was modeled after the Seelbach. Fitzgerald did stay at the Seelbach in 1918. Through the years, the Seelbach and the Brown Hotel were the capitals of different parts of Louisville. For one thing, the Brown (and its owner) were Republican, while the Seelbach was the traditional headquarters of Democratic campaigns. For a long time, Room 743 was the Democratic Party's own lucky room, and throughout the 1950's and 1960's, candidates would insist on having their headquarters in it. By 1971, though, the spell was over (or perhaps the G.O.P. had finally learned to rent room 744).

In 1975, the spell really was over, as the Seelbach Hotel closed. However, plans soon emerged to reopen it, as two investors joined with the Metropolitan Life Insurance Co. to finance a refurbishment, completed in 1982.

Amenities: Free airport and bus terminal shuttle; health club privileges; concierge.

Dining tip: The Oakroom is famous for Kentucky specialties such as Kentucky rack of lamb with black truffle sauce.

Location: The Seelbach is in downtown Louisville.

MARYLAND

Baltimore
THE CLARION   1928

612 Cathedral St., Baltimore 21201. Tel. 410/727-7101; 800/292-5500; Fax 410/789-3312. 103 rooms. Rates: rooms, $159-179.

Built in 1928, the Clarion has the small, wood-paneled lobby of a hotel in Brussels or Paris, a type that can be even more welcoming than a grandiose room. The hotel is part of Baltimore's classy Mount Vernon Square neighborhood, home to the Peabody Conservatory of Music.

Amenities: Valet parking; health club passes; in-room marble bathrooms; hair dryer; coffee-make; dataport. Some rooms have business amenities, refrigerators or live plants.

Dining tip: The Clarion has a casual restaurant of its own and is one block away from the Charles Street restaurant corridor offering many international cuisines.

Location notes: The Clarion is next to Mount Vernon Square in Baltimore, 1 1/2 miles from Johns Hopkins Hospital; 10 blocks from Camden Yards, and nine blocks from the Inner Harbor.

Berlin
ATLANTIC HOTEL   1895

2 N. Main St., Berlin 21811. Tel. 410/641-3589; 800/814-7672; web, http://www.atbeach.com/lodging/md/hotel/atlantic. 16 rooms. Rates: rooms, $65-150.

"It may be truly said that Berlin has one of the largest, handsomest, and best equipped hotels on the Eastern Shore," the paper in a nearby town reported in 1896, "It is a three-story structure, 40 by 90 feet, beautifully ornamented with galvanized iron cornices, and presents a most imposing appearance, attracting the attention of everyone who visits Berlin." What really impressed the neighboring towns was the determination with which Horace and Virginia Harmonson had built the new Atlantic

Hotel, finishing it in only six months after a fire destroyed their old hotel on the same spot.

Berlin is on Maryland's Eastern Shore, about ten miles from the ocean. It was a farm center, and the Atlantic Hotel was vital to commerce because traveling salesmen used it continually, for accommodation but also as a place to show their wares. Not many small town hotels of that type are left, yet they are a reminder of the days when much of the nation's commerce was conducted through the sample-case set out in a hotel lounge. The automobile changed that form of commerce, partly because it allowed a salesman to cover wider territory and stay in fewer hotels. The Atlantic attacked the problem in the 1920's, operating a bus solely to shepherd salesmen from the train station to the hotel, then on to calls around the county, and back again for supper.

Even despite such efforts, small town hotels suffered a direct hit from the advent of the automobile, as they lost the salesmen and never quite competed with tourist-camps and motels for the vacationers. That is why it is especially rare to have a fine, old small town hotel such as the Atlantic. Most of its contemporaries were long gone 50 years ago. The Atlantic was helped a little by the burgeoning resort business on the shore, 10 miles away, but it slid through the 1960's and barely stayed in business.

In 1986, Berlin resident named James Barrett could no longer resist the imperative of saving the hotel, for its own sake and that of the town. He gathered an investment group that, according to a record of the effort, "made inquiries about various subsidies and 'give-away' programs, but concluded that the restoration should be done in the 'tried and true' Eastern Shore method, emphasizing self-reliance and determination." The Atlantic Hotel reopened in 1988, its original paneling and wood floors refurbished. Nearly all of the furniture in the hotel is antique, purchased through local auctions. "We congratulate the people of Berlin upon having such a hotel as the Atlantic and such enterprising citizens ..." That was written in 1896.

Amenities: Complimentary breakfast; free parking; all rooms have private bathroom, air conditioning, television and telephone.

Dining tip: The hotel dining room makes Atlantic Hotel Crabcakes, with lump crabmeat on tri-color orzo.

Location notes: Berlin is about 10 miles from the ocean on the Eastern Shore.

Chestertown
THE IMPERIAL HOTEL   1903

208 High St., Chestertown 21620-1633. Tel. 410/778-5000; Fax 410/778-9662. 13 rooms. Rates: rooms, $125; suites, $200-300.

Long verandahs and white pillars distinguish the front facade of the Imperial Hotel, a three story brick building in the oldest part of Chestertown. Sycamore trees line the street, and many of the hotel's rooms overlook the relaxed traffic of the town. The Imperial has been restored in its original Victorian style, an award-winning effort in which many local crafts people participated. The courtyard garden on a side lawn is used for jazz concerts in the summer.

Amenities: Free parking; in-room cable television, telephone, individual climate control.

Dining tip: The hotel hosts wine tastings in conjunction with the Imperial Wine Society.

Location: Chestertown is on the Eastern Shore on the Chester River, an estuary of Chesapeake Bay.

Easton
THE TIDEWATER INN   1949

101 E. Dover St., Easton 21601 410/822-1300; 800/237-8775; Fax 410/820-8847. 114 rooms. Rates: (seasonal) rooms, $75-170; suites, $110-300.

In 1944, Talbot County, Maryland, suffered a community tragedy when its hotel burned to the ground. Most communities have a hotel that serves as a hub, a natural choice for local gatherings, no less than for accommodating visitors. In 1944, Talbot County lost its Avon Hotel. The Tidewater Inn was built on the same site in the late 1940's. Georgian in style, with a determined country elegance, it is reproduction, top to bottom, which is to say that every generation since the first in the 1940's has been free to reinterpret 18th century with its own eye. Within a few years, the Tidewater will fully adopt the mantle left by the storied old Avon, because it will finally have been in business on the spot for an even longer term.

Amenities: Free valet parking, complimentary morning coffee and newspaper; turndown service, swimming pool.

Dining tip: The Tidewater will serve breakfast at 4:30 a.m. for those on their way out to hunt.

Location notes: Easton is located on the Delmarva Peninsula, across the Chesapeake Bay from Annapolis.

PENNSYLVANIA

Hershey
THE HOTEL HERSHEY   1933
Hotel Rd., Hershey 17033. Tel. 717/533-2171; 800/533-3131; Fax 717/534-8888; web, http://www.800hershey.com/hotel/index.html. 240 rooms. Rates: $89-129.

In the early, hard years of the Depression, Milton S. Hershey was a good-hearted man who had piles of money. His mother told him to keep it. His friends begged him to keep it. Milton, however, decided to use some of his money to give local construction workers employment; he had made a fortune making chocolate, and felt an obligation toward the people who lived around him. The Rockefellers had the same inclination in building Rockefeller Center in New York City. Milton Hershey, however, had in mind a hotel: a grand hotel for his town.

First, he picked out a site called Pat's Hill, on the outskirts of his namesake town. Then he considered the question of architecture. A long time before, he and his late wife, Catherine, had admired a hotel they'd seen in Alexandria, Egypt. Somehow, his associates talked him out of building an exact copy of the Egyptian Hotel on Pat's Hill. However, the workers were waiting for jobs on the project, and so Hershey rummaged around and found a postcard of another hotel he and Catherine had liked: a small, Mediterranean place. The architect took the postcard away and returned with a design. Hershey made many suggestions as the building took shape, one of which was rather funny and certainly self-incriminating. He wanted to make sure that every table in the dining room had a good view of the rolling hills. "In some places," he confided to the architect, "if you don't tip well, they put you in a corner. I don't want any corners."

The Hershey Hotel opened in 1933, a stone and stucco building with a bell tower, tile floors, arched doorways, and an indoor courtyard, like the plaza in a Spanish town. However, the guestrooms reverted to the look of Pennsylvania country houses, with print wallpaper and reproduction antique furniture. The hotel grew into a resort over the years, with the addition of formal gardens, swimming pools, tennis courts and other recreation facilities.

Amenities: Complimentary shuttles to local attractions; swimming pool; tennis; free parking; 24 room-service; free chocolate bar.

Dining tip: The Circular dining room has stained-glass walls all 'round, with the hotel gardens on the other side.

Location notes: Hershey is in central Pennsylvania, about 85 miles from Philadelphia.

Jim Thorpe
INN AT JIM THORPE   1864

24 Broadway, Jim Thorpe 18229. Tel. 717/325-2599; 800/329-2599; Fax 717/325-9145; web, http://www.innjt.com; e-mail, innjt@ptd.net. 29 rooms. Rates: rooms, $65-115; suites, $150-250.

When the Inn at Jim Thorpe was built, it was the finest hotel in the anthracite coal region south of Scranton. Slow-burning anthracite coal was highly valued in the late 19th century and it had made millionaires out of many of the local residents. It also drew John D. Rockefeller, who stayed at the Inn at Jim Thorpe, as did U.S. Grant, Buffalo Bill Cody and Thomas Edison.

However, it may occur to you that the Inn at Jim Thorpe wasn't called that, back in the 1800's ... before the great athlete was even born. That would be too much of a coincidence. Actually, it was the "American Hotel." And the town was Mauch Chunk back then. "Mauch Chunk" being a name well worth changing, the town became "Jim Thorpe" in 1954. It has been making itself attractive to tourists ever since, a Victorian village with a stately hotel. The Inn at Jim Thorpe is a four story brick building with ornate ironwork forming the front porch and balconies, a style known as "New Orleans Victorian."

Amenities: Air conditioning; cable television; telephones; complimentary continental breakfast.

Dining tip: The hotel restaurant is operated by chefs from Ireland, a high recommendation nowadays. There is also an Irish-style pub on the premises.

Location notes: The Inn is in downtown Jim Thorpe, close to antique shops, galleries and boutiques. It is near to the Asa Packer Mansion, and other historic sites in town.

Philadelphia
PARK HYATT PHILADELPHIA
AT THE BELLEVUE   1904

1415 Chancellor Ct., Philadelphia 19102. Tel. 215/893-1776; 800/678-8946; Fax 215/732-8518. 170 rooms. Rates: $210-320; suites, $395-1,850.

George Boldt was running his own relatively small but fashionable hotel in Philadelphia at the turn-of-the-century, when the Astors summoned him to New York to whip their Waldorf-Astoria into shape. Boldt was a superb hotelier, attentive to every minute detail, and he was such a success in New York that he was able to turn his eyes back to Philadelphia in 1902. Eight million dollars later, he had a masterpiece of a hotel, the Bellevue-Stratford.

Thomas Edison himself oversaw the installation of electric lighting in the hotel: those in the ground-floor lobby are the *original* Edison lights. After the hotel closed in the 1970's, under the specter of the Legionnaire's Disease outbreak, it was completely renovated. The entire infrastructure was replaced and most of the floors turned over to office space. The top eleven floors, however, were reclaimed as the Bellevue: a luxury hotel now managed by Park Hyatt.

Amenities: Refreshment upon arrival; 24-hour room service; concierge; complimentary coffee; use of health club.

Dining tip: In its "Brunching with the Chef" program on Saturdays, diners can watch their food being prepared and chat with the cooks.

Location notes: The hotel is located in downtown Philadelphia.

WARWICK   1926

1701 Locust St., Philadelphia 19103. Tel. 215/735-6000; 800/ 523-4210; Fax 215/790-7766. 200 rooms. Rates; rooms, $189-209; suites, $290-360.

"In one of the wettest and worst heavyweight championship title battles in the long history of the prize ring," wrote Bill Corum in the *New York Journal,* September 25, 1926, "Gene Tunny, the Marine of Destiny, knocked the coveted crown of gold off the battered, bloody head of a tired and worn old man – Jack Dempsey." It was the fight of the decade, a seminal moment of the 1920's, and 135,000 people were in Philadelphia to see it.

Across the city, assuming that anyone was left over there, the same rain was falling on the grand opening of the new Warwick Hotel. It was, in its own way, as much a symbol of its times. It was a hotel for rich travelers, those so rich that it is not necessarily relevant to describe the room decor ... should a guest specify a preferable style for one of the suites, the Warwick was known to commission the services of a decorator, and make the change in time for the guest's arrival. The very, very rich were not affected by the Great Depression, and the competition for their business became all the more fiercesome among couturiers, automakers, jewelers and, of course, hotels.

The Warwick's crowd was very loyal, fortunately, and insulated the hotel from the troubles many others faced during the 1930's. In fact, according to the hotel's own historical notes, rooms in the 22 story tower were often all booked up for months in advance, even during the Depression. The hotel was able to draw prosperous, cheerful people largely because it was a prosperous, cheerful respite from the general mood of the times. The interiors are decorated in English Renaissance style, streamlined by an art deco sensibility. The Warwick has been periodically refurbished, most recently in 1994.

Amenities: Concierge; fitness club with pool; valet service; voice-mail; business services; hair-dryers, dataports, refrigerators; room service.

Dining tip: Shrimp Lamaza has been on the menu almost since the hotel opened: it is shrimp cocktail with special sauce.

Location notes: The Warwick is in the Center City neighborhood. It is two blocks from the Academy of Music, six blocks to the Pennsylvania Convention Center, and ten blocks from Independence Hall.

Pittsburgh
WESTIN WILLIAM PENN   1916
530 William Penn Pl. on Mellon Sq., Pittsburgh 15219. Tel 412/ 281-7100; 800/937-8461; Fax 412/553-5239. 595 rooms. Rates: rooms, $99-189; suites, $250-1,600.

The William Penn Hotel opened in 1916 with 1,000 rooms: a big hotel that grew even bigger a dozen years later, when the total number of rooms jumped to 1,600. That made it the biggest hotel anywhere between New York and Chicago. A triple tower of red brick, it was shaped like an "E" standing on its side: altogether a massive enterprise, in which conventioneers by the thousand swirled around the very center of Pittsburgh's social life.

The bandleader Lawrence Welk was foundering in the late 1930's when he got a break and signed for a stand at the William Penn. Before Welk was through at the hotel, however, a broadcaster had come up with the name "Champagne Music" for the orchestra's sound; a customer had contributed the song title, "Bubbles in the Wine," and a staff engineer had done no less than invent the first bubble machine. With a hotel like that, who needs Florenz Ziegfield? According to a history of the hotel by Marianne Lee, Jackie Gleason was another popular figure: "Employees remember Jackie Gleason driving up to the hotel in an open convertible, surrounded by the June Taylor dancers. The hotel literally rolled out the red carpet for him, and his friendliness impressed everyone."

Still, according to Lee, the most popular person in the whole hotel was Sugar Silverblatt, the woman who owned the florist shop in the lobby. Celebrities staying at the hotel lined up to see *her* – as did quite a number of Pittsburghers. She was charming, and that is not a characteristic that can be quantified after so many years. However, there is one way to put a number on Sugar Silverblatt's personal charisma. That florist shop sold 100 boutonnieres a day, a half-century after boutonnieres went out of style! Apparently, they weren't yet out of style in Pittsburgh. The William Penn itself gave a lesson in charm on one of President Dwight Eisenhower's visits. Mamie couldn't accompany him, but the hotel didn't forget her. Even while her husband was still in Pittsburgh, she received a box of the hotel's chocolate cookies and a bouquet.

The William Penn was sold in 1964 to a man who planned to raze it as soon as possible. He was going to build a giant skyscraper in its place, but the Hotel and Restaurant Employees Union chose that moment to mention that with or without a hotel, the owner had to pay the employees their wages. On a contract with about three years to run, the obligation equalled $7 million. It razed the deal, so to speak, but left the hotel standing. In 1971, the Alcoa Corporation saved the William Penn and restored it, reducing the number of guestrooms to make each more spacious (a usual practice in hotel restoration). Subsequent owners have made frequent refurbishments since, and the lobbies and lounges are brighter now than ever.

If you want to read a first-rate and very lively article about the William Penn, ask the hotel for a reprint of Marianne Lee's article, "A Grande Dame Named William Penn."

Amenities: Valet parking; 24-room service; in-room dataport.

Dining tip: The hotel's main restaurant is still the Terrace Room, where Lawrence Welk had his break (and where even Sugar Silverblatt sang a song or two on special occasions).

Location notes: The William Penn Hotel is close to downtown shopping. It is five blocks to the David Lawrence Convention Center and three blocks to the Benedum Center.

VIRGINIA

Richmond
THE JEFFERSON   1895

Franklin and Adams Streets, Richmond 23220. Tel. 804/788-8000; 800/424-8014; Fax 804/344-5162; web, www.jefferson-hotel.com. 275 rooms. Rates: $140-195; suites, $225-850.

The Palm Court at the Jefferson Hotel should be considered a second Jefferson Monument. It has the grandeur and the dignity of the one in Washington, but considerably more warmth, with its statue of the patriot standing on a pedestal in the middle. The Palm Court is a square room of good proportion – it had better be, with him standing in the middle of it – lit mainly through Tiffany stained-glass in the ceiling and windows. Instead of walls, twin pillars define the room, and the statue of Jefferson is surrounded, fittingly enough, by places to talk, comfortable furniture uphol-stered in dark red or blue to compliment the stained glass. It is almost as though, after a hard day at the Monument in Washington, Jefferson comes home to the Palm Court to relax a little. And to listen to what people are saying.

The tribute to Jefferson is deeply important to the origins of the hotel, which was built by a born Yankee and adopted Virginian named Lewis Ginter. Having made a fortune in Richmond, trading in textiles, he joined the Confederate cause wholeheartedly in the Civil War. He felt, as many Virginians did, that he was fighting to preserve the nation – the United States as Thomas Jefferson had intended them to be. Having lost the war to Northerners (who felt, of course, that it was they were preserving the nation, as it was intended to be), Ginter went home to Richmond and made another fortune, in pre-rolled cigarettes.

Fortunes came easily to Lewis Ginter; he made four, altogether. When he decided in the 1890's to build a hotel in Richmond, he spent $2 million, at least twice the cost of any other hotel of the same size at the time. Ginter named his new hotel for Thomas Jefferson, a decision that ultimately cost a great deal of money, not only for the Palm Court statue, but for all the small details. It isn't easy to honor a Renaissance man: the artwork had to be great, the inventions had to be great, the architecture had to be great, the *library* had to be great. Ginter might have saved millions if he had just named the hotel after Patrick Henry.

Among the inventions at the hotel was a telephone type of communications system called the "Teleseme" that connected every guestroom by voice to room service. In search of decorations, Ginter traveled widely, buying antiques, rare books and serious art. "Strikingly original in design, with not a single square foot of defect to mar the harmony ..." a newspaper wrote of the hotel on its opening day in 1895, but in 1901, a fire marred everything and destroyed three-fifths of the hotel. Ginter had died in 1897, but others rebuilt the Jefferson Hotel around what was left of the original. One of the strange improvements that was made, as long as there was the opportunity, was a pond, or moat, around the statue of Thomas Jefferson. It was stocked with live alligators until 1948. Alligators are beautiful creatures in their own right, but it is hard to picture them going with Edwardian decor.

The most extraordinary room at the hotel is the Rotunda. The Grand Staircase at one end is said to have been the model for

Scarlet O'Hara's bruising staircase in *Gone With the Wind*. The Rotunda is an enormous room, a rectangle in actuality, held in place by rows of faux-marble pillars, with a stained-glass skylight in the middle of a ceiling 70 feet high. Scarlet O'Hara might well look at home flopping her way down the Grand Staircase, but the rest of the Rotunda seems more befitting Anna Karenina, just standing in the middle.

Among the famous guests of the Jefferson were President Benjamin Harrison, Helen Hayes, Sir Edmond Hilary, and Sir Anthony Hopkins, just to name a few of those listed under "H," in the hotel's long list of celebrities. The Jefferson was closed for six years in the early 1980's, but it reopened in 1986, with the benefit of a sensitive restoration, widely admired at the time.

Amenities: Concierge; valet parking; exercise room; in-room mini-bar, dataport.

Dining tip: The hotel serves afternoon tea.

Location notes: The Jefferson is in downtown Richmond.

WEST VIRGINIA

BLENNERHASSETT   1889

Fourth and Market Streets, Parkersburg 26101. Tel. 304/422-3131; 800/262-2536; Fax 304/485-0267. 104 rooms. Rates: rooms, $69-79; suites, $85-105.

The business of Parkersburg was business, which may be why the history museum is the Oil and Gas Museum, located in the old W.H. Smith Hardware building. William Chancellor was one of those who made his fortune in Parkersburg, and in 1889 he built a hotel on a corner downtown to show the world that Parkersburg was blessed not only with oil, natural gas, and abundant lumber, but with exquisite taste, as well.

Now known as the Blennerhasset, the hotel is a four story redstone building that would be at home in Austria, with its gables and its peaked turret at the corner. The interiors have been augmented by museum-quality antiques, though an inventory of the important furnishings still reads as though it were a shopping list in Mr. Chancellor's own hand, with a Steinway grand piano, clocks made in Germany or England over a hundred years ago, and a Hepplewhite desk in the Library. The reproduction furniture in the guestrooms leans toward Chippendale, rather than Hepplewhite, actually. That was not the sort of debate heard much in Parkersburg, until the Blennerhassett opened its doors.

Amenities: Complimentary breakfast, airport shuttle; in-room coffee.

Dining tip: Harman's, in another historic building next door to the hotel, is one of West Virginia's best spots for beef, though the planked Salmon is probably the single most popular dish.

Location notes: Parkersburg is on the northwest border of West Virginia. The hotel is downtown, about five blocks from the Ohio River.

Morgantown
THE MORGAN   1927

127 High St., Morgantown 26505. Tel. 304/292-8401; Fax 304/292-4601. 96 rooms. Rates: $43.60 per room.

The Morgan is a seven story red brick building located in downtown Morgantown. It is distinguished on the interior by oak wood paneling and molding.

Amenities: Television, telephone, free parking.

Dining tip: There is a deli on the premises.

Location: The Morgan is walking distance to the University of West Virginia campus.

9. THE NORTHEAST

"One guest, from out-of-town, on her several visits-a-year to the hotel, always insisted upon rehanging all the pictures in her room upside down. When asked why she did this, her reply was simple: "I like them better that way!"

– *Essex House Fifty Years* (unpublished manuscript)

MAINE

Camden
CAMDEN HARBOR INN   1874

83 Bayview St., Camden 04843. Tel. 207/236-4200; 800/236-4266. 20 rooms. Rates (seasonal): $95-225.

The Camden Harbor Inn was built in 1874, overlooking Penobscot Bay from a hillside. When it was new, most of its guests came from the steamships that ferried passengers between Boston and Bangor. The ships stopped for the night in Camden Harbor, where horse-drawn carriages picked up passengers who wanted to spend the night in a hotel.

A clapboard building with dormitory windows in the mansard roof, the Inn is a quintessential New England Victorian building. Most of the guestrooms today are furnished with antiques.

Amenities: Complimentary breakfast; rooms are individually decorated, all have private bathrooms.

Dining tip: Lunch is not served at the Inn, but dinner can be served either in the dining room or, in fair weather, on the porch overlooking the harbor.

Location notes: The Inn is about a block (downhill) from the harbor, where tourboats are available. The Inn is about three blocks from center of town.

Southwest Harbor
THE CLAREMONT HOTEL   1884

Box 137 Southwest Harbor 04679. Tel. 207/244-5036; 800/244-5036. 43 rooms. Rates: $115-192.

In the 1870's, Capt. Jesse Pease sailed his ship, the *Caroline Grey*, all over the world from his home in Southwest Harbor, a town on Mt. Desert Island off the coast of Maine. In 1877, Pease married a fashionable woman named Grace Clark, and she went with him on a long journey aboard the *Caroline Grey*. She hated it. No doubt, there was a lot to hate about being on a working ship, but Grace tried again. She still hated it. She tried again and in 1883, Capt. Pease sold the ship and retired from the sea.

Looking around for something new, he noticed that Southwest Harbor was becoming a popular tourist spot. The Peases built a hotel, the Claremont. It was not a grandiose place, but it was supposed to reflect the island's rustic way of life. On that basis, at any rate, they were able to consider hot baths a luxury and charge extra for them. Mrs. Pease took a firm hand in managing the Claremont and continued to do so, even after her husband's death in 1900, and even after she sold the property to a local doctor.

The Claremont Hotel looks like a very large yellow house, with a porch all the way around. It presides over a five-acre compound in which other houses and cabins have been carefully placed, so as not to intrude on each other.

Amenities: Business services; tennis. Baths free!

Dining tip: Every table in the dining room overlooks the water.

Location notes: The Claremont Hotel is on the mouth of Somes Sound. Acadia National Park is also on Mt. Desert Island.

MASSACHUSETTS

Boston
THE BUCKMINSTER   1903

645 Beacon St., Boston 02215-3201. Tel, 617/236-7050; 800/727-2825; Fax 617/262-0068. 100 rooms. Rates (seasonal): rooms, $79-139; suites, $109-229.

Homely on the outside, homey on the inside, the Buckminster is a quiet hotel, especially suited to longer stays, since cooking facilities are available on each floor. Built at the turn-of-the-century, the hotel has been gently restored in 18th century English style.

Amenities: cooking and laundry facilities on premises.

Dining tip: Meals are not served at the hotel, though it is near many restaurants and take-away places on Kenmore Square.

Location notes: The Buckminster is one block from Fenway Park; four blocks from the start of the Back Bay neighborhood and six blocks from the Longwood Medical area.

FAIRMONT COPLEY PLAZA HOTEL   1912

138 St. James Ave., Boston 02116. Tel. 617/267-5300; 800/527-4727; 617/267-6681. 440 rooms. Rates: rooms, $299 and up; suites, $650 and up.

In 1916, John Singer Sargent wrote a letter to Isabella Stewart Gardner and concluded, "I wish we were dining tonight at the Copley Plaza." It doesn't get much more *Boston* than that. Sargent, a veritable poet among portrait painters, lived in a corner suite at the Copley Plaza Hotel for the last eight years of his life and had the same table reserved in the dining room every day for lunch and dinner. He had a lumberjack's appetite and would disdain anyone who didn't, according to a biography by C.M. Mount, sometimes pausing in the conversation to say deeply and sadly, "You eat like a bird." Sargent's favorite dining companions were his sister, Emily, and his niece, Reine. At the end of World War One, Reine was sitting in a church in Paris when it was hit by a shell launched from miles away by the Germans' "Big Bertha" gun. Reine was killed, and Sargent's letter to his friend Mrs. Gardner was written with the news. It was Reine, too, that he included when he said, "I wish we were dining tonight at the Copley Plaza."

Henry Janeway Hardenbergh, the architect responsible for the Willard Hotel in Washington and the Plaza in New York, also designed the Copley Plaza. The broad granite building is the backdrop of the Boston's Back Bay: its broad gray facade is literally the backdrop for all of Copley Square, and the interiors are the fantastic backdrop for a slice of the whole city's social life. The lobby and several of the other public halls sparkle with mirrors, gilt and cut-glass in the style of France before the Revolution. Whether you stay here or just make it your business to walk through – bring sunglasses. The dining rooms and the Oak Bar settle into more subdued, Edwardian surroundings, while the guestrooms are traditional in an up-to-date way.

When the Copley Plaza was three years old, the actress Bette Davis was seven, and her family stopped there for dinner on the way to the train station a few blocks away. Mrs. Davis was taking the children away on vacation. "It was festive with a string orchestra, hot rolls on a silver wagon and lemon sherbet. The scene is still vivid to me," Bette Davis wrote in her 1962 autobiography. The family never had dinner together again, however; by the time the vacation ended, Mr. Davis had moved away. Bette Davis stayed away from the hotel until years later, when she was a big success and her father asked her out to lunch. The Copley Plaza was her idea.

In 1941, the Copley Plaza was acquired at a bargain price by the founders of the Sheraton chain. By the 1950's, the hotel was called the Sheraton Plaza, with its rich interiors masked or replaced by tile ceilings, vinyl flooring and painted plasterboard. It was a dispiriting make-over, but at least the Copley Plaza remained viable in an era that generally despised historic hotels. Fortunately, the John Hancock Mutual Life Insurance Co. was a longtime neighbor on Copley Square. By 1972, it had lost patience with the Sheraton Plaza's sliding standards. The insurance company went into the hotel restoration business, purchasing the Copley Plaza and initiating its renaissance. Subsequent owners continued the process of returning the hotel to its original state, but it was the Hancock company that, even before the boom for historic hotels, recognized the imperative to save the Copley, while there still *was* a Copley.

Amenities: Valet parking; exercise room; concierge; 24-hour room-service; valet service; business center.

Dining tip: There is live music every evening in the Oak Bar, one of the best places in Boston to meet or to linger. According to the hotel, it is supposed to look like a World War II British Officers' Club in India. That seems rather nostalgic for an unhappy time and place, so let it suffice to say that the Oak Bar is an immensely comfortable living room with the occasional statue of an elephant about.

Location notes: The Copley Plaza is in the midst of Boston's Back Bay, about one mile from the financial district or Faneuil Hall. It is five blocks from the Hynes Convention Center.

COPLEY SQUARE HOTEL   1891

47 Huntington Avenue, Boston 02116. Tel. 617/536-9000; 800/ 225-7062; Fax 617/236-0351. 143 rooms. Rates: $135-185; suites, $299.

It's quite easy to confuse the Copley Square Hotel with the Copley Plaza Hotel by their names. But they are, of course, very different. That is to say, every hotel is quite different from the grandiose Copley *Plaza* Hotel. In the case of the Copley *Square* Hotel, the result is a place more genteel than grand. It is a 19th century hotel, with rooms that benefit from vintage architectural details. The guest rooms are well-appointed, though they tend to be snug in size. The lobby is old-fashioned, in that the central part is a small front hall for transacting business, such as registering, while a spacious room on the corner is the lounge, with some peace and quiet.

Amenities: Adjacent indoor parking; complimentary use of nearby gym; in-room safe.

Dining tip: The hotel has a number of restaurants on-site; a take-away place called Tennessee's may be the best, if you want to spread towels all over the table in your room and have a BBQ picnic.

Location notes: The hotel is located one block from each of the following: Copley Square itself, Copley Place shopping/office/hotel complex, and the Prudential Center. It is four blocks from the Hynes Convention Center.

THE ELIOT   1925

370 Commonwealth Ave., Boston 02215. Tel. 617/267-1607; 800/443-5468; Fax 617/536-9914. 91 suites. Rates: $205-450.

Harvard University was feeling uncommonly good about itself in 1912, in the afterglow of the presidency of Charles W. Eliot, who had assumed the job while in his twenties and held it for forty years, until 1909. Eliot was nationally famous for his writings, his judgment and his leadership. In 1912, Harvard built a Club on Commonwealth Ave. so that alumni would have somewhere to dine and stay for short periods. It was a great success, to the extent that it became hard to get a room reservation.

In 1925, Charles Eliot's family took the opportunity to build a hotel next door, at the corner of Commonwealth and Mass. Ave., to catch the overflow of business and to permanently align the names "Harvard" and "Eliot." For a long time it was a residential hotel, where Harvard old boys and Radcliffe old girls could live out their years comfortably. It is no longer the old slipper it was then. In 1990, the family that owned the hotel (the Eliots having sold it in the 1930's) decided to turn it into a luxury "little hotel," a

European-flavored hotel category of which Boston then had none. The whole place was renovated, inside and out.

The improvements keep coming: a new ironwork portico, worthy of Brussels; new uniforms for the doormen; better planters, new fur hats for the doormen in the winter. Some people look to the top of the old John Hancock building to see what the weather is going to be; some just look to the headgear of the Eliot doormen.

Amenities: Valet parking, in-room kitchenettes.

Dining tip: Cleo's is the hotel's swank bistro.

Location notes: The Eliot is located at the western end of the Back Bay, one block from the Hynes T-stop; three blocks from the Hynes Convention Center, and about four blocks from Fenway Park.

THE LENOX   1900

710 Boylston St., Boston 02116-2699. Tel. 617/536-5300; 800/ 225-7676; Fax 617/266-7905. 212 rooms. Rates: rooms, $220-295; suites, $350-475.

The Lenox is a small but formal hotel, built in the last century, and renovated in 1996. Perhaps it is the Lenox's combination of antiques and good reproductions – no, it is probably the way the wallpapers seem to have been handpressed in some cottage somewhere, that makes such an urbane hotel feel so much like a hillside inn once you're well inside.

Amenities: Valet parking; room service; exercise room; in-room fax and dataport.

Dining tip: The Samuel Adams Brewhouse at the hotel taps a dozen beers, porters, and ales from the popular brewery.

Location notes: It is in the midst of the Back Bay: across the street from the modern addition to the Public Library, two blocks from Copley Place, and about four blocks to the Prudential and the Hynes centers.

THE MILNER HOTEL   1895

78 Charles St. South, Boston 02116. Tel. 617/426-6220; 800-453-1731; Fax: 617/350-0360. 64 rooms. Rates: $65-85.

The Milner was built as a little charmer, with its dainty lobby so fully detailed in plasterwork, and so content with good proportion. The current owners keep the lobby in very good repair, but they seemed to go to great lengths to pick out a front desk made of some brown laminate invented but to depress dainty plasterwork. However, the breakfast nook off the lobby at the Milner is set up with cast-iron furniture on the original mosaic floor and it does suggest the old dignity of the place.

As refurbished in 1995, the rooms would be very nice at a ski lodge; they are quite plain for the city of Boston, but the hotel is respectable throughout. It could, however, be the jewel of the city.

Amenities: Complimentary shuttle to Logan Airport, continental breakfast.

Dining tip: Breakfast is the only meal served at the Milner.

Location notes: The Milner Hotel is in the Theater District, about two blocks from the Boston Common and the Public Garden.

THE PARK PLAZA HOTEL   1927

64 Arlington St., Boston 02116-3912. Tel. 617/426-2000; 800/ 225-2008; Fax 617/423-1708. 960 rooms. Rates: rooms, $155-215; suites, $375-1,500.

Staying at the Park Plaza is like traveling with an elegant great-aunt who happens to be prepared for any eventuality. And, while other hotels may well be willing to send out for anything that a guest might need, the Park Plaza may not have to do more than send downstairs, because so many of the major airlines, travel companies and other services have storefronts in the same building. The Park Plaza is a big, bustling hotel, seemingly seen every night on the local news as the backdrop for some political or social event.

Amenities: Concierge; exercise room; room service; business center.

Dining tip: The hotel has on-going seasonal and holiday events at the Swan's Court, usually variations on Afternoon Tea.

Location notes: The Park Plaza is located about three blocks from the Theater District, and across the street from the Public Garden and the start of the Back Bay.

OMNI PARKER HOUSE   1927

60 School St., Boston 02108. Tel. 617/227-8600; 800/843-6664; Fax 617/742-5729. 535 rooms. Rates: $119-249.

The original Parker House Hotel was built in 1855, and it is only a slight exaggeration to state that everybody in the world stayed there. It was central to Boston's social, political, and literary worlds, at a time when all were formidable. One man who was stopped at the old Parker House was John Wilkes Booth, who was recalled looking handsome and relaxed at a sunstreaked breakfast table, April 8, 1865, just before leaving for Washington to shoot Abraham Lincoln. But much better people than that loved the old Parker House through the years, and loved its restaurant – and loved its rolls, too, enough to make them famous throughout the country. There was a time when the hotel regularly received mail addressed to the "Parker Rolls House."

The new Parker House, built in 1927 to replace the first one, is now one of the city's most venerable hotels in its own right. In fact, it is the oldest grand hotel in the country, in terms of continuous operation. There are older minor hotels, but the Parker House has the distinction that in 1856 and still today people came to Boston from all over the country with the bustling entity called the Parker House on their minds. The richly paneled lobby has that air of importance, bolstered by the continuing tradition that every U.S. President since Coolidge has been a guest.

Amenities: Valet parking; room service; business services.

Dining tip: They serve the rolls, if that is your question. They also serve Boston Cream Pie, likewise invented at the hotel.

Location notes: The Parker House is downtown, two blocks away from the Common or the State House. It is along the Freedom Trail.

THE RITZ-CARLTON   1927

15 Arlington St., Boston 02117. Tel 617/536-5700; 800/241-3333; Fax 617/536-1335. 275 rooms. Rates: rooms, $320-445; suites, $395-2,000.

Richard Rogers and Lorenz Hart were inspired to write "Ten Cents a Dance" in a suite at the Ritz-Carlton. That must say something about the creative process: namely, that there is nothing more inspiring to an artist than to have a big hotel bill mounting and a play in trouble. Boston was an important "try-out" city for productions on their way to Broadway, and so the Ritz has a list of 40 plays and musicals that were drastically rewritten within the walls of the hotel. They could probably tell just how drastic by the room-service orders. Rodgers claimed that he thought of the melody for "Edelweiss," while taking a shower at the Ritz. Neil Simon wrote the third act of "The Odd Couple" while he was at the hotel.

The Ritz-Carlton, built in 1927, has no pronounced sense of that era: most of an original set of art-deco murals were removed a dozen or so years ago, while the dining areas seem, if anything, turn-of-the-century in their high-ceilinged grace. The overall scheme is that pastel known as French Provincial. What is historical about the Ritz is the air about it, as though it were a high-horsepower engine that hums only very softly.

Amenities: Valet parking; exercise room and passes to European health spa; 24-hour room-service; complimentary morning shuttle to financial district, shoeshine; in-room safes and honor-bars.

Dining tip: From Memorial Day through autumn, the Roof is open. Overlooking the Public Garden, it offers dinner and dancing, along with a Jazz brunch on Sundays.

Location notes: The Ritz-Carlton is located on Newbury Street, the city's trendiest shopping area. It is across the street from the Public Garden, seven blocks from the Hynes Convention Center and about one mile from the financial district.

Salem
THE HAWTHORNE   1925

The Common, Salem 01970. Tel. 508/744-4084; 800/729-7829; Fax 508/745-9842; web, www.hawthornehotel.com. 89 rooms. Rates: rooms, $99-151; suites, $240.

The Hawthorne presides over the Common in one of Massachusetts' oldest cities. It is a neat looking brick building in Colonial style, with cheerful New England interiors. Named for Nathaniel Hawthorne, who lived in the neighborhood, the hotel was built in 1925 on a swell of enthusiasm from local residents, who financed it themselves one share of stock at a time. Many people even donated artwork or antiques to help the hotel properly reflect Salem's colorful spirit. A number of locals chose to live at the hotel, since it was the hub of the city's social life. According to the hotel's own history, one such permanent guest was a businessman named Larry Haverty: "Known as the 'official greeter' by the other residents, he was at the center of the group who could usually be spotted on the second floor mezzanine balcony watching the comings and goings below. A cocktail in the Brace Lounge was named after him despite the fact that he was a teetotaller ..."

Out-of-state businessmen gained control of the Hawthorne in the early 1970's and did a poor job of managing it. On the verge of bankruptcy, they sold many of the hotel's treasured antiques. In the actual bankruptcy that followed, the Hawthorne was sold to a company that started to restore it. In 1986, the hotel finally came full circle and landed in local hands – very local, one of the new partners is a former Congressman. They completed the restoration, concurrent with a renewal of tourist interest in Salem, its seafarers, its witches and its colonial mansions.

Amenities: Business services; exercise equipment; valet service.

Dining tip: Nathaniel's, the hotel restaurant, serves fresh seafood.

Location notes: The Hawthorne is one block from the waterfront or the Peabody Essex Museum. It is eight blocks to the House of the Seven Gables.

Northampton
THE HOTEL NORTHAMPTON   1927
36 King St., Northampton 01060. Tel. 413/584-3100; 800/547-3529; Fax 413/585-0210. 77 rooms. Rates: rooms, $105-150; suites, 138-250.

The Hotel Northampton was built in 1927 by a dedicated antiquarian named Lewis Wiggins. A five story building in red brick, it was a fairly standard design for the era, although there was certainly an echo of the Federal era in the pillared entrance, with its flanking verandahs. They have since been glassed-in, to make an elegant conservatory out of the entrance.

However, it was the interior of the hotel that Mr. Wiggins cared about most. He turned it into a veritable repository for fine antiques: a recreation of colonial era in a 20th century great-house. Not many hotels can boast of a curator, but the Northampton had one in the 1930's – and the curator had a staff of no less than 15 assistants. The hotel retains many of the pieces Wiggins collected, though the guestrooms are decorated today with fine reproductions.

After Lewis Wiggins was satisfied with the atmosphere in his museum-hotel, he collected just one more piece. But it was a deusie: he took title to the Wiggins Tavern, an authentic relic of Yankee hospitality, opened in 1786 in New Hampshire by one of his ancestors. He had it moved to Northampton, brick by brick, and augmented it with more (of course) antiques. It became the hotel's official dining room. Some New Englanders could claim to have dined at the same table in the same Wiggins Tavern in two different states.

Amenities: Complimentary breakfast; business center; exercise room; television, telephones.

Dining tip: The Wiggins Tavern sets out an extensive buffet for Sunday brunch.

Location notes: The hotel is located within four blocks of Smith College.

NEW YORK

Buffalo
HOTEL LENOX   1897

140 North St. at Delaware Ave., Buffalo 14201. Tel. 716/884-1700. 800/825-3669; Fax 716/885-8636. 156 rooms. Rates: $59-69; suites, $79-120.

When the Lenox was under construction in 1897, the Buffalo Courier sent a reporter over for a look. "In the office of the building on the first floor will be long-distance telephones, messenger calls, and similar conveniences," wrote the reporter, "The passenger elevators will be run 24 hours each day, every day in the year. The elevator on the west side of the building runs to the roof, which is railed off for security and may be arranged as a roof garden or verandah; Buffalo is peculiarly attached to the verandah, and on the roof of the Lenox may be found, it is claimed, the grandest verandah in Buffalo, fitted up with seats, awnings, and plants, and from which Lake Erie, Niagara Falls and all of the country about Buffalo may be seen."

The Lenox flourished during Buffalo's Pan-American Exposition in 1901, an event now more famous for tragedy than amusement. President William McKinley was shot while visiting the Exposition. He seemed likely to recover, but when his condition turned grave, Theodore Roosevelt was summoned to Buffalo from a hunting trip in the Adirondacks. After McKinley succumbed to the wound, Roosevelt took the oath of office in a house right across the street from the Lenox. During World War Two, the hotel thrived with the local aircraft industry, and the lobby was often filled with cots full of pilots waiting to fly new planes out of Buffalo.

Changes have attempted to update the hundred-year-old architecture – wood panels obscure the marble pillars in the lobby, for example – but the Lenox still retains the details of a hundred year-old hotel. It still has that roof, if the owners would just reopen it to the public. Because it certainly still has that view.

Amenities: Free parking; business services; complimentary coffee, self-service laundry facility.

Dining tip: The hotel's dining room is closed for renovation, but Elmwood Avenue, two blocks away, has a wide choice of restaurants.

Location notes: The Lenox is in the historic Allentown neighborhood of Buffalo. The Theodore Roosevelt Inaugural Site is across the street. The Erie County Convention Center about a half-mile away.

Cazenovia
THE LINCKLAEN HOUSE   1836

79 Albany St., Cazenovia 13035. Tel. 315/655-3461; web, www.cazenovia.com/linklaen. 18 rooms. Rates: rooms, $99-125.

Little towns can hold a palace of the people, whether they describe it that way or not. On November 11, 1836, the Cazenovia Democrat announced: "The Lincklaen House is now finished and open for the reception of company ... the building is spacious, durably constructed and elegantly finished." It is still all of those things.

From the outside the three story brick building has barely changed at all; just about the most glaring difference is that the signpost that once faced north-south now faces east-west. Recruits collected at the Linklaen House to leave for the Civil War. The actual outbreak inspired 24 enlistees, but in the summer of 1862, when the President needed 300,000 more soldiers, 101 of them came from Cazenovia, which raised enough bonus money to offer a $25 sum to each man. They showed up at the Lincklaen House on August 14, went outside, formed a line at the signpost, prayed, said goodbye, and headed south to the ringing of bells.

The Linklaen followed the new grand hotel example of such hotels as Boston's Tremont House in many respects, including the one that allowed American hotels to develop so much faster than European hotels: it was built by a group of investors, operating as a stock company, capitalized at $23,000 (the Astor Hotel, opened the same year in New York City, cost $400,000). In all these years, the ground floor has had only one major renovation, resulting in a comfortable 1916 version of 1836.

Amenities: Complimentary continental breakfast; free parking; air conditioning; in-room private bathroom, telephone, television.

Dining tip: The hotel's main restaurant is in an uncommonly elegant dining room, creamy white and well-proportioned, with lots of light from the windows and a fireplace at one end.

Location notes: Cazenovia is about 19 miles southeast of Syracuse. The hotel is adjacent to shopping in the town, and within one block of the Cazenovia College campus.

East Aurora
THE ROYCROFT INN   1905
40 South Grove St., East Aurora 14052. Tel. 716/652-5552; Reservations 800/267-0525; Fax 716/655-5345. 22 rooms. Rates: $120-210.

In the early 19th century, industry suddenly grew big enough to dwarf the human spirit, wherever and however it wanted. Junk was turned out by machine so meaninglessly that the workers and even the consumers all became part of the junk, too, at least in the view of English philosophers such as Ruskin and Morris. They were more than philosphers, however; they were brakemen, trying to slow the mechanical age by turning back to the inefficient ways of the village crafter – inefficient but caring ways. It took hold as a movement, called the Arts and Crafts Movement. Fittingly enough, though, its leading proponent in America was a man who couldn't help but make it big business.

Elbert Hubbard was a unique American. As effective a salesman as Professor Harold Hill in *The Music Man*, he was a homespun philosopher and humorist who left his own executive highlife to promote a way of life in which people felt good about themselves, and in which they did their work as a sort of gift for their fellow man. His essay, "A Message to Garcia," is still in print, having sold 80 million copies since it was first published in 1899. In establishing the Roycroft community in East Aurora, a suburb of Buffalo, Hubbard started by lovingly printing books, sometimes with handmade paper and bindings. At the same time, he sold hundreds of thousands of subscriptions to his two magazines, *The Philistine* and *Fra*.

Other Arts and Crafts Movement adherents also tried to form colonies of careful artisans: Hubbard succeeded, because he was equal parts businessman and idealist. His Roycroft community kept almost a hundred artisans employed in its heyday from 1900-1925, turning out furniture, ceramics, lamps and books in the attractive Arts and Crafts style, at once folksy and cunningly modern. In 1904, Hubbard built the Roycroft Inn in East Aurora, as a full statement of the style he prescribed as an antidote to the standardized world all around.

The Inn is a long three story hotel, painted mossy green. Located on a side street, it is surrounded by other vintage buildings of the Roycroft colony, which continues to operate. A shop across the road from the inn sells furniture, pottery and jewelry made by the Roycroft artisans. Inside and out, the Roycroft takes on the personality, though not the actual lines, of a rustic cottage: the sense of comfort lent by grainy wooden furniture, stained-glass lamps, leaded glass windows and painted tiles. A central garden court and a long front porch lined with rockers allow the cottage atmosphere to expand into the open air. An $8 million restoration, completed in 1995, left the inn so immaculate, as a living museum, that volunteers from town give daily tours. The guestrooms are new, though vintage 1905 in decor, from the simple square oak furniture to custom wallpapers, tiles and carpets, in tones of beige. One of Hubbard's sayings is chiselled into the wide, oaken front door: "The love you liberate in your work is the only love you keep."

Amenities: Television with VCR, free parking, complimentary breakfast.

Dining tip: The Inn has a wide choice of dining areas, indoors and out.

Location notes: East Aurora is 30 minutes by car from downtown Buffalo. The Inn is within two blocks of Roycroft shops and exhibits, and the Millard Fillmore Museum.

New York City
THE ALGONQUIN   1902

59 W. 44th St., New York City 10036. Tel. 212/840-6800; 800/228-3000; Fax 212/944-1419. 165 rooms. Room rates: rooms, $230-250; suites, $375-550.

"In America, there are two classes of travel – first class and with children." That, in case you couldn't tell for sure, is wit (from Robert Benchley), and wit is a phenomenon so closely associated with the Algonquin Hotel that a half-dozen books have been published and a couple of movies produced, just to repeat the funny things once said there.

The original manager was Frank Case, a hotelier of the old school who considered himself a host, not a businessman. He would do anything for his guests – he was even known to loan shirts to actors who needed presentable ones for auditions. He gave generous credit to writers and fatherly advice to the likes of Tallulah Bankhead. Neither the shirts, the credit, nor the advice had much lasting effect on most of his wards, but nonetheless, Frank Case took care of his guests. By the 1920's, when he purchased the Algonquin outright, it was the favorite of any such Case alums who did manage to make good in the theater or publishing. So it was that the "Wits of the Round Table" collected in the hotel's Rose Room in the 1920's and 1930's to spray epigrams like aerosol. It is a fragrance that obviously still lingers about the place.

The Algonquin is a beautiful hotel in its own right, with a large lobby and rather small rooms, most of them decorated with English cottage decor, along with some with theatrical or literary memorabilia. The best part of the place is the lobby, a bit of old New York that still wakes up every day: filled with comfortable seats and sofas, it is the perfect place to alight for a tall glass of fresh orange juice. Just ring a bell and a waiter appears – what technology could be easier than that? For a place that has belonged to five generations of celebrities, including many a Barrymore, Noel Coward, and Helen Hayes, it still meets Frank Case's original standard, seeming like home even to first-time visitors. Among the celebrities known to stay at the Algonquin these days are Maya Angelou, Jeremy Irons, Liza Minelli and Sandra Day O'Connor.

Amenities: Complimentary copy of *The New Yorker* (founded at the Round Table and still edited in offices only across the street); Continental breakfast; in-room safe, dataport, and hair dryers; available business services.

Dining tip: Well-known nightly cabaret in the Oak Room.

Location Notes: Midtown Manhattan, two-to-three blocks to the theater district and the department stores on Fifth Avenue.

THE ESSEX HOUSE   1931

160 Central Park South, New York City 10019. Tel. 212/247-0300; 800/645-5687; Fax 212/315/1839. 595 rooms and suites: Rates: rooms, $350-380; suites, $425-3,000.

What could be worse than to be stuck with a half a hotel, just as the county settled into its worst Depression?

The "Sevilla Towers" was only one of 26 New York hotels under construction at the time of the Crash and beached by the Depression. Somehow or other, it managed to open in 1931 with a new name, "The Essex House." It had sparkling Art Deco furnishings, along with 1,286 rooms that remained largely empty for the first year, awaiting guests who were simply staying home. For awhile, the deed to the place seemed to ricochet among every bank and real estate company left in New York, but in 1932, the bouncing mortgage fell to the Federal government, which would own the super-Deco skyscraper for the following fifteen years. Not generally known for its *savoir faire* or continental ways, the government did a good job of hiring managers who made The Essex House one of New York's hot nightspots, nationally known for Big Band radio broadcasts made from the hotel-nightclub, the Casino on the Park. Determined managers also constructed a giant neon sign on the roof in 1932, though it hasn't been lit since 1945 when arts groups complained that it marred the cityscape. The real problem, say the oldtimers, was that pranksters sometimes managed to switch off the first two letters in the hotel's name, to the great amusement of sophomores everywhere. The sign is still there, though unlit.

The Essex House survived by renting many of its rooms on a longterm basis, and among those who made it their address were Bing Crosby and his family, Eleanor Roosevelt, Casey Stengel, Sinclair Lewis, and Joe Louis. Eddie Cantor also lived there, taking up a whole floor with his wife and five daughters. Many families chose to live or stay at the Essex House because it is across the street from Central Park. In fact, the hotel insists that it invented the buffet brunch, originally to attract the many New Yorkers who took walks in the Park on Sunday mornings, and worked up a big appetite by the time they started for home.

In 1991, The Essex House was renovated. More accurately, it had its Art Deco lines and surfaces re-sharpened after years of wear. The lobby is fitted in black marble and white, as shiny as a movie set. The guestrooms are much more traditional, with country print fabrics and soft colors. In the renovation, the number of rooms was pared down to 595, making each more spacious than originally.

Amenities: Television with VCR; mini-bar, safe, fax, dataport, complimentary shoeshine, 24-hour room service, health spa.

Dining tip: The main dining room, Les Celebrities, seats only 55, a very intimate setting.

Location notes: The Essex House is across the street from Central Park; it is five to eight blocks to Rockefeller Center, the Times Square theater district, or Lincoln Center.

GRAMERCY PARK HOTEL   1924

2 Lexington Ave. at 21st St., New York City 10010. Tel. 212/475-4320; 800/221-4083; Fax 212/505-0535. 509 rooms. Rates: rooms, $145-160; suites, $190-220.

To describe Gramercy, either the Park or the Hotel: it is a close-knit place in New York, rather dark in a comforting way and remnant of old New York. The park is fenced and requires a key to get in, but guests staying at the hotel can borrow one at the desk.

Amenities: Reduced-price parking nearby; in-room direct-access telephone, individual climate control.

Dining tip: The dining room serves a three-course continental buffet including such dishes as beef stroganoff, Yankee pot roast, and homemade desserts ($35.75).

Location notes: The Gramercy Park Hotel between midtown and downtown Manhattan, three blocks east of Fifth Avenue and just east of the now-fashionable Union Square area.

THE PLAZA   1907

Fifth Ave. at Central Park South, New York 10019. Tel. 212/759-3000; Res. 800/678-8946; Fax 212/759-3167. 815 rooms. Rates: rooms, $235-625; suites, $650-1,950.

The Plaza opened in 1907, an improbable French Chateau that dominates a neighborhood as no other New York hotel does, making it hard to tell exactly where the plaza out front ends and the Plaza takes up. Built by three New York businessmen, the Plaza generally lookslike something left behind by Louis XIV, the Sun King, on one of his infrequent visits to New York.

At a cost of $12 million, it appealed to Alfred G. Vanderbilt, at any rate, and he was the first guest. George M. Cohan, F. Scott Fitzgerald and the Beatles also favored the Plaza. The emininet architect, Frank Lloyd Wright (who designed buildings that looked absolutely nothing like the Plaza) chose to live in the hotel for six years in the 1950's. However, the most famous person ever to stay at the Plaza was its perfect guest, Eloise, the character in a series of books by Kay Thompson (in addition to stories about Eloise, the books offer an expert tour of the hotel). Eloise was the daughter of a glamorous mother who was usually away somewhere, leaving the little girl to raise herself at the hotel. The first book in the series was published back in 1955, but Eloise's descriptions are still accurate: "There is a lobby which is enormously large with marble pillars and ladies in it and a revolving door with ℙ on it."

When the hotel opened, it catered to people who needed a permanent place to stay – a *pied à terre* – in New York and the rooms were much more spacious than was usual for hotels. The guestrooms still seem big. They are very traditional in decor, and fortunately many of them still have original features such as crystal sconces or chandeliers, fireplaces, and elaborate moldings. In fact, the hotel is surprisingly unchanged throughout, considering that it seems to have been mobbed constantly since the moment the revolving door with the ℙ first budged.

The Palm Court at the Plaza is one of New York's most famous interiors: an Edwardian restaurant where tradition is as light as a feather. Palm trees and greenery separate the tables from the bustle of the city (and the time of day), while piano and violin music wafts into the airy space of the room with an acoustic not quite heard anywhere else. The room is open all day, from breakfast to after-theater dining.

The Oak Bar, a wood-paneled old pub, is as intimate as the Palm Court is public. Long restricted to men only, it is still an adventurous little pocket of the city: you never quite know who will be there. In the late 1980's, the Plaza was associated with the Trump regime, which undertook a major restoration. Today, it is part of the Fairmont Hotel group.

Amenities: Valet parking; exercise room; business center; concierge; 24-hour room service; in-room dataport.

Dining tip: "I have lunch at the Palm Court if it is too rainy." – Eloise

Location notes: The Plaza is adjacent to Central Park, within 10 blocks of Rockefeller Center, Lincoln Center and Times Square.

THE ST. REGIS   1904

2 E. 55th St. at Fifth Ave. New York 10022. Tel. 212/753-4500; 800/759-7550; Fax 212/787-3447. 313 rooms; rooms, $455-565; suites, $695-5,000.

The St. Regis was built – and, more important, paid for – by John Jacob Astor IV, known in his day as the richest man in America. His idea was to open "not so much a hotel as a temporary home for those who are used to the best of everything and who appreciate artistic surroundings." As a location, he chose a spot that is possibly the epicenter of life on Manhattan Island: 55th Street at Fifth Avenue.

In 1894, he and his mother had purchased the lot on the southeast corner for $500,000 – a fortune even in that day. At 17 stories, Astor's St. Regis would be the first skyscraper-hotel when it opened in 1904, serviced by state-of-the-art inventions such as elevators, air conditioning, central vacuuming, and in-room telephones. But it was the decor that could embarrass practically any castle, its lobbies lit almost from within by the gloss of imported French marble, the glitter of 22-karat gold leaf trimming and the glint of crystal chandeliers. All still remain.

Colonel Astor was famously rigid in maintaining his standards – but he was just as adamant about his personal standards and eight years after his glorious hotel opened, he sailed with the *R.M.S. Titanic.* He was to become part of its lore: told that he would have to go down with the ship, he changed into evening dress and calmly announced that he would, at any rate, go down as a gentleman. Apparently, he did. From the first, an international clientele adopted the St. Regis as a sort of headquarters. The hotel had an on-going struggle with the late Salvador Dali, who always insisted on bringing his pets with him. Once he and his bear stayed at the hotel. There is also a letter from Dali in the files, in which he agreed, under duress, not to bring his ocelot. The Duke and Duchess of Windsor; Fred Astaire, and Lady Mountbatten were also regular guests.

Over the first eighty years, the St. Regis never fell into disrepute, exactly, but it was a tired old star by 1988, when ITT Corp., the owner, initiated a $100 million renovation worthy of Astor's original dream. The public spaces on the first and second floors were generally restored to original condition, while the guest floors were completely rebuilt. The rooms have silk wall coverings and original art, with a blend of antique-style and modern furniture, true to the 1904 hotel only in that they are still supposed to be merely par ... for people who are used to the best of everything.

Amenities: 24-hour butler and room-service; complimentary ironing service, local calling, newspapers, snacks and beverages; in-room fax; fitness club.

Dining tip: Lespinasse, the hotel's main dining room, is often ranked as New York's most respected restaurant.

Location notes: The hotel is within five blocks of Rockefeller Center, Carnegie Hall and Central Park.

THE WALDORF-ASTORIA   1931

301 Park Ave., New York City 10022. Tel. 212/355-3000; 800/445-8667; Fax 212/872-7272. 1,219 rooms. Rates: rooms, $260-410; suites, $400-1,000.

When George C. Boldt opened the old Waldorf Hotel on Fifth Avenue, he graciously invited other hotelmen to the grand opening. Frank Case, later of the Algonquin Hotel, recalled that he and his friends were impressed with the facility, but thought Boldt was a "damn fool" for lining the halls and lobbies with Oriental rugs. Smart hoteliers would never waste money like that. Finally, Case was sent to ask Boldt what he would so when the expensive rugs wore out from all the crowds trampling on them. "I'm more concerned for fear they may not wear out," Boldt replied.

The turn-of-the-century history of almost anything or anyone is likely to include an episode at the old Waldorf-Astoria. Most notoriously, though, it was at the core of that Fifth Avenue "lobster society" that considered the cheapskate the only real sinner. Peacock Alley became the nickname (later copied elsewhere) for a wide hallway that rustled late every morning with expensive clothes and fresh gossip.

The Waldorf also had a bar.

J.P. Morgan stopped in for his daily Manhattan, while John (Bet-a-Million) Gates ordered milk and crackers. Manhattans and milk were available elsewhere, of course, but special drinks concocted at the Waldorf Bar commemorated what seemed at the time to be great events. Ninety years later a listing of these drinks is like a faint and scratchy recording of talk around the Waldorf bar: about war (the Santiago Sour, the Dewey Frappe, the Schley Punch, the Shafter Cocktail), about monetary issues (the Single Standard Rickey, the Double Standard Sour, and the Free Silver fizz), hit plays, (the Floradora, the Chanticleer, the Soul Kiss), scandals (the Bradley-Martin), and other phenomena so obscure that possibly they were not great events, after all.

In 1929, the old Waldorf-Astoria was demolished to make space for the Empire State Building. The new Waldorf-Astoria Hotel opened in 1931, two enormous, connected towers at home on Park Avenue. It is, as ever, at its best when it's busiest, still seeming to judge itself on how fast the carpets can be worn out. They weren't worn out very quickly the first year, in the middle of the Great Depression; it is said that one night, fewer people were registered in the 2,200 rooms than were playing in the orchestra on the Starlight Roof.

The hotel gathered momentum, though, by thinking of practically everything. Eighty-six chefs trained in French cooking made one million meals in 1938, but there were always some guests who looked down on haute cuisine, and for them the hotel hired American women to serve up American cooking, made in a regular kitchen. The thorough and eminently practical Waldorf Manuals became standard texts in hotel-management schools, with tips like this, in the chapter on breakfast: "Anything lukewarm in the morning is an invitation to trouble." The art deco Waldorf-Astoria has been well-maintained throughout its life, one of the few hotels in the country that never grew old, in looks or in spirit.

Amenities: Concierge; business center exercise room; steam room; in-room refrigerators, dataport.

Dining tip: Cole Porter used to live in the Waldorf Towers and his piano is in the Peacock Alley.

Location notes: The Waldorf is on Park Avenue on Manhattan's East Side. It is within eight blocks of Grand Central Station, the New York Public Library and Rockefeller Center.

Saratoga Springs
THE ADELPHI   1877

365 Broadway, Saratoga Springs 12866. Tel. 518/587-4688; 800/ 860-4086; Fax 518/587-0851; web, web, www.adelphihotel.com. 39 rooms. Rates: $110; $210 during August. Note that the hotel is only open during the summer.

The reaction of many Yankees on the home front during the Civil War was to become very tired of the news: either the violent specter of too many battles or the dreary stalemate of too few of them. Those with means marched north and Saratoga Springs suddenly sprang up as their destination. The mineral waters cured their thirst, if nothing else, but the very insouciance of the place cured their blues. Hotels of a thousand rooms and more were hammered together as fast as planks could be brought in. Gambling was rampant, but the stakes were just as high in the area of fashion, as the hotels built long front porches: fashion runways in actuality, where ladies and gentlemen showed themselves like prize poodles.

The big hotels were the Congress, the United States and the great Grand Union – still lamented, its old place on Broadway is a gaping parking lot. But a local builder named John McAfee realized that the town needed a smaller, boutique hotel, in contrast to the giants. In 1877, he opened the Adelphi Hotel, with just 77 rooms. It is a three story brick building with a long front porch of its own. After thriving with the rest of the town for the next 40 years, it fell with the rest of the town in the 1920's, when Prohibition combined with changing fashion to stop the party in Saratoga. The current owners purchased the Adelphi in 1978, just to save it from imminent destruction. Having used all their money for the purchase, they set about restoring the hotel by themselves, two or three guestrooms a year. In 1996, they finished the job.

Amenities: Complimentary continental breakfast; swimming pool; television.

Dining tip: The hotel serves breakfast and there is a bar in the lobby, leading out to a terrace in the back.

Location notes: The Adelphi is in downtown Saratoga Springs, near many shops and restaurants. It is about three blocks to Congress and about one mile to either the Performing Arts Center or the thoroughbred races.

Syracuse
THE HOTEL SYRACUSE   1924

500 S. Warren St. 13202. Tel. 315/422-3440; 800/255-3892; Fax 315/422-3440. 472 rooms. Rates: $74-115; suites, $125-275.

A well-preserved city hub, the Hotel Syracuse is a handsome brick hotel that takes up its own triangular block in downtown Syracuse. Despite considerable financial confusion in the late 1980's, the hotel has emerged with its perennial aura of bustling prosperity. The guestrooms have been refurbished in a traditional style. The Hotel Syracuse is fortunate to have especially beautiful meeting and party rooms, including the Grand Ballroom and Persian Terrace, still in their original Second Empire grandeur. It has been the best hotel in town ever since they tore down the storied old Yates Hotel decades ago.

Amenities: Free enclosed parking; room and valet service; fitness center; business services.

Dining tip: Coach Mac's, a sports bar for Syracuse University fanatics, is affiliated with former S.U. football coach Dick MacPherson.

Location notes: The hotel is within two blocks of the OnCenter and War Memorial convention halls. It is located downtown, about one mile from the S.U. campus.

West Point
HOTEL THAYER   1926

U.S. Military Academy, West Point 10996. Tel. 914/446-4731; 800/247-5047; Fax 914/446-0338. 189 rooms, Rates: rooms, $80-100; suites, $110-185.

It is hard not to notice that West Point's Thayer Hotel looks rather a lot like a fortress. Chiseled in red brick and granite, it is buttressed by two wings angled backward a bit, as though to secure the central section from getting pushed too hard from the front. If it were pushed a hundred yards or so, it would go into the Hudson River, because the Thayer is built on the actual west-point for which the vicinity is named. And so, far from being a fortress, the Thayer is actually just a clever hotel trying to give as many rooms as possible a view of the gentlemanly Hudson River.

Red brick on the outside, the hotel lobby has rooms decorated with homelike prints and antique reproduction furniture. Generals Eisenhower and MacArthur took in the Hudson views from guestrooms at the Thayer, as have most U.S. presidents. (One exception is Franklin Roosevelt, who only lived across the river and up the street at Hyde Park, New York.) The Thayer Hotel has been owned by the Federal government since 1943, and so it is the official bunkhouse for guests of the U.S. Military Academy. However, the hotel is certainly open to the public and can help visitors get the most out of a visit to West Point – a place like no other. For example, the Military Academy Band stages ambitious summer concerts at the amphitheater on the grounds, and the hotel can help guests arrange to attend.

Amenities: Concierge, business services; television.

Dining tip: The garden terrace, commanding a wide view of the Hudson, is one of the most breathtaking dining spots in the country, when it is open in summer.

Location notes: The Parade Ground at the Military Academy is one-and-a-half miles from the hotel. The West Point Museum and the Visitor's Information Center are each about one-half miles away. There is a ski hill two miles away.

RHODE ISLAND

Newport
THE HOTEL VIKING   1926

*One Bellevue, Newport 02840. Tel. 401/847-3300; 800/556-7126.
184 rooms. Rates (seasonal): rooms, $59-269; suites, $99-799.*

Make no mistake: the great mansions that line Newport's cliffs
and shores were not homes. They were big toy-hotels, offering
room and board at a bargain price (nothing). Reservations were
tough to get, of course. For a long time, however, Newport was one
town in America that didn't have need of a hotel: you either had a
room already or didn't belong, anyway.

By the 1920's however, when the mansions were starting to
fade from prominence, social equality found a foothold in Newport at the Hotel Viking. It was built in an unabashedly Georgian
style, with antiques and reproductions throughout the hotel and its
guestrooms. The hotel mentions Jack and Jacqueline Kennedy at
the top of its list of famous guests. But it claims Astors and
Vanderbilts, as well. It is either deeply satisfying or else rather sad
to think of a for-real Vanderbilt needing a hotel room in Newport.

Amenities: Amenities: indoor pool; exercise room; free parking; business services, exercise room.

Dining tip: The hotel's rooftop bar overlooks Newport harbor.

Location notes: The Viking is within two blocks of the Tennis
Hall of Fame, the Newport Library and the Art Museum. The
Newport mansions are about one mile away.

Providence
PROVIDENCE BILTMORE   1922

*Kennedy Plaza, Providence 02903. Tel. 401/421-0700; 800/294-
7709; Fax 401/455-3040. 245 rooms. Rates: rooms, $160-180; suites,
$200-1,000.*

"This hotel we've got, there's no place like it in Rhode Island;
it's like no place you'll ever see again," said Jimmy McDonnell, who

started working at the Providence Biltmore in 1948. He was still there in 1998. Designed by the architectural firm responsible for Grand Central Station in New York, the Biltmore is similarly massive and intelligent.

Constructed of red brick rising 17 stories, the hotel is set on a V, so that every room has an open-air view. The Biltmore may be a conservative building from the outside – it could be part of the Brown University campus, not far away – yet it is still known for its longtime flirtation with the Navy. Sailors and officers from ports all along the coast stationed themselves in Bacchante Room. As former Rhode Island governor Bruce Sundlun recalled for the Associated Press, "It was a shocking place because, if you can believe it, the waitresses in the Bacchante Room wore transparent skirts. It shocked the community to its core." (But not the Navy.) "The Bacchante Room in the Biltmore was the place to go on Friday and Saturday nights," he said of its heyday before and just after World War Two.

Throughout the 1960's, the Providence Biltmore was sorely neglected, but when it closed in 1974, the city realized with a jolt the truth of Mr. McDonnell's sentiment: *it's like no place you'll ever see again*. People within the community bought the property in 1979 and renovated it without erasing the feel of a vintage hotel. There were 600 rooms when it opened in 1922; today there are 245 more spacious rooms. That *haute* symbol of 1920's glamour – the rooftop cafe – is still considered part-two of the hotel's lobby, but now it is a glass enclosed elevator that makes the trip from one to the other.

Amenities: concierge; in-room ironing facilities, dataports, voice mail; Heritage Executive Level rooms.

Dining Tip: Known for excellent seafood – in a city getting to be very well known for fine cuisine.

Location Notes: Rhode Island Convention Center across the street; Waterplace Park is a half-mile away; Brown University is one mile, and Roger Williams Park and Zoo is five miles away.

VERMONT

Brattleboro
THE LATCHIS HOTEL   1938
50 Main St., Brattleboro 05301. Tel. 802/254-6300; 802/254-6304; web, http://www.brattleboro.com/latchis. 30 rooms. Rates: rooms, $55-95; suites, $120.

When Peter Latchis decided to create a memorial to his father in 1938, it was not a block of stone, and it was not a little plaque somewhere. It was Brattleboro-sized Rockefeller Center, a building of business and life: encompassing a theater, hotel, shops, ballroom, restaurant and cocktail lounge. Peter's father, Demetrius, might have approved: he started out in business at the turn-of-the-century as a pushcart merchant, selling fruit. As a recent immigrant (from Greece), he had the worst possible territory for a pushcart merchant: Brattleboro, Vermont, a city on a tilt, on the side of a Green Mountain. Anyone who can push a cart of fruit three feet in Brattleboro deserves a memorial, but Demetrius did even more than that, and managed to establish several stores. Eventually, he and his sons went into the theater business and built a string of 15 theaters.

Peter's memorial to his father was not a sentimental exercise, looking wistfully backward in style – in 1938, it was the most modern building in Vermont. It may still be: a high art deco complex that has changed very little since the grand opening. The three story building fans out from a corner downtown, with large, paned windows. The interiors include the original terrazzo masonry, patterned in geometric images; hand-painted murals that are stylized depictions of Vermont wildlife, and hidden lighting from the original fixtures. The guestrooms still have much of the original furniture from the opening, re-upholstered, and the bathrooms still have the original tiling and chrome fixtures.

The restoration of the hotel was a hands-on project for Spero Latchis, Demetrius' great-grandson, and his wife, Elizabeth Vinyard. The Latchis Memorial Building was down, but not out, when they started work in the 1980's: it still had much of its own furniture and furnishings, and they were both trained in the decorative arts and restoration. Today, guests at the hotel can see a new movie or live performance at the Latchis Theater (a 1,200-seat gem) or at one of the other two theaters added more recently, and then dine at the Latchis Grille – all without leaving the building. Or, more important, going up or down a hill.

Amenities: Complimentary continental breakfast in the room; in-room private bathroom; telephone; television; refrigerator, and coffee maker.

Dining tip: The Latchis has its own brew-pub, known as the Windham, in addition to the restaurant, the Latchis Grille.

Location notes: The Latchis is in lower downtown Brattleboro.

Middlebury
THE MIDDLEBURY INN   1827

14 Courthouse Sq., Middlebury 05753-0798. Tel. 802/388-4961; 800/842-4666; Fax 802/388-4563; internet, www.middleburyinn.com; e-mail, midinnvt@sover.net. 80 rooms. Rates: rooms, $70-156; suites, $124-185.

Middlebury, Vermont, takes itself seriously as the crossroads of ... practically the whole world, but at least of Routes 7 and 125. And in the middle of Middlebury, there has been a tavern or inn on the same spot since the 18th century. The current incarnation, a handsome red brick building, was built in 1827 and has grown by fits and starts through the years, without losing its Georgian character.

One of the historical attractions today is a vintage Otis elevator, still doing its job after nearly a century. An even older and better invention – a front porch – overlooks a town green. Guests should request a room in the main hotel, as the more recent motel addition would not represent much of a historical adventure – the Otis elevator definitely won't take you there, for one thing.

Amenities: continental breakfast included; afternoon tea for guests; in-room telephones, cable television, and hair-dryers; free parking.

Dining Tip: New England cuisine. In fair weather diners take to tables on the front portico.

Location notes: Greyhound and Vermont Transit buses stop a block away; not far from Middlebury College.

White River Junction
HOTEL COOLIDGE   1879

White River Junction 05001. Tel. 802/295-3118; 800/622-1124. 33 rooms. Rates: $39-69.

When the Junction House in White River Junction, Vermont, burned to the ground in 1878, neighbors had scant pity for the owner and attributed the fire to "the unrestricted looseness that characterized his system of running the Public House." The site, however, was still ripe for a hotel, since five railways crisscrossed White Water Junction, and in 1879 a large new hotel opened. In fact, for a small town, the new Junction House was enormous, with no less than 200 rooms.

The new owners knew what they were about, though, serving both trainmen and tourists on their way to resorts – and tourists willing to treat the Junction House itself as a resort. The new owners made sure that their hotel was almost constantly celebrating something or other, some occasion or visit from a famous personage. It worked: the big hotel in the little town hosted 38,000 guests in an average year around the turn-of-the-century, according to an engaging brochure, *A Short History of the Hotel Coolidge,* which quotes the locals of the time as saying, "the beds never cool down at the Junction House." In 1923, Calvin Coolidge was sworn in as President of the United States in a town not far from White River Junction. Even so, that was still the biggest thing ever to happen in White River Junction, and the owners of the Junction House renamed their place the Hotel Coolidge. (Officially, it is named after the President's father, Colonel John Coolidge.)

The Hotel Coolidge sits amid a downtown block in White River Junction, a town just barely big enough to have a downtown. Today, Amtrak's Vermonter stops daily at White River Junction.

Amenities: Individually decorated rooms, each with private bathroom, television, telephone.

Dining tip: There is a coffeeshop in the lobby, convenient for breakfast and lunch. White River Junction is a compact village with a handful of restaurants, including A Taste of Africa, the owner of which is from Kenya.

Location notes: The hotel is across the street from the train station. The town is four miles from Dartmouth College.

10. THE GREAT LAKES

"One night there was a fellow smoking in bed evidently, and he started the mattress on fire. He had a good bean on, I suppose. He took the mattress, rolled it up, shoved it out the window and went back to bed. And there we had a burning mattress on the building next door!"

–Art Lillyblad, speaking of the St. James Hotel, Red Wing, Minnesota, as quoted in *If Walls Could Talk*

ILLINOIS

Brussels
THE WITTMOND HOTEL   1885
108 Main St., Brussels. Tel. 618/883-2345. 7 rooms: Rates: $40-70.
Where were your ancestors in 1847? The Wittmond family, proprietors of the Wittmond Hotel in Brussels, Illinois, can answer that question in a single word. "Here." When Conrad and Mary Wittmond first started turning a dollar on the property, they sold supplies to settlers on their way out west. Of course, a settler – by the very nature of the word – mainly needs a place to stay, for a night as well as a lifetime, and so the Wittmonds built a small hotel and started offering accommodations in 1863. In 1885, the family built a bigger hotel, the one still in use. It's a red longhouse of a building: two stories, sashed by a verandah running the whole length for the sake of the second-story rooms.

Amenities: Free parking; no television or telephones; complimentary breakfast.

Dining tip: Dinners are served family-style, with such specialties as country sausage and homemade desserts, including cobblers.

Location notes: Brussels is on the Mississippi River in western Illinois. Brussels Ferry, eight miles south, is a prime spot for eagle-watching.

Chicago
THE AMBASSADOR WEST 1924

1300 North State Parkway, Chicago 60610. Tel. 312/787-3700; 800/300-9378; Fax 312/640-2967. 220 room and suites. Rates: $200-800.

The Ambassador West was planned after World War One, and opened in 1920, a twelve story hotel always glancing back at 18th century England. Antique beveled mirrors, marble floors and tapestries decorate the public spaces in a place where the main ballroom was named the Guildhall, after the one in Bath, England. And the actor Brian Aherne was hired to dress up like Beau Nash on the night it opened officially in the late 1950's.

The Ambassador West is located on the so-called Gold Coast, the dignified part of downtown reaching north along Lake Michigan. The area was developed in the 1920's and the Ambassador West was such a success in its first years that it spawned the Ambassador East across the street in 1927. Bankrupted a few years later by the Depression, the hotel rebounded with the successful World's Fair, the Century of Progress, that was staged in Chicago in 1933-34. The Ambassador West was renovated in 1989.

Amenities: Fitness room, valet parking.

Dining tip: Ballroom dancing is still very much in fashion in the hotel's Guildhall Room.

Location notes: The hotel is within a three blocks of the Magnificent Mile shopping district or Lake Michigan beaches.

BLACKSTONE 1910

636 S. Michigan Ave. 60605. Tel. 312/427-4300; 800/622-6330; Fax 312/427-4736. 220 rooms. Rates: rooms, $139-169; suites, $159-195.

The most venerable of Chicago's hotels, the Blackstone was the big noise in 1913, when the Republican Convention came to town. Theodore Roosevelt and William Taft were not known to agree on much, but they both stayed at the Blackstone during the convention. In fact, the Republicans came to town for their convention in 1920, too, and it deadlocked between candidates, until Warren G. Harding's campaign manager took it upon himself to hold a private meeting with several influential delegates in his suite – number 408/10 – a heated meeting made hotter by billows of nervous cigar smoke. Harding carried the ballot soon thereafter and, according to hotel lore, that tense caucus gave rise to the expression, "smoke-filled room."

Associated with the 1920's in Chicago, the Blackstone Hotel was used in the movie *The Untouchables*, which was about that era, because it has changed so little, with marble floors and crystal chandeliers. The rooms have been newly refurbished in traditional decor. The play *Sheer Madness* has been running in the hotel theater for over 15 years.

Amenities: Television, telephone.

Dining tip: The Blackstone Grill is an upscale restaurant on the premises.

Location notes: The Art Institute is two blocks away, the shopping area of State Street is about six blocks away.

CHICAGO HILTON & TOWERS 1927

720 S. Michigan 61605. Tel. 312/922-4400; 800/445-8667; Fax 312/922-5240. 1543 rooms. Rates: rooms, $240-355; suites, $575.

Even a hotel that has 10 rooms is an invention. A hotel with 100 rooms is an accomplishment, and a hotel with 1,000 is called a "city within a city." But what does that make a hotel with 3,000 rooms? You may say "big," but James W. Stevens said "just right," because the gargantuan Stevens Hotel was his idea and it came to reality in 1927.

Four connected towers, each one at least 28 stories high, the hotel took up all of a large block on Michigan Avenue in Chicago. It had its own movie theater (1,200 seats) and its own golf course on the roof. On one record-breaking occasion, 7,200 people sat down to dinner, more or less together. Even on an average day, the hotel had to wash 300,000 plates. Stevens looked at the growth of conventions in the 1920's and noticed how 10 or 15 hotels would handle the delegates for a single convention: he proposed to take them all in under one roof and also to give them the meeting space in which to convene. In fact, one of the towers rests entirely on a Grand Ballroom built without pillars. Instead, structural engineers calculated that four steel trusses over the room, and hidden behind the ceiling, would hold just as well as 55 pillars. They calculated correctly. Stevens didn't: the hotel/convention center was a tricky balancing act.

In 1945, Conrad Hilton purchased the property, named it after himself, and used his company's marketing strength to keep the rooms filled. In 1962, the number of rooms was reduced and the amount of convention space was increased. Changes continued along the same lines in the course of a massive (needless to say) restoration of the Towers in the mid-1980's. The Grand Ballroom and Grand Stair Hall are still original to 1927, as are aspects of the other public rooms and lobbies. The guestrooms are down to half their original number, through enlargements; they have been fully modernized. The Chicago Hilton is very much a historic hotel, not as a decor, by comparison to others, but as a stupendous variation on the old invention.

Amenities: Exercise room with lap pool and track; 24-hour room service; business center; valet parking.

Dining tip: Kitty O'Shea's, the hotel pub, has live Irish music on weekends.

Location notes: The hotel is across the street from Grant Park; four blocks from the Art Institute and four from the Field Museum (although it is still necessary to drive, due to traffic).

THE DRAKE   1920

140 E. Walton Pl., Chicago 60611. Tel. 312/787-2200; 800/445-8667; Fax 312/787-1431. 535 rooms. Rates: $265-2,150.

Ben Marshall was outlandish in the way he dressed, wearing a sombrero on the golf course, for example, and ruffled shirts everywhere he went. He was certainly outspoken in the way he carried himself: as an architect, his motto was, "I can build a better one." But then he did build a better one, the perennial "better one."

The Drake Hotel can match any in the country and it was Ben Marshall who built it. In 1917, he talked the Drake family of hoteliers into investing in a major project in a newly developing part of town: then called the Near North Side, now known more commonly as the Magnificent Mile. The surprise, however, was that the Drake, as Marshall designed it, was refined and conservative, even hushed, considering it was a hotel of 700 rooms.

The Drake is a 13 story building, broad shouldered to use a Chicago sort of compliment, and it overlooks Lake Michigan almost as though it were a beach hotel. The guestrooms are large and furnished with more personality than would be found at many big hotels: good furniture and fetching fabrics that would be found in a well-run home. According to Marshall's original plan, a visitor is insinuated into the Drake Hotel, as a pair of wood-paneled lower lobbies lead up to a main lobby, raised above the fray of the street level. The Drake opened in 1920, not much different than it is today, and just as smooth. Ben Marshall couldn't stay away, as he continued to work at the hotel, managing it and also decorating some of the restaurants, including the glamorous dinnerclub called the Gold Coast Room. Being Ben Marshall, he then directed the floor show there.

Amenities: Valet parking; 24-hour room service; fresh fruit on every floor; in-room mini-bar, iron.

Dining tip: The Cape Cod Room opened for the 1933 Century of Progress. It is still fresh, and specialties include seafood.

Location notes: The Drake is adjacent to designer boutiques on Oak Street; it is about two blocks from the Water Tower shopping center and one mile from the Art Institute.

PALMER HOUSE HILTON   1924

17 E. Monroe, Chicago 60603. Tel. 312/726-7500; 800/445-8667; Fax 312/263-2556. 1639 rooms. Rates: rooms, $169-189; suites, $450 and up.

The Palmer House was the most famous hotel in the country, perhaps in the world, when it opened in 1873: the very name became a synonym for a grand hotel. Today, one might say, of a fleabag, "Well, it's not exactly the Ritz," but in the days when Cesar Ritz was just another Swiss waiter in Paris, it would not even have been surprising to hear him say of a fleabag, "Well, it's not exactly the Palmer House."

In 1926, the original was replaced (one tower at a time – the hotel never ceased operations) by a large hotel, a good hotel that still enjoys the luster of the name. The main lobby is a blaze of gilded light (it's the cover shot of this book), although the guestrooms and much of the rest of the hotel may as well be in a much newer hotel.

Amenities: Room service; concierge.

Dining tip: The hotel's restaurant, the Big Downtown, recaptures the 1940's in Chicagoland, with vintage movies, and even an overhead El-train. Portions are huge.

Location notes: The hotel is adjacent to extensive shopping. The Art Institute and Federal buildings are one block away; financial markets are with three blocks, and most major theaters are within five blocks.

THE REGAL KNICKERBOCKER   1927

163 E. Walton Pl., Chicago 60611. Tel. 312/751-8100; 800/678-8946; Fax 312/751-0370. 254 rooms: Rates: $205-245.

When people talk about the Regal Knickerbocker, the subject starts with the Crystal Ballroom. The floor was made of glass when it was new, and 760 fluorescent lamps underneath lit the very steps of the dancers. Meanwhile, the ceiling was 28 feet high, and gilded to reflect another type of light entirely. A flapper's paradise, the Crystal Ballroom has changed most notably only in that the floor

is now made of plexiglass. The Knickerbocker was opened as the
"Davis Hotel" in 1927, one of a handful of hotels built at the time
to help to establish the newly fashionable neighborhood around
North Michigan Avenue in Chicago. However, when the Great
Depression took hold, the Davis fell out of popularity for a time, in
part because it had become associated with a fast, perhaps danger-
ous, crowd. One of the hotel legends is that the rooftop ballrooms
were built specifically for use as casinos, with both limited access
going in, and secret passages leading out.

A new owner, Allan Hurst, took over in 1931. He dispensed
with the old name, and came up with a pointedly non-Chicago
word, "Knickerbocker," to describe his hotel in its new era. Hurst
presided over the hotel and its respectable new image until 1959,
when he died. In 1970, Playboy Enterprises bought the hotel.
Known for almost 10 years as the Playboy Towers, its reputation
was once again rather questionable, as the magazine's version of
the good life was put on display, in the nightclub, of course, but also
in the restaurants and the giftshop. By the 1980's, the hotel once
again clung to the name Knickerbocker and a more sedate style of
business. A Regal hotel since 1995, the old Knick has been
renovated, though most of its original details had long since been
rubbed out by owners in intervening years. Not the Crystal ballroom, though. That is still something.

Amenities: Dual telephones, room service, mini-bar, fitness
room.

Dining tip: The Martini Bar offers 40 variations on the theme.

Location notes: The hotel is within blocks of the Magnificent
Mile shopping district and Lake Michigan beaches.

Galena
DESOTO HOUSE HOTEL   1855

*230 South Main St., Galena 61036. Tel. 815/777-0090; 800/343-
6562; Fax 815/777-9529. 55 rooms. Rates: $75-185.*

In most respects, the DeSoto House is the oldest grand hotel
still operating in the United States, having opened for business in

1855. The record is even more remarkable, considering that in all that time, the place almost never turned a profit, in good times and bad, in peace and in war. And yet, it remained. And it still remains, a strapping brick building on Main Street, with an ironwork gallery all the way across the second story. It was easily the biggest, best hotel in the "West" when it opened. But did little Galena, population 8,000, really need a better hotel than St. Louis or Chicago?

While hotels are private enterprises, they make a very civic statement, and when the DeSoto was launched, it was supposed to point to the biggest possible future for the little Mississippi River town. The dining room proudly served "Frenchified" food to the locals and traders bustling through. (That's *Frenchified*, not French-fried.) Abraham Lincoln made a speech from the hotel's balcony in 1856, ringing out in favor of the Republican candidate for President (John Fremont) and against Slavery.

The year 1855 may have been the DeSoto's very first year, but the year 1859 brought an event just as important, the hotel's first bankruptcy. Galena didn't appear to need the biggest, best hotel in the region, and though a new owner was found, business only dropped to yet a new low. "All this talk about the dissolution of the Union is humbug – nothing but folly," Lincoln had declared from the gallery of the DeSoto in 1856. He wasn't exactly right about that, as it turned out. When the Civil War started in 1861, the Mississippi River closed to commercial traffic, part of the South's effort to choke the North into submission. It mostly seemed to choke the DeSoto House. Commerce and westward expansion both stalled on the Upper Mississippi during the war, leaving Galena with few people passing through, and the hotel with few guests.

Ultimately, the hero of the Union cause was Ulysses Grant, a native of Galena. The General made the hotel his political head-quarters when he staged a successful run for the presidency in 1868, but he was weary and so was the hotel, according to a reporter from Vermont, who stayed at DeSoto House: "I knew it was ancient because I saw sure proofs of its antiquity all about. The spots on the table cloth were of no recent date. The towels and other equipments in my room had been worn quite thin. I made an estimate and calculated from the amount of custom I saw there it would have taken several hundred years to have worn them to their present condition." The DeSoto House was then 13 years old. If a dog is said to age seven years for each human year, then a hotel undoubtedly ages 70 years for each one.

A new owner in 1870 faced the fact that Galena had overestimated itself with the DeSoto House, and simply removed the top two stories: not too simply actually, but the result was a three story building where there had once been five. In that form, the DeSoto House lurched through a hundred years of optimistic owners – and realistic bankers. Wrenchingly enough, it didn't quite reach the 1980's, the golden era of hotel restoration, intact. In 1978, a local developer gutted the old DeSoto House. "Gutted" is a horrifying verb when dealing with hotels or other living things. The result is a stunningly preserved hotel, from the outside. On the inside, though, the DeSoto is all new. The lobby is faithful to the mid-19th century, but the guestrooms and most of the rest of the interiors pay little homage to the past. Even if is only a shell of its former self, though, the DeSoto is still a treasure, the oldest of the nation's extant grand hotels, and the grandest of survivors in any species.

To read a keenly researched history on the subject, ask the hotel about buying a reprint of the 1986 booklet called *Galena's DeSoto House*.

Amenities: Free indoor parking; cable television, telephones; suites have fireplaces.

Dining tip: Little Galena gave nine generals to the Union effort in the Civil War; the casual main dining room is named for them. Oddly enough, it is decorated in pink.

Location tips: Galena is in the northwest corner of Illinois, close to the border with Iowa and across the Mississippi from Wisconsin. The hotel is walking distance to museums regarding U.S. Grant and lead mining. Riverboat gambling is available 15 minutes away, by car.

Peoria
HOTEL PÈRE MARQUETTE   1927

501 Main St., Peoria 61602. Tel. 309/637-6500; 800/447-1676; Fax 309/637-5211. 288 rooms. Rates: rooms, $94-104; suites, $175-500.

"Hotel Père Marquette – The Monocled Ambassadors," reads the marquee over the main entrance of the building in a 1940's photograph. Heaven knows what that is supposed to mean, but on another side, it reads, "Hotel Père Marquette – Center of Social Activities," and that is just what the hotel has been in Peoria since 1926.

In the 1950's and 1960's, the Pere Marquette had a clever manager named Ferdinand Sperl. Of course, it is easy to be clever, when one is perfectly suited to a job, and Sperl, a devoted gourmet, made his hotel into something of a school for budding gourmets on the Illinois plain. Spreading his own enthusiasm in any way he could, he started the "Quando Manducamus Fraternity" in his main dining room. The Fraternity was a loose-knit gourmet club: Sperl's engaging way of introducing haute cuisine, and of making his hotel something special, as well.

The Père Marquette never quite sagged or fell by the wayside, perhaps in part because it was a part of the Hilton chain during the 1960's, when vintage hotels needed all the help they could get. Admittedly, Hilton modernized the building, *streamlined* it, even. However, Hilton left in 1981, when it no longer needed the Père and the Père no longer needed it. The new owners reversed the streamlining: the gracious lobby, with its half-pillars leading up and up to a high ceiling, looks almost as it did in the 1920's, when the hotel opened.

Amenities: Free parking and airport shuttles, exercise room, free local calls; business services available.

Dining tip: People come from all over the Midwest for New Year's Eve at the Père.

Location notes: Peoria is in Central Illinois, about 120 miles southwest of Chicago. Located near antique stores and offices in downtown Peoria, the Père Marquette Hotel is across the street from the Peoria Civic Center.

INDIANA

Indianapolis
THE CANTERBURY   1928

123 S. Illinois St., Indianapolis 46255. Tel. 317/634-3000; 800/ 538-8186; Fax 317/262-8111. 99 rooms. Rates: rooms, $195-245; suites, $325-1,400.

There has been a hotel at the corner of Illinois and Chesapeake streets in Indianapolis since 1858. The first was the Oriental, which was replaced in 1928 by the more Anglophilic Lockerbie Hotel. It was recently renamed the "Canterbury." Twelve stories in brick and granite, the hotel is veddy veddy English inside. The public rooms and the two story lobby are proportioned to be intimate, rather than grand, with subtle, elegant decor worthy of an embassy.

Amenities: Valet parking; complimentary continental breakfast; 24-hour room service; concierge; shoeshine; in-room minibar, hair dryer, telephone and television in bathroom.

Dining tip: The Canterbury restaurant, serving American cuisine, is highly respected. In addition the hotel is next door to the St. Elmo, a steakhouse dating from the turn-of-the-century.

Location notes: The Canterbury is in downtown Indianapolis, two blocks from Union Station or the Indiana Convention Center and RCA Dome, and three blocks from the State Capital.

MICHIGAN

Dearborn
DEARBORN INN   1931

20301 Oakwood Blvd., Dearborn 313/271-2700; 800/321-2049; 313/271-7464. 242 rooms. There are also five houses. Rates: $69-179.

The Dearborn Inn claims, with very peculiar pride, to have been the world's first airport hotel. It is a pleasing building, quaintly colonial in architecture and relaxed in atmosphere: it couldn't possibly be an airport hotel. However, Henry Ford was standing around the Ford Airport in Dearborn one day in 1930, when it occurred to him that as passenger flights proliferated, a hotel would be needed at the air field. He spotted the perfect site, across the street from the airport. Being Henry Ford, the magnate, he called in Albert Kahn, one of the nation's most eminent architects, to start the job. And being Henry Ford, the traditionalist, he specified that the new hotel should look like it was already nice and old. The Dearborn Inn opened a year later, a red brick building in early Georgian style. A year after that, the airport across the street closed, but the Inn rolled along nicely without it. It has always been owned by the Ford Motor Corp.

In addition to the guestrooms in the main building, the Dearborn Inn offers five historic homes as accommodations. Most were built in 1937, and each one is an exacting replica of the actual house of a great American. The five people, listed with the sites of their homes, are: Walt Whitman (Huntington, Long Island); Edgar Allen Poe (New York City); Patrick Henry (Red Hill, Virginia); Oliver Wolcott (Litchfield, Connecticut), and Barbara Fritchie (Frederick, Maryland). Barbara Fritchie, the subject of a poem by John Whittier, was 95 years old when she hung out the window of her house and waved a U.S. flag at Confederate troops riding through Frederick; as a much younger patriot, she had been enthusiastic in her support of George Washington.

Amenities: Free parking; swimming pool; tennis courts; exercise room; valet service; room service; in-room television, radio and individual climate control.

Dining tip: As in Henry Ford's day, the Early American Room features many old-fashioned favorites.

Location notes: The Dearborn Inn is about 10 miles from either the Detroit Metro Airport or downtown Detroit. It is about a half-mile to the Henry Ford Museum & Greenfield Village.

Grand Rapids
AMWAY GRAND PLAZA   1913

*187 Monroe NW, Grand Rapids 49503. Tel. 616/774-200; 800/
253-3590; 616/776-6496. 682 rooms. Rates: rooms, $150-165.*

The Amway Grand opened as the Pantland Hotel in 1913, a
moment at the very zenith of Grand Rapids' long history as the
furniture capital of the country. The builders had guts, opening
their showplace in a city of showrooms. It is one thing to try and
wow people with the decor of a hotel in Texas, where they pump
oil and raise cattle, or in Washington, D.C., where they write
reports and sometimes read them, but visitors to Grand Rapids in
1913 knew their furniture – and everybody else's. They looked at
a chair and its serial number flashed across their eyes. They didn't
wow easily. However, the Pantlind succeeded, bringing in a few
items not normally seen in Michigan, including a sunburst wall
decoration made in France in the 17th century.

The hotel was purchased by the Amway Corp. in 1979 and
beautifully restored as part of the Amway Grand Plaza, a complex
of shops, restaurants, and a new hotel tower that augments the
former Pantlind.

Amenities: Air conditioning; exercise room; indoor pool;
tennis courts; in-room dataport, hair dryer, climate control.

Dining tip: The richly paneled 1913 Room is the original hotel
dining room.

Location notes: The Grand Plaza is on the Grand River. The
Gerald R. Ford Museum and the Van Andel Museum are both
accessible across a pedestrian bridge over the river.

Petoskey
STAFFORD'S PERRY HOTEL   1899

*Bay & Lewis St., Petroskey 49770. Tel. 616/347-4000; 800/456-
1917; Fax 616/347-0636. 80 rooms. Rates (seasonal): $70-185.*

Dr. Norman J. Perry met with a tragedy, when he was practicing
dentistry in the late 1890's. Possibly, he even contributed to it. He
pulled several teeth from a patient's mouth, but something went

wrong and the patient died. Dr. Perry abandoned the profession and looked for something else to do, something positive. He chose the hotel business: a good living and a cheerful one, by and large. In 1899, Dr. Perry opened a three story hotel in the town of Petoskey, which had been incorporated a few years before.

The hotel sat on a rise overlooking a placid bay in Lake Michigan. The building is Georgian in style, painted yellow, with a columned cornice that seems to step right over the downhome porch. However, the back of the hotel looks out over the water and it was rebuilt the very minute that picture windows were invented. Nowhere could they have been put to better use than on that rise overlooking the bay.

Amenities: Private bathrooms; cable television; spa.

Dining tip: The Rose Room overlooks the lake; in the summer, meals are also served on the front porch.

Location notes: Petoskey is on Lake Michigan in the northwest part of the state. The hotel is in a historic shopping district.

Plymouth
MAYFLOWER HOTEL   1927

827 W. Ann Arbor Trail, Plymouth 48170. Tel. 313/453-1620; Fax 313/453-0775. 87 rooms. Rates: rooms, $55-175.

In the mid-1920's, the Plymouth Rotary Club raised the money to build the Mayflower, a three story brick hotel. Actually, it was supposed to be five stories, but the Rotary's efforts came up a little short and so then did the building. A seasoned hotelier named Ralph Lorenz took over in the early 1930's and he slowly changed the interior decor to the Victorian look that it still carries. Instead of growing upward, the popular hotel grew all around, into neighboring buildings. Because the hotel rambles, there is some doubt as to whether it is worth a full, structural restoration. Unfortunately, one of the plans on the table is to raze the old Mayflower and build a new one in its place.

Amenities: Air conditioning; television; telephone; in-room safe and refrigerator.

Dining tip: There is no dining room in the hotel, but there is an Irish pub directly across the street.

Location notes: The Mayflower is in downtown Plymouth.

St. Ignace
BOARDWALK INN   1928

316 N. State St., St. Ignace 49781. Tel. 906/643-7500. 16 rooms. Rates: rooms, $39-79; suites, $84-99.

The great debate around St. Ignace, Michigan in the late 1920's was about the bridge. There wasn't a bridge – but people talked about it anyway, and most were leery at the very thought of a direct connection between St. Ignace (Upper Peninsula) and Mackinaw City (the rest of the world). Oliver Vallier was in the midst of the debate, because he opened a hotel in St. Ignace in 1928. He called it the Traveller's Hotel and tried to make it a worldly establishment, both as a destination for tourists and as a reflection of St. Ignace. Vallier's opinion on the issue of the bridge wasn't noted, though some people who wrote letters to the newspaper insisted that it would "destroy the tourism business." The bridge was finally built in the 1950's and if what followed was destruction, then the hotel thrived on it. Later though, as the hotel's own history points out, "age took its toll on both the Valliers and the hotel and it fell on hard times."

Steve Sauter was a real estate agent when he walked into the empty hotel one day in the 1980's, but he was a hotelier when he walked out. He and his wife, Lanie, bought the place, fell in love with it, fixed it up, and renamed it the Boardwalk Inn. They have never stopped learning its secrets and revelling in them. "During one of our remodeling projects," they wrote, "we found the original stenciled finish, as well as the outline of a wall lamp matching a light fixture found in a closet. That light fixture is now over the telephone desk in the Fireside Room, and the stencil design has been duplicated and now decorates the Homestead Room." That is a succinct description of a lucky hotel.

Amenities: Private bathrooms, antique furnishings, complimentary coffee/tea; cable television.

Dining tip: Breakfast is the only meal served.

Location notes: St. Ignace is a quaint village. The hotel overlooks Lake Huron, with nearby boats to Mackinac Island, home to the great resort, the Grand Hotel (1887).

Saulte Ste. Marie
OJIBWAY HOTEL   1927

240 W. Portage Ave., Sault Ste. Marie 49783. Tel. 906/632-4100; 800/654-2929; Fax 906/632-4199. Rates: $99.

The moment the decision to build the Hotel Ojibway was reached, early in 1927, the architect knew what he wanted: something Egyptian. "The first impression that the visitor receives," a reporter wrote that same year, "is one of size, massive solidity, subdued refinement and grandeur, all of the attributes peculiar to Egyptian architecture." The hotel never was very Egyptian from the outside – being square for one thing – a six story brick building. And inside, it has become much more Upper Peninsula than Upper Nile: cherry furniture and floral patterns, rockers in the lobby, duck prints on the wall. There are still grand columns in the lobby, and at the very top, if you look, the capitals are rather Egyptian.

The Ojibway has been renovated and the guestrooms also feature the Upper Peninsula style, with traditional cherry or pine furniture.

Amenities: Free parking; exercise room; indoor pool, laundry facilities.

Dining tip: The hotel dining room has a wide-ranging menu, including whitefish caught in Lake Michigan.

Location notes: The Ojibway Hotel is across the street from the museum ship, *Valley Camp,* and three miles from a casino.

Yale
YALE HOTEL   1901
119 S. Main St., Yale 48097. Tel. 810/387-2710; Fax 810/387-2787. 20 rooms. Rates: $80-100.

The Yale is a small town hotel, three stories in brick and stone, with its original oak woodwork.

Amenities: Valet service, in-room refrigerator.

Dining tip: The dining room features prime rib.

Location notes: Yale is in eastern Michigan, north of Detroit.

MINNESOTA

Northfield
ARCHER HOUSE HOTEL   1877
212 Division St. Northfield 55057. Tel. 507/645-5661; 800/247-2235; Fax 507/645-4295. 36 rooms. Rates: $45-140.

No one knows how Northfield, Minnesota, came by its name ... and the mere fact that it was founded by a couple of men named "North" and "Field" does not lessen the controversy in the little college town. Mr. North was a New England abolitionist and he wrote glowing letters that drew a whole community of idealists out to Minnesota. They built a town so prosperous that the James Gang traveled all the way from Missouri in 1876 just to rob its First National Bank. When the bookkeeper wouldn't open the safe, they killed him on the spot. His name is worth remembering if the James' is: it was Joseph Heywood. The Northfielders retaliated by killing two of the gang members and that was the beginning of the end of the James Gang.

A town prosperous enough to attract the attention of nationally famous bankrobbers could surely sustain a good hotel, and the Archer House was built the following year, a three story building with a mansard roof and dormer windows: the height of sophistication, 1877. Situated right downtown, the new hotel included a portico on the east where guests could take in a breath of fresh air. A brass band played, Northfielders swarmed and the Archer House opened for a long run beginning August 23, 1877.

Among the most enterprising of the many owners were Henry and John Henry Kahler, who built Rochester's Kahler Hotel (see below). A writer named W.F. Schilling told an anecdote: "Old Henry Kahler was a right cocky individual and made himself quite conspicuous when the dining room was full of guests. He would busy himself picking up the soiled dishes, piling them on a large tray and then to show his prowess would hoist the tray over his head and do a few waltz steps for the amusement of the boarders. One day, as Mr. Kahler was doing his waltz stunt, big Emma gave the head dining-room door a vicious kick from the kitchen side and in doing so she caught Kahler off balance and he went down with his tray of dishes like a house of cards. He gathered himself and the broken dishes together but was not seen in the dining room for many weeks."

According to the hotel's historian, Susan Thurston Hamerski, the hotel had myriad owners through the years, including a man named Gordon who bought it five times in four years, and sold it five times too. In the 1970's, a local developer created a shopping mall adjacent to the old hotel, which was all but derelict by that point. He couldn't resist the hotel itself and purchased it in 1981. Although he turned the old dining room and lounges into retail space – an inclination obviously dear to him – he was careful in restoring the rest of the hotel. So-called improvements were removed from the facade and the front portico was rebuilt. The guestrooms were redecorated, using furniture commissioned for the hotel.

Amenities: Free parking; room service; television, local phone calls.

Dining tip: The hotel has three restaurants, including Treats, a European-style deli serving chilled soups in summer, unexpected specials, such as Cornish pasties, and homemade baked goods.

Location notes: The Archer House is a half-block from the Carleton College campus, and about nine blocks from St. Olaf's College. The old First National Bank – the one that Jesse James tried to rob – is now the Northfield Historical Society, and it is two blocks from the hotel.

Red Wing
THE ST. JAMES   1875

406 Main St., Red Wing 55066. Tel. 612/388-2846; 800/252-1875. 60 rooms. Rates: $115-165.

In about 1913, a young woman named Clara Nelson heard that St. James Hotel was hiring waitresses, and so she and a friend moved to Red Wing from a nearby town. She must have liked what she found at the bustling hotel, because she stayed for 59 years. In fact, she may not have liked what she found – because she spent most of those 59 years perfecting the place.

One of the St. James Hotel's doors leads to the street. And one leads to the Mississippi River. Red Wing is a river town, where wheat was once loaded onto lines of waiting boats for the trip down the Mississippi and then to points all around the world. The trade made Red Wing a prosperous town, and a group of businessmen raised the money for a first-class hotel, the St. James, in 1875. Four stories in red-brown brick, the hotel anchors the well-preserved downtown section of Red Wing. It is sedately decorated on the inside – a Victorian version of a colonial hotel, with palladian moldings and columns.

Clara Nelson married the owner of the St. James, Charlie Lillyblad, soon after meeting him. He died after about 15 years and Clara ran the hotel, and Red Wing to a certain degree, for the rest of her life. According to employees and relatives reminiscing in the book, *If Walls Could Talk*, she possessed every characteristic necessary for running a hotel: she could dress beautifully and be the grande dame when needed. There was not a job in the place that she could not or would not do. She didn't waste food. She didn't have an office, her workplace was the hotel itself. And she was a generous person who wanted to give and to serve. Ardeth Anderson, a longtime night clerk recalled that on Christmas Eve, when other restaurants were closed, "she'd put out a lot of eggs and bacon and all kinds of things, and say 'If anybody comes in and wants to know if they can get something to eat, you just go out and fix them something.' And I did that to lot of people, truck drivers and others. Never charged a thing for it."

Clara Lillyblad died in 1972 and her son ran The St. James hotel for a few years, but it needed an infusion of capital and a major restoration. The Red Wing Shoe Co. purchased the property in the community interest in 1977 – and so the hotel came full circle. It had been built by 19th century businessmen, also acting in the town's interest. What makes the company's participation rather unique, however, is that the hotel was not stripped back to its opening day in 1875. Clara and Charlie Lillyblad had not built the St. James, but they had worked it into a longstanding success. The hotel's popularity wasn't based on its initial novelty, anyway, and so the restoration recognized all 100 years of life at the St. James. The doors, wainscoting and tin ceilings remain. Included in the $2.2 million restoration were an addition and the renovation of the basement into meeting rooms.

Amenities: individually decorated rooms (named after steamboats), cable television, complimentary morning coffee brought to the room, welcoming bottle of champagne, free copy of the oral history, *If Walls Could Talk*, a story of the old St. James, edited by Patrice Avon Marvin and Nicholas Curchin Vrooman.

Dining Tip: an extensive Sunday brunch is served on the fifth floor, overlooking the River

Location Notes: Red Wing is located about 25 miles south of Minneapolis/St. Paul. Three blocks to Shelden Auditorium; the hotel is on the historical walking tour of Red Wing.

Rochester
KAHLER HOTEL   1921
20 S.W. Second Ave., Rochester 55902. Tel. 507/282-2581; 800/ 533-1655; Fax 507/285-2775; web, www.kahler.com. 700 rooms. Rates: rooms, $69-159; suites, $350-2,000.

All of the properties listed in this book had to have been built as hotels, that is the first rule. The Kohler was a little more. It was built as a "triple plan," hotel in the unique lexicon of the Kahler Realty Corp.: part hotel, part hospital. There aren't many communities in which that would be an attractive or necessary combination: in fact, Rochester, Minnesota, was the only one. It was a unique place, especially in the first decades of this century, as the Mayo Clinic grew by giant leaps.

Local businessmen tried to keep up with the various demands – but there were so many demands. People visiting the clinic needed accommodations, and so John Henry Kalher (see the Archer House, above) built the Zumbro House in 1912. The clinic needed clean sheets and so he built the Model Laundry. But when the Clinic just kept growing and generated the need for more hotel rooms, more hospital rooms, and more convalescing rooms, he came up with the Triple Plan and built the Kahler Hotel, which opened in 1921. In 1954, the hospital rooms were abandoned, and the Kahler retrenched as a hotel, adding a 257-room wing.

The hotel, built with an Old English atmosphere, has not emphasized preservation in the past couple of generations, since so many of its guests are otherwise distracted by hospital business. However, considering the hotel's unofficial role as adjunct to the Clinic, it is an especially historic, historic hotel. The lobby still has its vaulted Gothic ceiling, while the Elizabethan Room restaurant also has its original decor, including walnut paneling.

Amenities: Concierge; complimentary breakfast and cocktail hour; indoor swimming pool; pets welcome.

Dining tip: The Kahler's Spa menu is full of snappy dishes that have remarkably few calories. Baked fresh salmon with stir-fry vegetables and a salad ... 220 calories (or one handful of potato chips).

Location notes: The Kahler Hotel is connected by covered walkway to the Mayo Civic Center, the Mayo Medical Complex, and the Galleria Mall.

Sauk Centre
PALMER HOUSE   1901

228 Original Main St., Sauk Centre 56378. Tel. 320/352-3431; Fax 320/352-5602. 22 rooms, Rates: $39-99.

In 1901, there was a family living in a certain house on Main Street in Sauk Centre, and as the children in the family spied a new building going up next door, little by little and day by day, they couldn't imagine what it was going to be. Then they saw men installing stained-glass windows: to their certain knowledge, only churches had stained-glass windows. Ninety years later, one of those children still remembered their astonishment on learning that the new building was to be a hotel. A hotel with stained-glass windows!

Sauk Centre had a palace.

The new hotel was built by Mr. and Mrs. Richard L. Palmer, to replace the Sauk Centre House, which was lost in a fire in 1900. On the night of the blaze, according to the lore, the good townspeople of Sauk Centre stood and watched the old hotel burn, and they could hardly keep from cheering. Sentimental folk, they'd been wanting a new hotel for years and the fire made sure they'd get one. In response, the Palmers built a handsome three story brick building on a corner of Main Street, lined the public rooms with red oak, ordered a bank of stained-glass windows from Vienna, and installed electric lighting throughout. A year after the hotel opened, Mr. Palmer was forced to replace the switches in most of the guestrooms: people would just stand by their doors for hours, putting the lights on and off, on and off. Sauk Centre had a palace.

The Palmer House – having with some justification the same name as Chicago's world famous hotel – became famous in Central Minnesota as a sophisticated place to stay or eat. It became famous around the world, however, as "Minniemashie House," the hotel in Sinclair Lewis' novel *Main Street*. Lewis knew all about it, because he was from Sauk Centre and worked at the Palmer House one summer. As a matter of fact, Lewis was obsessed with hotels; he later lived at the Essex House and offered to buy the Algonquin (see New York City for both). He also wrote a whole novel about big hotels and little ones, often lingering in the plot just to talk hotel-talk – unfortunately, he talked more about the hoteliers than the guests, which gave the book the tone of a seminar, rather than scuttlebutt. (Some people liked the book, called *Work of Art*, but it didn't do as well as the quintessential scuttlebutt-novel, *Main Street*, not by a long shot.)

The Palmer House survived as a small town hotel, host to truckers and travelers pausing between buses. Salesmen writing up orders in the quiet of the lobby were a common sight long into the 1980's. Now, however, they can do their work to the live music from the baby grand piano in the lobby. The Palmer House has been gentrified: still a small town hotel, but recently refurbished to be as sophisticated as Mr. and Mrs. Palmer always intended it to be. Guestrooms, which were enlarged, have high ceilings and furnishings in turn-of-the-century style.

Amenities: Exercise room; business services; room service; in-room television, telephone, individual climate control, private bathroom.

Dining tip: In addition to the original restaurant, the hotel has a small pub off the lobby.

Location notes: The Palmer House is on Main Street, designated a historic district; it is three blocks from Sinclair Lewis' boyhood home.

OHIO

Cincinnati
THE OMNI NETHERLAND PLAZA   1931
35 W. Fifth St., Cincinnati 45202. Tel. 513/421-9100; 800/843-6664; Fax 513/421-4291. 621 rooms. Rates: rooms, $99-265; suites, $325-1,325.

Most grand hotels were built with the idea that historical decor was not only dramatic to behold, but a prudent business decision in the long run. A hotel built to look like a 15th century Italian palace or a Georgian townhouse would remain suspended in tasteful isolation, as other fashions grew dated. Only a few hotels had the sheer bravery to be absolutely of-the-moment – knowing that moments do pass, after all.

The Netherland Plaza Hotel, an art deco masterwork, was nothing if not brave, in many ways. It was part of a development called Carew Tower, which rose out of a downtown block in Cincinnati, 1927, looking from a distance like the Emerald City in *The Wizard of Oz* – a cluster of skyscrapers reaching up past one another. Containing stores, offices, and the Netherland Plaza Hotel, the development pioneered the concept of the multi-use complex in modern architecture. John Emery, heir to a meatpacking fortune, paid for the development.

In September of 1929, the project required an injection of a large amount of cash and Emery stoically started to sell all of his stocks and bonds, to raise capital. Friends frantically tried to stop him: the Tower was sheer speculation, in their eyes. Needless to say, after the Crash a month later, they were left with piles of pretty stock certificates, many of which were slightly worthless, while John Emery had a giant building and plenty of cash with which to finish it.

The hotel, in particular, had been planned as a showcase for art deco motifs. Later art deco became a machine-turned look, but the Netherland Plaza's style was drawn from the same famous Exposition in Paris that inspired super-modern ocean liners of the day, such as the *Ile de France*. The hotel was decorated with crafted details, intended to surprise the mind, even more than the eye, with images drawn from nature or primitive cultures. The materials were lustrous, rather than garish: mellow German silver rather than silverplate or sterling; frosted glasswork rather than crystal, and light-colored Brazilian rosewood rather than typical mahogany or cherry.

The Netherland Plaza *did* go out of style: if it didn't, it wouldn't have been modern in the first place. By the 1950's the rosewood was painted over or masked by vinyl; sconces were painted and complex lighting arrangements were replaced by ceiling panels better suited to a discount store. However, the Netherland Plaza survived and when its art deco derring-do was appreciated again in the 1980's, the new owners found most of the decoration still intact, beneath the vinyl. The restoration received important awards and the hotel is now considered a resource for those studying art deco design.

Sir Winston Churchill was the greatest fan the Netherland Plaza ever had. He stayed there in 1933. While he is now better known for saving democracy than for reviewing hotels, he did call the Netherland Plaza "an unsurpassed hotel." According to his private secretary, he had the hotel send him samples of the painted tiles from his bathroom, so that he could copy them. That is high praise, too, since he was a serious mason, in addition to once saving democracy and occasionally reviewing hotels.

Bing Crosby liked the hotel and one of the managers, Harry Nolan, recalled that he could walk around undisturbed, as long as he left off his hairpiece. According to the hotel's own history: "Nolan frequently talked of the day Bing was in town for a golf tournament. A crowd began to grow outside the hotel, anxious for a glimpse of the star. When offered an alternative escape route, Crosby replied, 'When they stop recognizing me, I'm in trouble' and walked out into the crowd, climbing on the back of his convertible to sing a few songs, the story goes, before the police finally needed to clear the road."

If you ever dreamed of being onboard one of the great oceanic super-liners of the 1920's or 1930's ... it's too late. But there is still the Netherland Plaza.

Amenities: Concierge; 24-hour room service; exercise room, with indoor pool; in-room dataport.

Dining tip: The hotel dining rooms are home to the Netherland Salad, invented at the grand opening in 1931 and still popular today.

Location notes: The Omni Netherland Plaza is in downtown Cincinnati, two blocks (accessible via Skywalk) from the Convention Center, four blocks from the Taft Theater, and seven blocks from Riverfront Stadium.

THE CINCINNATIAN   1882

601 Vine St., Cincinnati 45202. Tel. 513/381-3000; 800/942-9000; Fax 513/651-0256; internet, http://www.CincinnatianHotel.com; e-mail, info@CincinnatianHotel.com. 147 rooms. Rates: rooms, $210-255; suites, $270-1,500.

The Cincinnatian was called the Palace when it opened in 1882, a Second Empire building on a busy downtown corner. A seven story building in granite, it had the mansard roof and the gables popular in Paris or Brussels at the time. The Cricket Restaurant opened with the hotel and remained a tradition through five generations in the city.

By 1984, the old Palace, long since renamed The Cincinnatian, was standing in disrepute. It was scheduled for destruction to make way for a parking garage, when a local group stepped in with $25 million for a massive reconstruction. Much of the hotel was modernized, but the exterior and the lobby woodwork, in particular, still represent another time in the city's aspirations.

Amenities: Concierge; gym with sauna; 24 room service; overnight shoeshine; afternoon tea.

Location notes: Downtown: two blocks to the Convention Center or Aronoff Center for the Arts.

Cleveland
RENAISSANCE CLEVELAND HOTEL   1918

24 Public Sq., Cleveland 44113; Tel. 216/696-5600; Reservations 800/696-6898; Fax 216/696-3102; 491 rooms. Rates: rooms, $125-225; suites, $225-1500.

When the Cleveland Hotel opened, it was an eleven story time capsule of the year 1918, filled with ideas of the moment. "Food will be served in a hurry," promised the lunchroom, Cleveland's first quick-service restaurant. "No cabaret jazz here," sniffed the entertainment director, making a hopeless stand on a controversial issue of the day. And to show that the elevators were perfectly safe and smooth, they were operated exclusively by female employees.

The Hotel Cleveland offered innovations (and opinions) at every turn, but then, it was not merely a hotel. It was "the last proof that Cleveland is a great city and not merely a big town," according to the main newspaper in town. Considering that Cleveland is indeed a great city, it seems perenially insecure about the fact, but in 1918, the new hotel was its latest *last proof* of urbanity.

The Cleveland Hotel is built of light colored granite in an E-shape. Inside, the public rooms are also light in shade, lined in white marble with vaulted ceilings in blue tile. The rooms have been modernized in a generally traditional style. They no longer come equipped with a "Servidor" – a lockable cubby hole leading from the hall to each room, in which bellboys and room service waiters could leave items requested by guests without having to disturb them. It was a system so very modern that apparently it didn't work.

Amenities: Exercise room; indoor pool; 24-hour room service; complimentary coffee and paper, delivered to room; in-room mini-bar, iron, safe, three telephones.

Dining tip: The hotel dining room specializes in food from the Provence region of France. The lobster bisque is a favorite dish.

Location notes: The hotel is attached to Tower City Center. It is two blocks to the convention center; four blocks to Jacobs Field, and six blocks to the Rock 'n Roll Hall of Fame, which is on Lake Erie.

Columbus
WESTIN GREAT SOUTHERN   1897

310 S. High St., Columbus 43215. Tel. 614/228-3800; 800/228-3000; Fax 614/228-7666. 196 rooms. Rates: rooms, $119-185; suites, $155-500.

It wasn't just a hotel company, it was a fireproof hotel company, and not only that, it was the Great Southern Fireproof Hotel Co. Who wouldn't invest in it? Four hundred sensible residents of Columbus, Ohio, jumped at the chance and at shares priced at $100 each. They must have been delighted to learn that they were not only to own a new hotel, but a new theater, as well: the Southern. That was the plan, and it came to pass just as promised.

The Great Southern Hotel opened in 1897, with a center section slightly taller than its shoulders on either side. That center section was quite a lot more distinctive, too, with pillars between the windows and pretty arched windows on the top two stories. The atmosphere throughout the hotel was opulent. Even so, the Great Southern Fireproof Hotel Co. was in rough shape by the turn-of-the-century. The hotel failed.

A family named Lazarus brought the Great Southern back to life, to make a Biblical reference out of it: Frank and Ralph Lazarus bought both the hotel and the theater in 1901, and they proved to be excellent managers. Their family owned the properties for the next 68 years. The next owner intended to turn the hotel into apartments and the theater into a parking lot, but the old hotel stopped him, in its own way. Fortunately or unfortunately, the Lazaruses had made very few substantive changes to the hotel: they neither modernized the decor very much (that's good), nor tended to its plumbing, electrical or heating systems (that's bad). The hotel couldn't be made into apartments very easily and so it was sold again.

In 1982, subsequent owners started a restoration process that modernized the building systems and redecorated the guestrooms in a spanking new but traditional-looking way. The public rooms, left largely in their original condition, did not require as much work. In more recent years, the Southern Theater has followed its sibling's good fortune and is also a going enterprise again, the home of the Columbus Association for the Performing Arts.

Amenities: Valet parking; in-room safe, coffee-maker, irons.

Dining tip: The hotel features live jazz music on Friday and Saturday nights.

Location notes: The Great Southern is in downtown Columbus, three blocks from the State Capitol or the Brewery District, and two blocks from City Center Mall.

Wilmington
GENERAL DENVER   1928

81 W. Main St., Wilmington 45177. Tel. and Fax 937/382-7139; web, http://www.crinet.com/gendenver; e-mail, gendenver@erinet.com. 26 rooms. Rates:$39-49; suites, $79.

The General Denver is a four story hotel in Tudor style, recently purchased by a family long involved in both real estate development and historic preservation.

Amenities: Complimentary breakfast.

Dining tip: The Denver Tavern serves lunch and dinner.

Location notes: Wilmington is in southwestern Ohio.

WISCONSIN

Milwaukee
THE PFISTER   1893

424 E. Wisconsin Ave., Milwaukee 53202. Tel. 414/273-8222; 800/558-8222; Fax 414/273-8082. 307 rooms. Rates: rooms, $225-245; suites, $265-850.

The Pfister, like the Copley Plaza in Boston and the Palace in San Francisco, is a statement. Milwaukee ends at the door, and inside the setting is some other place, some other time, in gilt and polish. But of course Milwaukee does not end at the door of the Pfister, it pours in and out of the busy hotel so that the lobby of the Pfister may as well be the lobby of the city.

Guido Pfister came to America in the 1840's, determined to make a fortune. And he did. He started as a tanner and grew with the city of Milwaukee into other forms of trade. Next, Pfister determined to use part of his fortune to build a hotel in Milwaukee, a place that would show visitors and locals just how far the young city had come. He budgeted a hefty half-million dollars for the project. In 1889, Pfister had his general plan for the grand new hotel, but he died that year before construction started. In tribute, his son built the hotel to match anything else in the world, missing the original budget by three times in the process. The $1.5 million Pfister Hotel opened in 1893 in downtown Milwaukee, taking up a full block. Not especially eye-catching from the outside, described as "Romanesque Revival" but looking more or less like a light-colored office building, the hotel had eight stories, 200 rooms and grand proportions in the public rooms inside, where ceilings were high and hallways generous. Charles Pfister was a good hotelman, and the Pfister ranked easily as the best hotel in town.

Hotel artwork is often made and hung on the wall specifically to be ignored. The Pfister, however, opened with a collection of original oil paintings and sculptures considered the equal of practically any museum in 1893. The collection includes about 82 oil paintings in a classical style. Some are quite old, dating from the 16th century, though most were made in the late 19th century, often by artists working "after" or in a style influenced by a more prominent artist. The collection has become more than the sum of its parts, however, as the Pfister collection is considered an intact representation of the 19th century sensibility in art. Even for those less attuned to such junctures of art history, they add a vibrancy and humanity without compromising the basic formality of the Pfister.

In 1926, control of the Pfister passed to the general manager, Ray Smith, who had worked at the hotel since he was boy: a bellboy. According to hotel history, Smith was compelled by the situation in World War Two to offer accommodation at the Pfister to refugees. To leave any war-torn part of the world and end up at the Pfister must have been a blessing, if not a shock. The glorious Pfister seemed only old-fashioned in the 1950's when it was bankrupt by competition and its own steep upkeep.

Ben Marcus, a movie theater owner from Minnesota, purchased the place in 1963, the first of his corporation's extensive holdings in the hotel industry. It was not immediately obvious that it would make a good business investment, but Marcus matched the new hotels around Milwaukee by adding a modern tower, swimming pool, and meeting facilities. He also renovated the property, which was restored again recently.

Amenities: Indoor pool, room service, concierge, valet parking, shuttle to General Mitchell International Airport.

Dining tip: English Room is the city's longtime favorite place for steaks.

Location notes: The hotel is located downtown, six blocks from Milwaukee theaters or the lake.

INDEX

TRAVEL NOTES

TRAVEL NOTES